# Macroeconomics
## Income and Monetary Theory

Joseph Aschheim

Ching-Yao Hsieh

*The George Washington University*

Charles E. Merrill Publishing Co.

*A Bell & Howell Company*

Columbus, Ohio

Library of Congress Catalog Card Number: 69-19270

Standard Book Number: 675-09513-1

Printed in the United States of America

1 2 3 4 5 6 7 8 9 / 76 75 74 73 72 71 70 69

to LINDA and ROCHELLE

# Preface

This book is designed to fill a specific need of the first-year graduate student and advanced undergraduate in economics. What such students need at this stage of the learning process is not another textbook on macroeconomics, but rather a review of the major lines of thought in income and monetary theory which will facilitate the integration of their studies in these areas. This book can also be useful to the professional economist in that it can serve him as a handbook on the important post-Keynesian developments in income and monetary theory and their relevant theoretical antecedents.

What distinguish this book from the standard text on macroeconomics are the following features:

(1) This book includes a systematic treatment of the relevant historical antecedents of contemporary income and monetary theory. The rationale of our evolutionary approach is to give perspective to some important post-Keynesian developments in this area. The standard textbooks on macroeconomics typically devote a chapter or two to the contrast between the Keynesian system and the "Classical" system. The "Classical" model is generally meant to be a composite one, reconstructed by post-Keynesian writers. No attempt is made to trace systematically the classical and neoclassical components of the model. In going through the useful exercise of contrasting the two systems, the following unanswered questions frequently arise in the student's mind: Does the "Classical" model reflect the core views of the classical or the neoclassical writers? Since the classical writers were mainly interested in the long-run problem of economic growth, did they have anything to say on the short-run problems of income determination? As it is generally recognized that the main body of neoclassical economics is microeconomics, what were the neoclassical writers' views on macroeconomics? Furthermore, did the pre-Smithian writers make any con-

tributions to the development of macroeconomic theory? Answers to these questions are not readily given in the standard textbooks on macroeconomics; nor could they be found easily in the standard textbooks on the history of economic thought. It seemed to us, therefore, useful to aim at providing the answers to the foregoing questions systematically and succinctly in the space of one book. Such a treatment not only integrates contemporary income and monetary theory with the history of economic thought, but also should prove helpful to the student in organizing and drawing together his studies in several related fields.

(2) Since this book is designed to help the student to formulate a conceptual "filing system" for the organization and integration of his studies in macroeconomics, no attempt is made here to reproduce the Keynesian building blocks in the chapter on "The Keynesian Revolution." These essential building blocks of Keynesian economics have been stated and restated in contemporary textbooks. We presume that the student has already acquired familiarity with them. Our objective here is not to update the leading texts, but to highlight the overall impact of Keynesian theory and its interpretation.

(3) A third noteworthy feature of this book is that it includes a considerable number of quotations from both pre- and post-Keynesian literature. Lest this sound like a book of quotations, we must emphasize that this unorthodox treatment serves a twofold purpose: (a) A judicious selection of quotable passages from source readings and original texts helps to heighten the student's interest in and appreciation of the contributions made by the leading authors. There are many "pearls of wisdom" scattered among the pre- and post-Keynesian literature. They, undoubtedly, should be highlighted, for in a few well-chosen words they could open the mind's eye of readers and help to put all the seemingly unconnected pieces together into a meaningful whole. Yet these "pearls of wisdom" are often lost in the paraphrased versions of the scholarly treatise. (b) A judicious selection of relevant quotations will also save the interested reader a great deal of time. For it will provide a short-cut to the otherwise time-consuming process of searching and hunting for the relevant passages in the original writings. To a graduate student who is striving to consolidate his studies in preparation for comprehensive examinations in economics, such a volume is especially useful. It will provide him with an added measure of confidence in his familiarity with the words of the great writers themselves.

(4) This book is concerned with theory, and not with empirical studies and policy. Our objective is not to provide the student with a comprehensive survey of all aspects of macroeconomics. Thus the vast amount of post-Keynesian empirical work in connection with the extension or criticism of Keynesian economics is outside our purview. The reader will find that policy considerations are also abstracted from the present volume. Instead, we attempt to provide an exposition of the important post-Keynesian developments in income and monetary theory and their relevant antecedents.

(5) The text is divided into two parts: Part I deals with the theory of income and employment, and Part II contains a systematic study of monetary theory. We fully recognize that Keynes's *General Theory* is a theory of income and employment, as well as a monetary theory. The most widely accepted and taught IS-LM approach (or the Hicks-Hansen restatement) highlights the merger of these two theories. The reason for our classification is entirely pedagogical. By separating the different aspects of macroeconomic theory, we attempt to provide the student with a conceptual "filing system" wherein he can reshuffle and rearrange the relevant material in his own way.

In the introduction, the main ideas of the book are introduced by a summary of the major theoretical developments in both the pre- and post-Keynesian writings. A common format is then followed in both Part One and Part Two: first, the antecedents of modern theory are systematically traced back to the pre-Smithian period; second, the essentials of post-Keynesian developments are spelled out at length.

Our product is truly a joint one, and the listing of our names is merely indicative of the order of the alphabet. We are grateful to the Graduate Council of the George Washington University for financial support of our preparation of the manuscript, and to George Driscoll, who helped to proofread the text, and who compiled the indexes.

*Joseph Aschheim*

*Ching-Yao Hsieh*

# Contents

# Introduction

This volume is devoted to two aspects of macroeconomics: (1) the theory of income determination, and (2) the theory of money. It reviews major analytical contributions to these fields since the publication of J. M. Keynes' *The General Theory of Employment, Interest, and Money*,[1] within the framework of the historical antecedents of these ideas.

Part I is devoted to the theory of income and employment. It begins with a review of pre-Smithian theory. Three principal propositions emerge. (1) Most writers in the period (1650–1776) considered an adequate level of aggregate demand the key to full employment. Unlike the classical economists writing after them, they did not assume that aggregate demand would take care of itself. Hence, they emphasized the role of fiscal and monetary policies in the determination of the level of total spending. (2) They recognized different types of unemployment. Although they emphasized the elimination of voluntary unemployment due to indolence and sloth, they did recognize involuntary unemployment. It may sound a bit far-fetched to assert that some of the pre-Smithian writers had an inkling of involuntary unemployment; however, if we consider Petty's emphasis on public works and taxation, Berkeley's repeated complaints about emigration from Ireland in search of a livelihood, and Steuart's stress on using debt management as a tool to influence total spending, there is justification in such an assertion. (3) Although these writers stressed aggregate demand and full employment, they were not really precursors of Keynesian economics, for none of them had any notion of underemployment equilibrium.

---

[1] John M. Keynes, *The General Theory of Employment, Interest, and Money* (New York: Harcourt, Brace & World, Inc., 1936).

Chapter 2 deals with the essentials of the classical theory of output and employment. It points out that the classical writers recognized three types of unemployment, namely, short-of-capital unemployment (Professor Joan Robinson's "Marxian unemployment"), wage-too-high unemployment, and seasonal unemployment. The mainstream of classical economics overlooked both voluntary and involuntary unemployment due to inadequate aggregate demand, and technological unemployment. The explanation for their neglect of "Keynesian" unemployment lies in their acceptance of the conclusions of Say's Law.

The neoclassical theory of output and employment is discussed in Chapter 3 with the aid of the familiar reconstruction of the "Classical" model, which can be found in almost every contemporary textbook on macroeconomics. Like the basic classical model before it, the implicit theory of output and employment of the neoclassical economists was essentially a theory of "pure choice," i.e., choice abstracting from money as a store of value.[2] So long as we adhere to the assumption of "pure choice," the conclusions of Say's Law necessarily follow.

The "Keynesian Revolution" in the theory of income and employment is the subject matter of Chapter 4. Keynes shifted the center of economic analysis from the sphere of pure choice and certainty to that of "impure choice" and uncertainty. In theories of impure choice there is cognizance of money as a store of value. Thus, *The General Theory* contains a monetary theory of output and employment in which monetary theory, capital theory, and theory of interest are all brought into a coherent, though incomplete, union.

Chapter 5 is devoted to a review of important post-Keynesian developments relevant to the theory of income determination. These developments, of course, are intertwined with other aspects of macroeconomics, and any classification scheme would necessarily be somewhat arbitrary. Our scheme is based on the recognition that *The General Theory* left at least five gaps that post-Keynesian writers have sought to fill: (1) the respective roles of the public sector and foreign trade in the determination of the level of income; (2) analysis of the aggregate supply function; (3) the "wealth effect"; (4) analysis of the determinants of investment other than the rate of interest; and (5) types of unemployment other than demand induced. An exposition of

---

[2] Professor G. L. S. Shackle observed: "When a theory supposes the available alternatives to be perfectly known to these [acting] subjects in every respect which concerns them, I shall speak of a theory of *pure* choice." See his "Recent Theories Concerning the Nature and Role of Interest," in *Surveys of Economic Theory* (New York: St. Martin's Press, Inc., 1965), p. 109.

major post-Keynesian contributions in these areas is provided in this chapter.

Part II contains a systematic study of the principal developments in monetary theory. The five chapters in Part II are arranged in the same chronological order as those in Part I. Chapter 6 expounds the two strands of thought in pre-classical monetary theory. The first is the so-called "money-stimulates-trade" doctrine advocated by John Law, Jacob Vanderlint, and Bishop Berkeley; the second is the quantity theory of money formulated by John Locke, refined by Richard Cantillon, and restated by David Hume. It was at the hands of Hume that the quantity theory took its well-known form. It is interesting to note that neither Cantillon nor Hume had anything to do with the so-called "homogeneity postulate."[3] Although they lacked the notion of the "real-balance effect," they did not lose sight of the interdependence of the component parts of the economy. They stated explicitly that a change in the monetary sector would have repercussions in the real sector.

The main ideas of classical monetary theory are set out in Chapter 7. The emphasis in this chapter is on the contrast between the mainstream of classical monetary analysis—the quantity theory of money embraced by Henry Thornton, David Ricardo, and John Stuart Mill—and the dissenting views of Thomas Tooke and the "Banking School." In this active period we find the beginning of the income approach to monetary theory.[4]

Chapter 8 deals with neoclassical monetary theory, in which the quantity theory of money was still prevalent. There were three versions of the predominant view: the Fisherian Transactions-Velocity Approach, the Marshallian Cash-Balance Approach, and the Wicksellian restatement of the quantity theory, into which the basic framework of the income approach could easily be fitted. It was Marshall's objective to integrate monetary theory with value theory. He adopted the cash-balances approach and concentrated on the analysis of the demand for money. Unfortunately, because of the full-employment assumption, the valiant efforts of the Cambridge School to integrate the two theo-

---

[3] A lucid discussion of the "homogeneity postulate" and its background is given by Professors Gary S. Becker and William J. Baumol in their essay, "The Classical Monetary Theory: The Outcome of the Discussion," reprinted from *Economica,* n.s. XIX (November, 1952) in *Essays in Economic Thought,* Joseph J. Spengler and William R. Allen, eds. (Chicago: Rand McNally & Co., 1960), pp. 753–771.

[4] See Alvin H. Hansen, *Monetary Theory and Fiscal Policy* (New York: McGraw-Hill Book Company, 1949), Chap. 6.

ries were incomplete, for total output under full-employment conditions was held to be fixed. Therefore, there was neither the necessity to consider the relationship between money and output, nor the need to consider the elasticity of the supply of output. Furthermore, as pointed out by Professor Patinkin, the neoclassical writers failed to include an analysis of the stability of the dynamic system. "There is a basic chapter missing in practically all neoclassical monetary theory— the chapter which presents a precise dynamic analysis of the determination of the equilibrium absolute level of money prices through the workings of the real-balance effect."[5] Wicksell was the only exception. With a view to defending orthodoxy, Wicksell made a restatement of the quantity theory. In this restatement, Wicksell not only provided the orthodox monetary theory with the missing stability analysis, but also formulated an analytical framework into which the Keynesian theory could be fitted without difficulty. In any case, neoclassical monetary theory is still a theory of pure choice. Therefore, its hallmarks are: (1) zero interest elasticity of the demand for money and (2) constant or unitary income elasticity of the demand for money. It also follows that its theory of interest is a nonmonetary one, namely, the savings-investment theory of interest, which subsequently became the main target of Keynes' attack.

Chapter 9 is designed to set forth the salient points of *The General Theory* as a monetary theory. The Keynesian theory is demonstrably more general than neoclassical quantity theory; for it includes not only an analysis of the relationship between the quantity of money and the level of output, but also an analysis of the relationship between the quantity of money and the rate of interest. Since *The General Theory* presents a theory of impure choice, the fundamental issue raised by Keynes in the realm of monetary theory is the function of money as a store of value.

The last chapter concentrates on some of the important developments in post-Keynesian monetary theory. The material is grouped under four headings: (1) integration of monetary theory and value theory; (2) neutrality and non-neutrality of money; (3) theory of demand for money; and (4) theory of the supply of money. The first two topics flow directly from the fundamental issues raised by Keynes in his critique of classical monetary theory. *The General Theory* offers one version of the integration of monetary and value theory; Professor Patinkin's

---

[5] From *Money, Interest and Prices*, 2nd Edition by Don Patinkin, p. 168. Copyright © 1965 by Don Patinkin. Reprinted by permission of Harper & Row, Publishers.

*Money, Interest, and Prices* suggests an alternative approach to the subject. The issue regarding the assumptions required to establish the neutrality and non-neutrality of money has been greatly clarified by several post-Keynesian writers.[6]

The trend of the post-Keynesian developments in the theory of demand for money is toward a synthesis which has been most effectively summarized by Professor Harry G. Johnson:

> Contemporary monetary theorists, whether avowedly "Keynesian" or "quantity," approach the demand for money in essentially the same way, as an application of the general theory of choice, though the former tend to formulate their analysis in terms of the demand for money as an asset alternative to other assets, and the latter, in terms of the demand for the services of money as a good.[7]

The post-Keynesian trend in the theory of the supply of money has been towards treating the money supply as an endogenous, rather than an exogenous, variable. Some of the theoretical developments in this area are noted in the concluding chapter.

---

[6] See Lloyd A. Metzler, "Wealth, Saving, and the Rate of Interest," *Journal of Political Economy*, LIX (April, 1951); Patinkin, *Money, Interest and Prices;* and J. G. Gurley and Edward S. Shaw, *Money in a Theory of Finance* (Washington, D. C.: The Brookings Institution, 1960).

[7] Harry G. Johnson, "Monetary Theory and Policy," *American Economic Review*, LII (June, 1962), 344.

# PART ONE

## Theory of
## Income and Employment

# 1

# Pre-Classical Theory of
# Income and Employment

Our survey of the pre-classical theory of income and employment begins with Sir William Petty (1632–1678) and concludes with Sir James Steuart (1712–1780). The ideas of these writers, relevant to our subject matter, emerge in bold relief if they are viewed from the perspective of modern theory.

The student of economics is well aware that modern income theory in its simplest form can be succinctly stated by either a truncated model depicted by the Keynesian-cross diagram, or a general equilibrium model (the Hicks-Hansen model) represented by the *IS-LM* diagram. For our present purpose, a mere reminder of the basic ideas will suffice. The relationship between the two models is illustrated by Figure 1-1. The truncated model highlights the crucial role of aggregate demand $(C + I)$ in the determination of equilibrium real income $(Y)$. This Keynesian-cross diagram highlights the inverse of Say's Law. Whereas the caricatured version of Say's Law states that supply creates its own demand, "Keynes' Law" as depicted by the truncated model, asserts that demand creates its own equilibrium supply. The suppressed aggregate supply function is the 45° line. It will be recalled that this truncated model has also been frequently used to illustrate the following: (1) underemployment equilibrium output and involuntary unemployment, (2) the fickleness of $(C + I)$ owing to the volatility of investment expenditures, (3) the "Paradox of Thrift," (4) the consumption function as the kingpin of Keynesian theory, and (5) the rationale of a "mixed private enterprise" economy.

9

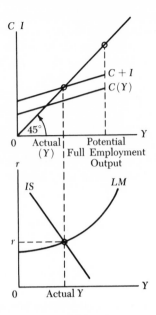

**Figure 1-1**

The *IS-LM* diagram neatly represents the integration of three theories: (1) monetary theory (depicted by the *LM* schedule), (2) income and employment theory (symbolized by the *IS* curve), and (3) theory of interest. It shows that the equilibrium level of (*Y*) and the equilibrium rate of interest (*r*) are simultaneously determined by both monetary (*LM*) and real (*IS*) forces. In other words, it depicts the level of output and employment as the central subject matter of monetary theory. Conceptually, income theory and monetary theory are indivisible. However, for clarity of exposition, it is sometimes useful to present the basic ideas under separate headings.

In this chapter, we are concerned with pre-classical theory of income and employment. The most important question involved here is whether or not the pre-classical writers had a precise theory of income determination such as the one described by the Keynesian system. The answer is an emphatic "no." None of these writers fashioned the Keynesian analytical tools which would have enabled them to state the problem of income determination rigorously. However, the basic idea of modern theory—that the levels of output and employment depend essentially on the level of aggregate demand—was clearly perceived by Petty and his successors. It is fair to say that the majority of writers of this period stressed full employment as the objective of economic policy and an adequate level of aggregate demand as the key to prosperity. With the exception of Sir Dudley North (1641–1691), and perhaps to a certain extent David Hume (1711–1776), the important writers of this period did not believe that aggregate demand would take care of itself and that full employment would automatically be achieved. They thought that government should play a positive role in bringing about full employment, as well as fostering economic development. In this sense they may be said to agree with Keynes. Furthermore, it is interesting to note that several modern concepts were anticipated by pre-Smithian writers. Table 1-1 summarizes some of their contributions.

**Table 1-1**

**Contributions Made by Pre-Smithian Writers**

| Concepts | Writers |
|---|---|
| Circular flow of income | Petty, Cantillon, the Physiocrats |
| National income | Petty, Gregory King |
| The crucial role of total spending | Petty, Barbon, Berkeley, Steuart, etc. |
| Paradox of thrift | Barbon, Mandeville |
| The multiplier | Recognized by practically all writers but not formalized due to the absence of the concept of a consumption function |
| Underconsumption | The Physiocrats |
| Involuntary unemployment | Petty, Berkeley |
| A mixed private-enterprise economy | Petty (fiscal policy) <br> John Law and Berkeley (monetary policy) <br> Steuart (debt management) <br> Commercial policies and other policies discussed by most of these writers. |

In the following sections of Part I, we discuss ideas of representative writers concerned with the theory of income and employment. Their monetary analyses will be considered in Part II.

## SIR WILLIAM PETTY (1623–1687)

Sir William Petty is generally recognized as the precursor of scientific economics in general,[1] and of modern income analysis and English national-income estimates in particular.[2] He clearly perceived the concept of a circular flow of income and expenditure, and explicitly conveyed this concept in his national-income estimates.[3] Petty approached the measurement of national income from the consumption point of view, adopting the basic assumption that the annual income of a nation is equivalent to its annual expenditures. He was aware of savings and capital accumulation, but did not estimate any of these.

From his national-income estimates it is clear that Petty recognized the relationship between consumption and income. But he did not perceive that these two variables could be related in a functional sense. In other words, the consumption function is missing in his economic writings.

Petty gave special emphasis to the role of fiscal policy in influencing aggregate demand:

> Taxes if they be presently expended upon our own Domestic Commodities, seem to me, to do little harm to the whole Body of the people, only they work a change in the Riches and Fortunes of particular men; and particularly by transferring the same from the Landed and Lazy, to the Crafty and Industrious.[4]

---

[1] See William Letwin, *The Origins of Scientific Economics* (Garden City, N.Y.: Doubleday & Company, Inc., 1964), Chapter 5.

[2] See Joseph A. Schumpeter, *History of Economic Analysis* (New York: Oxford University Press, Inc., 1955), p. 213; and Paul Studenski, *The Income of Nations* (New York: New York University Press, 1958), p. 26.

[3] Paul Studenski observes that Petty had two main objectives in mind in estimating the national income of England: (1) He tried to show that the government could raise its tax revenues by a more equitable form of taxation to meet its wartime and peace-time expenditures; and (2) he tried to show that, in spite of the civil and foreign wars, England was not ruined and could still compete with Holland and France. See Studenski, *Income of Nations*, pp. 27–28. Petty's first estimate may be restated as follows:

| Expenditures (Consumption) | Receipts (Income) |
| --- | --- |
| Food<br>Housing<br>Clothing<br>Miscellaneous | Labor income<br>Rental income from property |
| Total: 40 million pounds | Total: 40 million pounds |

See Studenski, *Income of Nations*, pp. 38–39.

Petty's estimates were elaborated upon by Gregory King. See Studenski, *Income of Nations*, pp. 30–37.

[4] See Charles Henry Hull, ed., *Economic Writings of Sir William Petty* (London: Cambridge University Press, 1899), I, 36.

With a view to maintaining full employment and to keeping up the spirit of industry among workers, Petty also advocated public works:

> Now as to the work of these supernumeraries, let it be without expence of Foreign Commodities, and then 'tis no matter if it be employed to build a useless Pyramid upon Salisbury plain, bring the Stones at Stonehenge to Tower-Hill, or the like, for at worst this would keep their mindes to discipline and obedience, and their bodies to a patience or more profitable labours when need shall require it.[5]

Petty recognized that hoarding by the rich or the State would cause a reduction in total spending and economic activity:

> That if the Sovereign were sure to have what he wanted in due time, it were his own great damage to draw away the money out of his Subjects hands, who by trade increase it, and to hoard it up in his own Coffers, where it is of no use even to himself, but lyable to be begged or vainly expended.[6]

However, he did not analyze the motives for or determinants of hoarding.

Petty explicitly recognized two types of unemployment: (1) technological unemployment, and (2) voluntary unemployment due to "indolence" or sheer laziness. Did Petty also recognize involuntary unemployment due to shortage of aggregate demand? Opinions have been divided on the question of whether these pre-classical writers had anticipated the Keynesian concept of involuntary unemployment.[7] On balance, the authors think it is fair to say that Petty did recognize involuntary unemployment. His advocacy of public works for the removal of unemployment evidences this view.

Petty discussed the problem of technological unemployment in connection with his emphasis on labor-saving devices. He contended that the wealth of a nation was "a result of the Lands, Art, Labour, and Stock."[8] In modern terminology, the inputs of Petty's aggregate pro-

---

[5] Hull, ed., *Economic Writings of Sir William Petty*, p. 31.

[6] Hull, ed., *Economic Writings of Sir William Petty*, p. 32.

[7] Heckscher, Blaug, and Ian D. S. Ward are of the opinion that the pre-classical writers had no concept of Keynesian involuntary unemployment. See E. F. Heckscher, *Mercantilism*, E. F. Soderland, ed. Appendix; also M. Blaug, *Economic Theory in Retrospect* (Homewood, Ill.: Richard D. Irwin, Inc., 1962), pp. 14–15; and Ian S. Ward, "George Berkeley: Precursor of Keynes or Moral Economist on Underdevelopment," *Journal of Political Economy*, Vol. LXVII (February, 1959). The opposite view is held by T. W. Hutchison. See his "George Berkeley as an Economist: A Comment," *Journal of Political Economy*, Vol. LXVIII (June, 1960).

[8] E. A. J. Johnson observed that the word "Art" was used by practically all the writers of the 17th and 18th centuries in explaining the production of wealth. It amounted to a fourth factor of production. *Predecessors of Adam Smith* (Englewood Cliffs, N.J.: Prentice–Hall, Inc., 1937), p. 264.

duction function are land, labor, technological progress, "Art", and capital stock, "Stock". Petty's view on "Art" is clearly revealed in the following passage:

> . . . if by such Simple Labour I could dig and prepare for Seed a hundred Acres in a thousand days, suppose then, I spend a hundred days studying a more compendious way, and in contriving Tools for the same purpose; but in all that hundred days dig nothing, but in the remaining nine hundred days I dig two hundred Acres of Ground; then I say, that the said Art which cost but one hundred days invention is worth one Man's labour for ever; because the new Art, and one Man, perform'd as much as two Men could have done without it.[9]

Petty believed that the introduction of labor-saving devices would generate unemployment.[10] The remedy he envisaged was an increase of aggregate demand to reabsorb the displaced labor—if necessary, through public works.

To attain the objective of full employment in the short run, Petty suggested fiscal and monetary policies. (His monetary theory is discussed in Part II of this book.) In addition to these policies, Petty stressed that England could increase her exports by surpassing rival countries in technological progress (advance in "Art"). His faith in technological progress made him a very moderate mercantilist. He was not in favor of import restrictions or restrictions on the export of bullion. It appeared to him that, so long as England could maintain her competitive position, there would be little fear of an adverse trade balance.

## Nicholas Barbon (1640–1698)

In *A Discourse of Trade* (1690), Barbon expounded the idea that prosperity and full employment depend upon an adequate level of aggregate demand.[11] An adequate level of aggregate demand, in turn, depends upon a high level of consumption. He pointed out that an increase in consumption requires "Liberality" or "the free usage of all

---

9 Hull, ed., *Economic Writings of Sir William Petty*, I, 182.

10 See Hull, ed., *Economic Writings of Sir William Petty*, I, 30.

11 An excellent study on Barbon's monetary theory is presented by Douglas Vickers, *Studies in the Theory of Money 1690–1776* (Philadelphia: Chilton Book Company, 1959), Chap. 5. Also see William Letwin, *The Origins of Scientific Economics* (New York: Doubleday and Company, Inc., 1964), Chap. 2.

those things that are made by the industry of the Poor."[12] The evil of thrift was explicitly stated by Barbon:

> The two extremes of this Vertue (liberality), are Prodigality and Covetousness. Prodigality is a Vice that is prejudicial to the Man but not to Trade. . . . Covetousness is a Vice, prejudicial both to Man and Trade: It starves the Man and breaks the Trader. . . .[13]

"Prodigality" means spending and "covetousness" means "thrift" or saving. Here Barbon anticipated the paradox of Mandeville. "But it was by Bernard Mandeville's *Fable of the Bees* that Barbon's opinion was mainly popularised."[14] The logic of the paradox of thrift was stated by Barbon as follows:

> . . . by the same way the Covetous Man thinks he grows rich, he grows poor; for by not consuming the Goods that are provided for Man's Use, there ariseth a dead Stock, called Plenty, and the Value of those Goods fall, and the Covetous Man's Estates whether in Land, or Mony, become less worth: And a Conspiracy of the Rich Men to be Covetous, and not spend, would be . . . dangerous to a Trading State . . . for though they themselves get nothing by their Covetousness, nor grow they Richer, yet they would make the Nation poor. . . .[15]

---

[12] Nicholas Barbon, *A Discourse of Trade*, Jacob H. Hollander, ed. (Baltimore: The Johns Hopkins Press, 1903), cited by Douglas Vickers in *Studies in the Theory of Money 1690–1776* (Philadelphia: Chilton Book Company, 1959), p. 83.

[13] *Ibid.*

J. M. Keynes in *The General Theory* (New York: Harcourt, Brace & World, Inc., 1936) pointed out:

Though complaints of under-consumption were a very subsidiary aspect of mercantilist thought, Professor Heckscher quotes a number of examples of what he calls "the deep-rooted belief in the utility of luxury and the evil of thrift. Thrift, in fact, was regarded as the cause of unemployment, and for two reasons: in the first place, because real income was believed to diminish by the amount of money which did not enter into exchange, and secondly, because saving was believed to withdraw money from circulation" [pp. 358–359].

[14] Keynes, *The General Theory*, p. 359.

William Letwin observed:

He was one of the first writers clearly to see that "prodigality" or a taste for luxury, however much it might run counter to established rules of State, Church or good morals, might easily benefit the economy. To make such a distinction between moral and economic consequences took a certain cynicism or wit; it might have drawn fuel from Barbon's own "foppishness", as Roger North put it; in any event, when writing on luxury, Barbon suddenly turns from schoolmaster into poet.

Fashion, or the alteration of dress, is a great promoter of trade because it occasions the expense of cloths before the old ones are worn out. It is the spirit and life of trade. . . . (Barbon, *Discourse*, 65)

See Letwin, *The Origins of Scientific Economics*, p. 68.

[15] Barbon, *op. cit.*, p. 84.

## SIR DUDLEY NORTH (1641–1691)

In his *Discourses Upon Trade* (1692), North pointed out that, in considering the problems of employment and the level of economic activity, primary attention should be directed toward aggregate demand. The level of aggregate demand, in turn, depends upon consumption spending. It should be noted that the mercantilist writers before Petty generally placed their emphasis on the foreign-trade component of aggregate demand. Their analyses have been called the "balance-of-trade" doctrine in the theory of international trade.[16] After the last quarter of the seventeenth century, attention had been shifted toward the domestic component of aggregate demand.[17] Reflecting this new trend of thinking, North emphasized consumption.

In the first place, North was of the opinion—shared by most of his contemporaries—that satisfaction of wants was an incentive toward the development of the spirit of enterprise and industry:

> The main spur to Trade, or rather to Industry and Ingenuity, is the exorbitant Appetites of Men, which they will take pains to gratifie, and so be disposed to work, when nothing else will incline them to it; for did Men content themselves with bare Necessaries, we should have a poor World.[18]

Secondly, North recognized that emulation was a strong subjective determinant of consumption:

> The meaner sort seeing their Fellows become rich, and great, are spurr'd up to imitate their Industry. A Tradesman sees his Neighbour keep a Coach, presently all his Endeavors is at work to do the like, and many times is beggered by it; however the extraordinary Application he made, to support his Vanity, was beneficial to the Publick, tho' not enough to answer his false Measures as to himself.[19]

Thirdly, North regarded luxury consumption as not only a stimulant to the spirit of industry but also a means of maintaining an adequate level of aggregate demand (see the following quotation).

---

[16] See P. T. Ellsworth, *International Economics* (1st ed.; New York: The Macmillan Company, 1938), pp. 14–15.

[17] Johnson, in *Predecessors of Adam Smith*, pointed out:
A real change of attitude, however, emerged almost dramatically in the last quarter of the seventeenth century. Coke, Barbon, North, Petty, and others began to praise luxury, antedating another group of writers, who saw indisputable benefits in greater consumption [p. 294].

[18] Sir Dudley North, *Discourses Upon Trade*, Jacob H. Hollander, ed. (Baltimore: The Johns Hopkins Press, 1907), p. 27.

[19] *Ibid.*, pp. 27–28.

Countries which have sumptuary Laws, are generally poor; for when Men by those Laws are confin'd to narrower Expence than otherwise they would be, they are at the same time discouraged from the Industry and Ingenuity which they would have employed in obtaining wherewithal to support them, in the full lattitude of Expence they desire.[20]

Finally, the emphasis on consumption led North to his celebrated defense of home trade:

It will be objected, That the Home Trade signifies nothing to the enriching a Nation, and that the increase of Wealth comes out of Foreign Trade.

I answer, That what is commonly understood by Wealth, viz, Plenty, Bravery, Gallantry, &c. cannot be maintained without Foreign Trade. Nor in truth, can Foreign Trade subsist without the Home Trade, both being connected together.[21]

Unlike the majority of his contemporaries, North was a firm believer in the efficacy of the price system:

That no Laws can set Prizes in Trade, the Rates of which, must and will make themselves: But when such Laws do happen to lay any hold, it is so much Impediment to Trade, and therefore prejudicial.[22]

In many respects, North anticipated the spirit of classicism. For instance, he held that consumption was the end of production; he thought that free domestic and foreign trade would be most conducive to the increase of national wealth. It is interesting to note that North based his espousal of free trade on a world-wide view: "That the loss of a Trade with one Nation, is not that only, separately considered, but so much of Trade of the World rescinded and lost, for all is combined together."[23]

---

[20] *Ibid.*, p. 27.

[21] *Ibid.*, p. 28.

[22] *Ibid.*, p. 13.

[23] *Ibid.*, p. 13.

This is a rather unusual viewpoint in North's time. Lionel Robbins observed that even among the classical economists, "there is little evidence that they often went beyond the test of national advantage as a criterion of policy, still less that they were prepared to contemplate the dissolution of national bonds." See his *The Theory of Economic Policy in English Classical Political Economy* (London: Macmillan & Co., 1952), p. 10.

## Bishop George Berkeley (1685–1753)

Like North, Berkeley emphasized the consumption component of aggregate demand as an important determinant of income and employment:

> Whether to provide plentifully for the Poor, be not feeding the Root, the Substance whereof will shoot upwards into the Branches, and cause the Top to flourish?[24]
>
> Whether there be any Instance of a State wherein the People, living neatly and plentifully, did not aspire to Wealth?[25]
>
> Whether comfortable living doth not produce Wants, and Wants Industry, and Industry Wealth?[26]

Berkeley regarded human labor as the "true source of wealth."[27] Hence, idleness and slothfulness were to be discouraged. One way to excite the spirit of industry was to allow people to enjoy the fruits of their labor. Thus "if our Peasants were accustomed to eat Beef and wear Shoes," they would be more industrious.[28]

Although Berkeley was in favor of increasing the consumption spending of the Irish people, he was against the consumption of luxury imports. He was conscious of the undesirable effects of such imports on the economic development of Ireland:

> Whether the imitating those Neighbours in our Fashions, to whom we bear no likeness in our Circumstances, be not one cause of Distress to this Nation?[29]
>
> Whether we are not undone by Fashions made for other People? And whether it be not Madness in a poor Nation to imitate a rich one?[30]

It is interesting to note that the so-called "demonstration effect" on the international plane is not a newly discovered phenomenon. It was recognized in eighteenth-century Ireland.

---

[24] George Berkeley, *The Querist*, Jacob H. Hollander, ed. (Baltimore: The Johns Hopkins Press, 1910), Part I, Query 64, p. 16.

[25] *Ibid.*, Qu. 65, p. 16.

[26] *Ibid.*, Qu. 113, p. 22.

[27] *Ibid.*, Qu. 44, p. 14.

"Whether if human Labour be the true source of Wealth, it doth not follow that Idleness should of all things be discourag'd in a wise State?"

[28] *Ibid.*, Qu. 20, p. 11.

[29] *Ibid.*, Qu. 17, p. 10.

[30] *Ibid.*, Qu. 146, p. 25.

Berkeley was very vehement about such a demonstration effect. He asked: "Whether a Woman of Fashion ought not to be declar'd a public Enemy?" Part I, Qu. 147, p. 25.

The type of unemployment that concerned him greatly was "voluntary" unemployment due to idleness and slothfulness:

> Whether the bulk of our Irish Natives are not kept from thriving
> by that cynical Content in Dirt and Beggary, which they possess to
> a Degree beyond any other People in Christendom?[31]

However, Berkeley was not unaware of "involuntary unemployment":

> Whether the Public hath not a Right to employ those who can not,
> or who will not, find Employment for themselves?[32]

The clause "those who cannot . . . find Employment" could refer only to involuntary unemployment. Berkeley's concern with this type of unemployment is also evidenced by his repeated complaints about emigration from Ireland in search of a livelihood.[33]

Following Petty, Berkeley stressed that the government should employ its tax and expenditure policies to influence aggregate demand and employment. In his opinion taxation could be a means of stimulating the spirit of industry and discouraging idleness.[34] With regard to transfer payments, he thought that poor laws and workhouses would only encourage idleness. He held that if unemployment compensation was set at a mere subsistence level, the idle would prefer work to leisure.[35]

Berkeley recognized the paradox of poverty in the midst of potential plenty:

> Whether we are not in Fact the only People, who may be said to
> starve in the midst of Plenty?[36]

However, he did not have a theory of underemployment equilibrium due to the shortage of aggregate demand. His concept of poverty in the midst of potential plenty was what modern writers would call "the vicious circle of poverty" in underdeveloped countries. He attributed the vicious circle mainly to the consumption of luxury imports on the part of the idle rich and the "cynical Content in Dirt and Beggary" of the masses.[37] Thus, it is fair to say that Berkeley recognized the signifi-

---

[31] *Ibid.*, Qu. 19, p. 10.

[32] Berkeley, *op. cit.*, Part II, Qu. 216, p. 72.

[33] See T. W. Hutchison, "George Berkeley as an Economist: A Comment," *Journal of Political Economy*, LXVIII (June, 1960), 304.

[34] Berkeley, Part II, Qu. 196, p. 70; Qu. 210, p. 71.

[35] Berkeley, Part II, Queries 202, 204, 205, 209, pp. 70–71.

[36] Berkeley, Part III, Qu. 101, p. 90.

[37] Berkeley, Part II, Queries 202, 204, 205, 209, pp. 70–71.

cant role played by aggregate demand in the determination of income and employment, but his main concern was the long-run problem of economic development of Ireland, and not the short-run problem of income determination.

## DAVID HUME (1711–1776)

David Hume was a synthetist. He accepted and refined some of the traditional ideas, such as (1) the glorification of the merchant, (2) the belief in the superiority of manufacturing, (3) the ideal of a strong national state, (4) the elimination of unproductive members of society, and (5) the improvement of a nation's competitive position in international trade through the reduction of production costs. Some of the earlier mercantilists' ideas rejected by him were: (1) the belief that low wages would excite the spirit of industry and lower production costs, (2) the balance-of-trade doctrine, (3) rigid state interventionism and beggar-thy-neighbor type of commercial policy, and (4) the purely monetary theory of interest.

In spirit, Hume was closer to the classical economists than to Keynes. He was not an underconsumption theorist. The paradox of Mandeville was bitterly denounced by him:

> . . . while men of libertine principles bestow praises even on vicious luxury, and represent it as highly advantageous to society; and, on the other hand, men of severe morals blame even the most innocent luxury, and represent it as the source of all corruptions, disorders. . . . We shall here endeavor to correct both these extremes, by proving, first, that the ages of refinement are both the happiest and most virtuous: secondly, that wherever luxury ceases to be innocent, it also ceases to be beneficial. . . .[38]

Hume completely rejected the suggestion of a "paradox of thrift." To him saving and investment were not separate functions. In his time, the merchant was both the saver and the investor; and employment was not determined in the labor market.[39] His justification of the con-

---

[38] Eugene Rotwein, ed., *David Hume: Writings on Economics* (London: Thomas Nelson & Sons, Ltd., 1955), p. 20.

[39] See Karl Polanyi, *The Great Transformation* (4th ed.; Boston: Beacon Press, 1963), Chapter 6.

Polanyi observes:

Mercantilism, with all its tendency towards commercialization, never attacked the safeguards which protected these two basic elements of production—labor and land—from becoming the objects of commerce. In England, the 'nationalization' of labor legislation through the Statute of Artificers (1563) and the

sumption of "innocent luxuries" was not based on the idea of inadequate aggregate demand but on the idea of increasing the rate of economic growth. Hume was of the opinion that the wealth of nations depended essentially on the spirit of industry of the people. Innocent luxury (refinement in arts and conveniences of life) encouraged the spirit of industry, thereby resulting in a higher rate of saving and a higher rate of capital formation.[40] The consumption of luxuries that did not encourage the spirit of industry was regarded by him as "vicious luxury." As his attention was focused solely on the long-run problem of economic growth, he could not see the possibility that spending on such vicious luxury might increase aggregate demand and employment in the short run.

Hume's classicism was further revealed in his views on money and on fiscal policy, especially on public debt. His monetary theory is discussed in Part II. We merely note here that it was at the hands of David Hume that the quantity theory of money took its commonly accepted form.

In his essay, "Of Taxes," Hume emphasized that taxation should not be allowed to destroy the spirit of industry by killing the incentive to save. He rejected the case for egalitarian distribution based on common ownership, but he favored diminution of inequality. How to reduce the prevailing inequalities? He was of the opinion that taxes levied on the poor had already reached the point where incentive for diligence was being threatened. Thus he suggested that taxes be levied on luxuries:

> The best taxes are such as are levied upon consumption, especially those of luxury; because such taxes are least felt by the people. . . . They naturally produce sobriety and frugality, if judiciously imposed. . . .[41]

The objective was encouragement of saving, and not the influencing of aggregate demand.

On the question of public debt, Hume anticipated the attitude of the classical economists. In his essay, "Of Public Credit," Hume

---

Poor Law (1601), removed labor from the danger zone, and the anti-enclosure policy of the Tudors and early Stuarts was one consistent protest against the principle of gainful use of landed property [p. 70].
Polanyi further points out:
Not until 1834 was a competitive labor market established in England; hence, industrial capitalism as a social system cannot be said to have existed before that date [p. 83].

[40] See Hume's essay, "Of Refinement in the Arts," in *David Hume: Writings on Economics*, Rotwein, ed., pp. 19–32.

[41] See Rotwein, ed., *David Hume: Writings on Economics*, p. 85.

warned against the undesirable effects of a growing public debt.[42] He pointed out that: (1) an increase in public debt has an inflationary effect; (2) a growing interest burden of public debt would necessitate raising taxes and increasing transfer payments to the *rentier* class; (3) when foreigners buy such securities, "they render the public, in a manner, tributary to them, and may in time occasion the transport of our people and our industry";[43] and (4) the growth of public debt would encourage the growth of *rentiers* and discourage the spirit of industry. Thus, Hume predicted the eventual breakdown of any economy which tolerated a growing public debt:

> It must, indeed, be one of these two events; either the nation must destroy public credit, or public credit will destroy the nation. It is impossible that they can both subsist, after the manner they have hitherto managed, in this, as well as in some other countries.[44]

Hume failed to distinguish the difference between internal and external debt; nor did he have any idea that debt management could be a powerful tool of fiscal policy.

## Sir James Steuart (1712–1780)

Like Petty and Berkeley, Steuart believed that government could play a positive role in maintaining full employment. He emphasized that fiscal policy could be a useful instrument for influencing aggregate demand:

> Now by the imposition of taxes, and the right employment of the amount of them, a statesman has in his power to retard or to promote the consumption of any branch of industry. By the imposition of duties he may either check luxury when he finds it calling for too many hands from other more necessary occupations; or by granting premiums, he may promote consumption or exportation upon any branches where it is expedient to increase the hands employed.[45]

---

[42] During the 18th century, England was involved in five wars. The public debt increased tremendously during this period. It was 16.4 million pounds in 1701, 78.3 million in 1784, and 252.5 million in 1793—almost sixteen times its original size. See Walter F. Stettner, "Sir James Steuart on the Public Debt," *Quarterly Journal of Economics*, LIX (1945), 451–476.

[43] Rotwein, ed., *David Hume: Writings on Economics*, p. 96.

[44] *Ibid.*, p. 102.

[45] Sir James Steuart, *Principles of Political Oeconomy* (London: 1767), I, 385.

For such purposes, he believed the statesman should carefully examine three variables:

> . . . the propensity of the rich to consume; the disposition of the poor to be industrious; and the proportion of circulating money, with respect to the one and the other.[46]

He also stated:

> The public treasure, by receiving from the amount of taxes, a continual influx of money, may throw it out into the most proper channels, and thereby keep that industry alive.[47]

On the question of debt management, Steuart's views had a decidedly modern ring about them. His position on debt management was opposed to that of Hume and the classical economists who wrote after him. Both Hume and Smith believed that a growing public debt would eventually break down. Steuart, on the other hand, insisted that internal debt would not burden the nation:

> That it is not necessary that public credit should ever fail, from any augmentation of debts, whatever, due to natives; and that it must fail, as soon as the nation becomes totally unable either to export commodities equal to all their imports and foreign debts, or to pay off a proportional part of their capital, sufficient to turn the balance to the right side. From this proposition two corollaries may be drawn. 1mo, That the most important object in paying off debts, is to get quit of those due strangers. 2do, That whatever circumstance has a tendency towards diminishing the burden of foreign debts, should be encouraged.[48]

Steuart emphasized that debt management could be a powerful instrument for influencing aggregate demand:

> That the effect of public borrowing, or national debt is to augment the permanent income of the country, out of the stagnating money, and balance of trade.
>
> If stagnation in one part is found to interrupt circulation in another, public borrowing, for domestic purposes, has the good effect of giving vent to the stagnation, and throwing the money into a new channel of circulation.[49]

---

[46] Steuart, I, 375.
[47] Steuart, I, 393.
[48] Steuart, II, 463–464.
[49] Steuart, II, 452.

There is no doubt that Steuart recognized the basic proposition that
the level of income and employment is determined by aggregate demand. In his discussion of the evolution of trade, Steuart distinguished
two principles of policy. (1) In a nation experiencing an export surplus,
frugality should be encouraged. The government should check consumption and bring down both the price of food and wages of labor in
order to increase the supply of exports. (2) Steuart believed that a nation which found that the balance of trade had turned against it should
abandon foreign trade. However, he held that full employment could
still be maintained at home if aggregate demand were kept up by
increasing consumption:

> . . . if the consequence should prove a general stop to exportation,
> then in foreign trade decently interred, without any violent revo-
> lution; because the statesman is supposed to have proceeded gradu-
> ally, and to have been all the while labouring to increase consump-
> tion at home, in proportion as the industrious have been forced to
> lie idle by the other operation.[50]

---

[50] Steuart, I, 506.

The discussion on the stages of foreign trade led Steuart to his "Listian" argument for protection. He pointed out that free trade would be detrimental to those
less frugal and less industrious countries. Unless countries were on the same foot-
ing, universal free trade would not be feasible. He wrote:

> Were industry and frugality found to prevail equally in every part of the
> great political bodies, or were luxury and superfluous consumption every-
> where carried to the same height, trade might, without any hurt, be thrown
> entirely open. It would then cease to be an object of a Statesman's care and
> concern [p. 506].

However, Steuart was mindful of belligerent nationalism:

> On the other hand, were all nations equally careful to check every branch of
> unprofitable commerce, a general stagnation of trade would soon be brought
> about [p. 506].

# 2

# Classical Theory of Income and Employment

## SUPPLY-ORIENTED THEORY

Classical economic theory was essentially macroeconomics. The problem of efficient allocation of given resources within a closed economy was a subsidiary theme, not the main concern. As observed by Professor Hla Myint, Adam Smith confined his exposition on the nature of competitive equilibrium to a very narrow section of *The Wealth of Nations*, namely, Chapters 7 and 10, Book I; and after Smith, few major classical writers developed this theme in a significant way.[1]

The economic problem considered paramount by the classical economists was the long-run problem of growth of the economy's productive capacity. Their analysis played down the demand side of the growth process and focused upon the supply side. In this chapter, however, our main concern is the classical theory of income and employment in the short run.

---

[1] See Hla Myint, *Theories of Welfare Economics* (New York: Augustus M. Kelley, Publishers, Reprint of Economic Classics, 1962), Chap. 4.

Professor Myint points out:

The main source of textual evidence for interpreting the classical concept of competition as the allocator of resources within a given closed economy is the *Wealth of Nations*. After Adam Smith, none of the major classical economists developed this trend of thought in any significant way. Ricardo and Malthus were content to accept Smith's theory of competition without further modification and amplification as far as its application to domestic trade within the closed economy was concerned. (Ricardo, *Principles*, Everyman's ed., p. 50.) The forerunners of the marginal analysis such as Senior and Longfield had important contributions to make to the theory of competitive equilibrium. They, however, exerted little influence on the main stream of classical tradition which continued undisturbed until Cairnes introduced his idea of "noncompeting groups" within the domestic economy [p. 55].

We have been brought up on the belief that classical analysis was aimed at the long run. As Professor Leontief has observed, "the classical approach suffers from what might be called theoretical farsightedness—the ability to appraise correctly the long-run trends, coupled with a singular inability to explain or even to describe the short-run changes and fluctuations."[2] The question facing us is whether we can meaningfully extract from the long-run classical analysis a short-run theory of income determination. To do so, we have to derive clues from three sources: the wages-fund doctrine, the "glut controversy", and Say's Law of markets. We shall find that the mainstream of classical analysis in this connection, too, was supply-oriented. Only the dissenters and heretics, such as Malthus, author of *Principles of Political Economy*, attempted to play up the role of effective demand.[3]

The supply-oriented theory of income and employment of the classical economists was based on the assumption that aggregate demand would always take care of itself. Adam Smith and the Ricardians all embraced this view.

### Adam Smith (1723–1790)

The adequacy of aggregate demand was implied in Smith's discussion of parsimony. Following Turgot, Smith stressed that voluntary saving created capital:

> Capitals are increased by parsimony, and diminished by prodigality and misconduct.
>
> Whatever a person saves from his revenue he adds to his capital, and either employs it himself in maintaining an additional number of productive hands, or enables some other person to do so, by lending it to him for an interest, that is, for a share of the profits. As the capital of an individual can be increased only by what he saves from his annual revenue or his annual gains, so the capital of a society, which is the same with that of all the individuals who compose it, can be increased only in the same manner.
>
> What is annually saved is as regularly consumed as what is annually spent, and nearly in the same time too; but it is consumed by a different set of people.[4]

---

[2] Wassily Leontief, "Postulates: Keynes' General Theory and the Classicists," in *The New Economics*, Seymour E Harris, ed. (New York: Alfred A. Knopf, 1947), p. 240.

[3] As generally recognized, there were "two Malthuses," namely, the Malthus of *The Theory of Population* and the Malthus of the *Principles*. The first Malthus was an architect of classical economics. Then he changed his mind and became the heretic of the *Principles*.

[4] Adam Smith, *The Wealth of Nations*, Edwin Cannan, ed. (New York: Random House, Inc., 1937), p. 321.

It is clear that the spirit of Say's Law permeated Smith's theory of saving and investment. Smith did not concede the possibility of over-saving, or shortage in aggregate demand under normal conditions:

> In all countries where there is tolerable security, every man of common understanding will endeavor to employ whatever stock he can command, in procuring either present enjoyment or future profit. If it is employed in procuring present enjoyment, it is a stock reserved for immediate consumption. If it is employed in procuring future profit, it must procure this profit either by staying with him, or by going from him. In the one case it is a fixed, in the other it is a circulating capital. A man must be perfectly crazy who, where there is tolerable security, does not employ all the stock which he commands, whether it be his own or borrowed of other people, in some one or other of those three ways.[5]

Smith's idea that what was saved would be expended was also reflected in his concept of the role of money. To Smith, money was under normal conditions a medium of exchange:

> Money, therefore, the great wheel of circulation, the great instrument of commerce, like all other instruments of trade, though it makes a part and a very valuable part of the capital, makes no part of the revenue of the society to which it belongs. . . .[6]

Only under abnormal conditions would money be hoarded:

> In those unfortunate countries, indeed, where men are continually afraid of the violence of their superiors, they frequently bury and conceal a great part of their stock, in order to have it always at hand to carry with them to some place of safety, in case of their being threatened with any of those disasters to which they consider themselves as at all times exposed.[7]

Recently, Professor Hicks called attention to the connection between the methodology employed by the classical writers and the postulates

---

This is what Schumpeter called the "Turgot-Smith theory of saving and investment." See Schumpeter's *History of Economic Analysis* (New York: Oxford University Press, Inc., 1955), pp. 324–327.

Schumpeter observed:

First . . . Turgot's theory proved almost unbelievably hardy. It is doubtful whether Alfred Marshall had advanced beyond it, certain that J. S. Mill had not. Böhm-Bawerk no doubt added a new branch to it, but substantially he subscribed to Turgot's propositions. Second, the theory was not only swallowed by the large majority of economists: it was swallowed hook, line, and sinker [p. 325].

[5] Smith, p. 268.

[6] Smith, p. 276.

[7] Smith, p. 268.

grouped under "Say's Law."[8] According to Professor Hicks, the classical economists employed the method of static equilibrium to explain the dynamics of economic growth. To make it applicable to dynamic theory, they introduced two simplifications: (1) the confinement of capital goods to circulating capital, and (2) the implicit assumption of homogeneous "capital." By means of these simplifications, the unit period of the basic classical model was made to be self-contained. The self-contained single period was the agricultural year; and the process of change was treated as a sequence of such self-contained unit periods. This was the methodology employed by Adam Smith.

> There is no fixed capital in Smith's (formal) model; but he does have something that corresponds to gross investment. This "gross investment" is (it has to be) net investment plus replacement of the using up of circulating capital. The labour which is employed in this "gross investment" he calls "productive labour." Thus it is productive labour that plays the same part in his system as gross investment does in ours. It is unproductive labor which corresponds to our consumption sector. . . .[9]

The initial capital stock was the previous year's harvest, a certain quantity of corn. This was the wages fund. If the corn-wage rate was given, the number of productive laborers employed would be determined by this wages fund. As a device for preliminary exploration of dynamic theory, this methodology is acceptable. However, the reverse side of the Smithian achievement is the birth of the classical doctrine of saving and investment. For "if there is just one homogeneous 'capital' there is nothing to do with our savings but to invest them in this 'capital'; there can be no problem of malinvestment—or of saving going to waste."[10]

The static method employed by Adam Smith and the classical writers also led them to overlook the role of expectations in economic decision making. They paid no attention to uncertainty and liquidity. Hence, the bridge between real theory and monetary theory remained unbuilt. The neoclassical writers did not break away from the classical heritage. Although Marshall clearly perceived the difficulties involved in the classical static method, he did not develop a dynamic analysis to take its place. Instead, Marshall invented the partial equilibrium analysis and concentrated on microeconomics.

---

[8] See John Hicks, *Capital and Growth* (New York: Oxford University Press, Inc., 1965), Chaps. 2 and 3.

[9] Hicks, p. 37.

[10] Hicks, p. 35.

Assuming that demand would take care of itself, Smith approached the problem of growth in the wealth of nations from the side of supply. In the "Introduction and Plan" of *The Wealth of Nations,* he pointed out that a nation's annual output was affected by two determinants:

> first, by the skill, dexterity, and judgement with which its labour is generally applied; and, secondly, by the proportion between the number of those who are employed in useful labour, and that of those who are not so employed. Whatever be the soil, climate, or extent of territory of any particular nation, the abundance or scantiness of its annual supply must, in that particular situation, depend upon those two circumstances.[11]

In other words, he maintained that annual output was determined by the state of technology, which increased the productivity of the labor force, and by the allocation of the labor force among productive and unproductive activity. Smith adopted and enlarged the Physiocratic distinction between productive and unproductive labor. In *The Wealth of Nations* he explained:

> There is one sort of labour which adds to the value of the subject upon which it is bestowed: there is another which has no such effect. The former, as it produces a value, may be called productive; the latter, unproductive labour. Thus the labour of a manufacturer adds, generally, to the value of the materials which he works upon, that of his own maintenance, and of his master's profit. The labour of a menial servant, on the contrary, adds to the value of nothing.[12]

---

[11] Adam Smith, *The Wealth of Nations,* p. lvii.

This is what Hla Myint calls "the labour theory outlook on the economic problem."

Professor Myint in *Theories of Welfare Economics* observes:

The labour theory depicts a primitive agricultural community, self-sufficient and having only a rudimentary system of exchange. In this setting it is natural to look upon production as the struggle of man against nature and to measure wealth in terms of the physical product of labour [pp. 2–3].

[12] Adam Smith, *The Wealth of Nations,* p. 314.

This is what Paul Studenski calls the "restricted production concept" of national income. See his *The Income of Nations* (New York: New York University Press, 1958), Part I, pp. 18–20.

Professor Studenski observes:

Adam Smith viewed the economic process not as a circulation of consumable and investible goods and income, but wholly as the circulation of entrepreneurial fixed and operating capital. The entrepreneur's advances of wages and other operating expenses are returned to him, and profits are created for him in the process of production, thereby insuring the continuation of the process. Only "productive labor" has this capacity of reproducing its own value and creating profit. Labor engaged in the rendering of services does not reproduce its costs or produce profits. Although such labor "has its value and

The key to the Smithian theory of income determination in the short run lies in the following passage:

> Both productive and unproductive labourers, and those who do not labour at all, are all equally maintained by the annual produce of the land and labour of the country. This produce, how great soever, can never be infinite, but must have certain limits. According, therefore, as a smaller or greater proportion of it is in any one year employed in maintaining unproductive hands, the more in the one case and the less in the other will remain for the productive, and the next year's produce will be greater or smaller accordingly; the whole annual produce, if we except the spontaneous productions of the earth, being the effect of productive labour.[13]

This passage clearly means that, given the state of technology and hence the productivity of labor, the annual national output depends upon the quantity of productive labor employed. If $(Y)$ represents the annual output [$(Y/L)$ signifies the average productivity of labor], and the quantity of productive labor is represented by $(L)$, then the Smithian idea of income determination may be summarized by the equation: $Y = (Y/L) \cdot L$.[14] It was, undoubtedly, a supply-oriented theory. Smith believed that $(Y/L)$ would be increasing over the course of time owing to the increasing division of labor and specialization.

The Smithian theory of income and employment is intimately related to his "wages-fund doctrine." This doctrine was one of the pillars of the classical system.[15] It was used by the classical economists both as a joint theory of capital and wages, as Professor Fellner puts it,[16] and

---

deserves its rewards," it represents the consumption and not the production of wealth [p. 19].

Professor Studenski further points out:

Adam Smith was also responsible for introducing new sources of confusion that were to plague economists for many years to come. Thus, he erroneously concerned himself with wealth primarily in terms of a "stock of goods," seriously neglecting its aspects as a "flow" of utilities, i.e., of national income. In this respect his analysis was a backward step. . . . Adam Smith's differentiation between productive and unproductive labor on the basis of the materiality or immateriality of its product, i.e., his restriction of the concept of production to material objects, viewed in a broad historical perspective, was also a major error [p. 19].

[13] Adam Smith, *The Wealth of Nations*, p. 315.

[14] For specific illustrations, see Hla Myint, *Theories of Welfare Economics*, pp. 18–26.

[15] See T. W. Hutchison, *A Review of Economic Doctrines 1870–1929* (London: Oxford University Press, 1953), pp. 12–13. Hutchison states the four pillars as follows: (1) The Wages Fund Theory, (2) The Malthusian Theory of Population, (3) The Ricardian Theory of Rent, and (4) The Labor Theory of Value.

[16] A lucid exposition of the wages-fund doctrine is given by William Fellner in his *Emergence and Content of Modern Economic Analysis* (New York: McGraw-Hill Book Company, 1960), pp. 56–59.

as an explanation for two types of unemployment, namely, (1) unemployment caused by excessively high wages, and (2) unemployment caused by insufficient capital stock.

The essence of the doctrine may be summarized as follows. The working capital existing at the beginning of any period has been saved out of the total output of the previous period. A part of this capital stock (savings) is used for wage payments of the current period. This is the so-called wages fund, which is the real or physical equivalent in the money-wage bill. Labor depends upon this wages fund for support. The money-wage rate is determined by the ratio obtained by dividing the number of laborers employed into the wages fund. Symbolically, this relationship may be stated as:

$$W_{(t-1)} = w_{(t)} \cdot L_{(t)}$$
$$w_{(t)} = W_{(t-1)}/L_{(t)}$$

where $W_{(t-1)}$ is the wages fund at the beginning of the period (which is equivalent to savings of the previous period); $w_{(t)}$ denotes the current money-wage rate; and $L_{(t)}$ symbolizes the number of laborers employed in the current period $(t)$. This relationship is depicted in Figure 2-1.

In Figure 2-1, the wages fund (savings) is plotted on the vertical axis; the volume of employment is plotted on the horizontal axis. The vector from the origin defines the current money-wage rate. A rise in the money-wage rate will be indicated by rotating the vector counterclockwise. A lowering of the money-wage rate will be indicated by rotating the vector clockwise. The volume of employment evidently depends upon two factors, namely, the wages fund (savings) and the money-wage rate. Given the money-wage rate, employment is an increasing function of savings (wages fund). Given the wages fund, em-

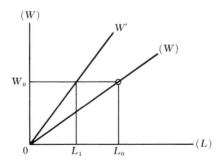

**Figure 2-1**

ployment is a decreasing function of the money-wage rate. If the money-wage rate is set too high, as represented by the vector $(0W')$ in the diagram, the given wages fund $(W_o)$ can only employ fewer workers, resulting in unemployment of $(L_1L_o)$ workers.

An increase in the wages fund (savings) would increase employment. Thus one of the practical maxims of classical economists was that encouragement of saving and control of the birth rate would be two feasible ways of uplifting the laboring poor.[17]

Adam Smith states the wages-fund doctrine in Chapter 8 of *The Wealth of Nations* as follows:

> The demand for those who live by wages, it is evident, cannot increase but in proportion to the increase of the funds which are destined for the payment of wages. These funds are of two kinds; first, the revenue which is over and above what is necessary for the maintenance; and, secondly, the stock which is over and above what is necessary for the employment of their masters.[18]

> The demand for those who live by wages, therefore, necessarily increases with the increase of the revenue and stock of every country, and cannot possibly increase without it. The increase of revenue and stock is the increase of national wealth. The demand for those who live by wages, therefore, naturally increases with the increase of national wealth, and cannot possibly increase without it.

> It is not the actual greatness of national wealth, but continual increase, which occasions a rise in the wages of labour. It is not, accordingly, in the richest countries, but in the most thriving, or in those which are growing rich the fastest, that the wages of labour are highest. England is certainly, in the present times, a much richer country than any part of North America. The wages of labour, however, are much higher in North America than in any part of England.[19]

It is evident from the preceding passages that the Smithian theory of income and employment is closely related to the wages-fund doctrine and the doctrine of productive labor. Total output $(Y_t)$ is determined by the quantity of productive labor $(L_t)$, given the productivity of labor $(Y/L)$. A part of this total output is destined to be the wages

---

[17] See R. F. Harrod *Towards A Dynamic Economics* (London: Macmillan & Co., 1956), p. 17. The three practical maxims listed by Harrod are: (1) Free Trade, (2) "saving by those of means would confer more lasting benefit on the labouring poor than charity, and (3) that the main method open to the poor for self-improvement was to raise their concept of a proper standard of living and by consequence reduce the birth rate."

[18] Adam Smith, *The Wealth of Nations*, p. 69.

[19] *Ibid.*

fund, which determines the volume of employment in the next period $(L_{t+1})$, given the money-wage rate.

### Jean Baptiste Say (1767–1832)

Say's law of markets was fundamental to the mainstream of classical economics. Say's law implies denial of the possibility of underemployment equilibrium.[20] Following Smith, Say, in his *Treatise on Political Economy* (1803), held that over-saving was impossible:

> It must on no account be overlooked, that, in one way or another, a saving such as that we have been speaking of, whether expended productively or unproductively, still is in all cases expended and consumed; and this is a truth, that must remove a notion extremely false, though very much in vogue—namely, that saving limits and injures consumption. No act of saving subtracts in the least from consumption, provided the thing saved be reinvested or restored to productive employment. On the contrary, it gives rise to a consumption perpetually renovated and recurring. . . . Capitalists have nearly the same advantage: they invest their whole savings in the same manner as their former capital is invested. . . .[21]

Say further pointed out that money was merely a medium of exchange and had no utility of its own:

> I say, you want other commodities, and not money. For what, in point of fact, do you want money? Is it not for the purchase of raw materials or stock for your trade, or victuals for your support? Wherefore, it is products that you want, and not money. . . . For after all, money is but the agent of the transfer of values. Its whole utility has consisted in conveying to your hands the value of the commodities. . . . Money performs but a monetary function in this double exchange; and when the transaction is finally closed, it will

---

[20] Say directed his law of markets against the underconsumption thesis of the Physiocrats and the oversaving thesis of Lord Lauderdale and other dissenters. See J. J. Spengler, "The Physiocrats and Say's Law of Markets," reprinted from *Journal of Political Economy*, LIII (September-December, 1945), in *Essays in Economic Thought*, Spengler and Allen, eds. (Chicago: Rand McNally & Co., 1960), pp. 161–214.

Prof. Spengler observes:

Perhaps as a result of Smith's inspiration, Say generalized the physiocratic thesis—that men need not be spurred to produce by the prospect of obtaining manufactures—into the thesis that men need not be excited by luxuries, since wants multiply at least as fast as they can be supplied [p. 195].

[21] J. B. Say, "A Treatise on Political Economy," in *Readings in Economics*, K. William Kapp and Lore L. Kapp, eds. (New York: Barnes & Noble, Inc., 1946), pp. 170–171.

always be found, that one kind of produce has been exchanged for another.[22]

Since, in Say's view, savings would always be offset by investment and since hoarding would always be zero, aggregate demand would always suffice.

It is worth while to remark, that a product is no sooner created, than it, from that instant, affords a market for other products to the full extent of its own value.[23]

Temporary over-production of a particular commodity was possible, but general over-production was not:

I answer, that the glut of a particular commodity arises from its having outrun the total demand for it in one of the two ways; either because it has been produced in excessive abundance, or because the produce of other commodities has fallen short.[24]

Such transient particular gluts could be corrected, should there be laissez faire in economic affairs:

No sooner is the cause of this political disease removed, than the means of production feel a natural impulse towards the vacant channels, the replenishment of which restores activity to all others.[25]

The total supply of products and the total demand for them must of necessity be equal, for the total demand is nothing by the whole mass of commodities which have been produced: a general congestion would consequently be an absurdity.[26]

Unfortunately, none of the classical writers provided a logical and adequate proof of Say's Law, nor did the neoclassical economists.[27] It was not until recently, after the post-Keynesian re-evaluation of the

---

[22] J. B. Say, "A Treatise on Political Economy," in *Readings in the History of Economic Thought*, S. Howard Patterson, ed. (New York: McGraw-Hill Book Company, 1932), pp. 66-68.

[23] *Ibid.*, p. 68.

[24] *Ibid.*, p. 68.

[25] *Ibid.*, p. 69.

[26] Say's *Treatise*, 1st ed., II, 175, cited by C. Gide and C. Rist in *A History of Economic Doctrines* (2nd English ed.; New York: D. C. Heath & Company, 1948), p. 131.

[27] This point is based on the observations of William Fellner. See his *Emergence & Content of Modern Economic Analysis*, pp. 80–83; also Mark Blaug, *Economic Theory in Retrospect* (Homewood, Ill.: Richard D. Irwin, Inc., 1962), Chap. 5.

logical consistency of classical monetary theory, that the concept was clarified.[28]

Upon re-examination of Say's Law, post-Keynesian writers concluded that two different concepts of the law should be distinguished: "Say's Identity" and "Say's Equality." The term "Say's Identity" was coined by Oscar Lange.[29] In the words of Professors Becker and Baumol, Say's Identity refers to the idea that "the supply of commodities will create its own demand irrespective of the behavior of the stock of cash and the price level."[30] This means that the output and the money markets will always be in equilibrium. The following example illustrates how this notion is derived from a general equilibrium framework:

Assume that there are $(n)$ goods in exchange in a closed economy. If the $(nth)$ good is selected as the *numéraire*, the price of the $(nth)$ good is determined. $P_n = 1$. This equation means that a dollar is a dollar; it is money of account.

There will be $(n-1)$ equilibrium prices left to be determined. In the determination of the equilibrium price for each of the $(n-1)$ goods, three equations will be involved:

A demand equation ........... $D_i = D_i(P_1, P_2, \ldots P_{n-1})$
A supply equation ............ $S_i = S_i(P_1, P_2, \ldots P_{n-1})$
An equilibrium condition ....... $D_i = S_i$, or $D_i - S_i = 0$
$$(i = 1, 2, 3, \ldots n - 1)$$

General equilibrium requires that all the $(n)$ number of excess demand equations be equal to zero. If money is only a unit of account, then the following identities hold:

Demand for goods $\equiv$ Supply of money

Symbolically,

$$\sum_{i=1}^{n-1} P_i D_i \equiv S_n, (i = 1, 2, 3, \ldots, n)$$

---

[28] The so-called post-Keynesian doctrinal controversy is lucidly summarized by Gary S. Becker and William J. Baumol in "The Classical Monetary Theory: The Outcome of the Discussion," reprinted from *Economica*, XIX (November, 1952), in *Essays in Economic Thought*, Spengler and Allen, eds. (Chicago: Rand McNally & Co., 1960).

[29] See Oscar Lange, "Say's Law: A Restatement and Criticism," in *Studies in Mathematical Economics & Econometrics*, Lange, McIntyre, & Yntema, eds. (Chicago: University of Chicago Press, 1942).

[30] Becker & Baumol, "The Classical Monetary Theory," in *Essays in Economic Thought*, p. 759.

Supply of goods $\equiv$ Demand for money

Symbolically,

$$\sum_{i=1}^{n-1} P_i S_i \equiv D_n, (i = 1, 2, 3, \ldots, n)$$

Total demand measured in money value for the $(n)$ goods:

$$\sum_{i=1}^{n} P_i D_i \equiv \sum_{i=1}^{n-1} P_i D_i + D_n \equiv S_n + D_n$$

Total supply measured in money value for the $(n)$ goods:

$$\sum_{i=1}^{n} P_i S_i \equiv \sum_{i=1}^{n-1} P_i S_i + S_n \equiv D_n + S_n$$

It follows that the total money value of all items supplied must equal the total money value of all items demanded. In algebraic notation,

$$\sum_{i=1}^{n} P_i S_i \equiv \sum_{i=1}^{n} P_i D_i$$

This identity is called "Walras' Law." It is used to indicate that one of the general-equilibrium equations is redundant. For instance, if we find prices which satisfy all but one of the supply and demand equations of the general equilibrium system, Walras' Law then tells us, by subtraction, that the supply and demand of the remaining item must necessarily be equal. Symbolically, Walras' Law [identity] is:

$$\sum_{i=1}^{n} P_i S_i \equiv \sum_{i=1}^{n} P_i D_i \, (i = 1, 2, 3, 4, \ldots, n)$$

Subtract the following equation from Walras' Law [identity]:

$$\sum_{i=2}^{n} P_i S_i = \sum_{i=2}^{n} P_i D_i \, (i = 2, 3, 4, \ldots, n)$$

The desired result is obtained:

$$P_1 S_1 = P_1 D_1$$

Thus, Walras' Law permits us to drop any single equation of our choice.[31]

---

[31] The reader will recall that this is the methodology adopted in any general equilibrium theory. For instance, Professor Patinkin in his "Keynesian Economics and the Quantity Theory" writes:

If the matter is left here, there is no problem concerning the internal logical consistency of the general equilibrium system. Unfortunately, as pointed out by Professor Baumol, "a number of more or less plausible-sounding assumptions have been made about the real sector which, without its being realized by those who made them, served effectively to destroy any mechanism for the determination of the price level. For *these assumptions make it impossible for any change in the price level to produce equilibrium or disequilibrium.*"[32]

One of the pitfalls in the determination of the price level has come to be known as Say's Identity, which is a caricature of Say's Law found in most modern references. It amounts to the stronger assertion that money has no utility of its own. Hence, people do not want money except to buy goods at once. It follows that general overproduction of commodities is impossible and that the total supply of goods (excluding money) must be identical to the total demand for goods. Using the notation of Walras' Law [identity], Say's Identity may be written as shown in Table 2-1.

Table 2-1

| Real Sector | Money Sector |
|---|---|
| $$\sum_{i=1}^{n-1} P_i S_i \equiv \sum_{i=1}^{n-1} P_i D_i$$ | $S_n \equiv D_n$, or in the more familiar symbols: <br> $M \equiv L$, or <br> $M \equiv kPY$ |

As aptly put by Professor Baumol, "Since Say's Identity requires that the goods markets, taken as a whole, must always be in equilibrium (total supply for all goods equals total demand) it follows by Walras' Law that the remaining market, the money market, must also always be in equilibrium. It is impossible for any change in the price level (or

---

Let us assume that the economy consists only of four markets: those for finished goods, labor services, bonds, and money, respectively. In each of these markets we have a demand function, a supply function, and a statement of the equilibrium condition: namely, a statement that prices, wages, and the interest rate are such that the amount demanded in the market equals the amount supplied. By virtue of what has come to be called Walras' Law, we know that if equilibrium exists in any three of these markets, then it must also exist in the fourth. Hence, in examining the equilibrium of the system as a whole, it suffices to concentrate on the markets for finished goods, labor services, and money, respectively, and to exclude from our explicit consideration the market for bonds.
See K. K. Kurihara, ed., *Post-Keynesian Economics* (New Brunswick, N.J.: Rutgers University Press, 1954), p. 125.

[32] William J. Baumol, *Economic Theory and Operations Analysis* (2nd ed.; Englewood Cliffs, N.J.: Prentice-Hall, Inc., 1965), p. 343.

any change in anything else, for that matter) ever to produce disequilibrium in the money market. As a result, Say's Identity also pre-
cludes the determination of any price level by any relationship of
monetary theory."[33] This is the essence of the Lange-Patinkin argument
that Say's Law is inconsistent with the quantity theory of money.

The concept of Say's Identity clearly ignores both monetary theory
and business cycle theory. It is the main target of Keynesian economics.

On the other hand, Say's Equality refers to the idea that the equilibrium conditions for both the output and money markets are genuine
equations and not identities. This is presented symbolically in Table
2-2.

**Table 2-2**

| Output Market | Money Market |
|---|---|
| $\sum_{i=1}^{n-1} P_i S_i = \sum_{i=1}^{n-1} P_i D_i$ | $S_n = D_n$, or, <br> $M = L$ [in Keynesian terminology] <br> or, <br> $M = kPY$ [The quantity theory of money] |

The meaning of Say's Equality is that the output market will be
in equilibrium, *if, and only if*, excess demand in the money market is
zero. Thus, Say's Equality is consistent with the quantity theory of
money. The absolute price level is determinate and there is no dichotomization of the pricing process. The essence of Say's Equality is that
price flexibility will automatically assure full-employment equilibrium.
The classical writers recognized this proposition, but none of them
spelled it out consistently. The result of this neglect is the misleading
impression that they upheld the concept of Say's Identity.

### David Ricardo (1772–1823)

The supply-oriented theory of income and employment was perpetuated by Ricardo and his followers. The Ricardians argued that a
general glut was impossible because savings would automatically flow
into investment and supply (production) would create its own demand
via Say's Law. The Ricardian version of Say's Law follows:

> M. Say has, however, most satisfactorily shown that there is no
> amount of capital which may not be employed in a country, be-
> cause a demand is only limited by production. No man produces

---

[33] Baumol, p. 346.

but with a view to consume or sell, and he never sells but with an intention to purchase some other commodity, which may be immediately useful to him, or which may contribute to future production. By producing, then, he necessarily becomes either the consumer of his own goods, or the purchaser and consumer of the goods of some other person. It is not to be supposed that he should, for any length of time, be ill-informed of the commodities which he can most advantageously produce, to attain the object which he has in view, namely, the possession of other goods; and, therefore, it is not probable that he will continually produce a commodity for which there is no demand.[34]

Productions are always bought by productions, or by services; money is only the medium by which the exchange is effected. Too much of a particular commodity may be produced, of which there may be such a glut in the market as not to repay the capital expended on it; but this cannot be the case with respect to all commodities. . . .[35]

Like Smith, Ricardo approached the problem of determination of income and employment from the supply side. He believed that, given the productivity of labor $(Y/L)$, total output $(Y)$ was determined by the quantity of productive labor embodied in its production $(L)$. However, he qualified the Smithian vision of unlimited expansion and increasing returns by introducing the concept of diminishing returns from land. He pointed out:

Adam Smith constantly magnifies the advantages which a country derives from a large gross, rather than a large net income.[36]

The difference of opinion between Smith and Ricardo may be illustrated by the following numerical example: Given $(Y/L = 1000/600)$, the total output will be 1000, if the quantity of productive labor embodied in its production is $600[Y = Y/L \ (L)]$. Suppose the wage rate is equal to one unit of total output. Then the total output of 1000 will command or employ 1000 productive laborers. Adam Smith considered this value of total output to be a positive index of the economic welfare of society.[37] But Ricardo argued that a positive index should be the net income, which was derived by deducting the total wage bill (in our numerical example, this should be $600 = w \cdot L = 1 \cdot 600$, where $w$ de-

---

[34] David Ricardo, *The Principles of Political Economy and Taxation*, Everyman's Library, No. 590 (London: J. M. Dent & Sons Ltd., 1955), pp. 192–193.

[35] Ricardo, p. 194.

[36] Ricardo, p. 234.

[37] This idea is based on the views of Hla Myint. See his *Theories of Welfare Economics*, pp. 26–33.

notes the wage rate) from the total output $(1000 - 600 = 400 = \text{net income})$.

Although Ricardo emphasized net income, his prescription for increasing wealth followed the Smithian line:

> . . . the wealth of a country may be increased in two ways: it may
> be increased by employing a greater portion of revenue in the
> maintenance of productive labour, which will not only add to the
> quantity, but to the value of the mass of commodities; or it may
> be increased, without employing any additional quantity of labour,
> by making the same quantity more productive, which will add to
> the abundance, but not to the value of commodities.[38]

In other words, total output $(Y)$ could be increased either by increasing savings (the wages fund) or by technological progress, which increases labor productivity.

In embracing Say's Law, Ricardo denied the possibility of a general glut and the type of unemployment caused by a chronic shortage of effective demand.[39] However, this is not to say that Ricardo was unaware of other types of unemployment in his time. The types of unemployment recognized by Ricardo and his contemporaries may be classified under the following headings: (1) seasonal unemployment, (2) structural unemployment caused by changes in demand, (3) unemployment caused by setting the money-wage rate too high, (4) unemployment caused by insufficient capital stock, or lack of savings, and (5) technological unemployment.

The first type, seasonal unemployment, was explicitly recognized by the pre-Smithian writers.[40] The second type, structural unemployment, was considered by Ricardo in his *Principles*, Chapter 19, "On Sudden Changes in the Channels of Trade." The third and fourth types, as mentioned before, were explained by the wages-fund doctrine.

---

[38] Ricardo, *op. cit.*, pp. 185–186.
It should be noted that Ricardo distinguished between "abundance" and "value." "Abundance" signifies "riches" which is represented by the physical magnitude of the total output; whereas "value" depends upon the quantity of labor embodied in the production of the total output.

Professor Myint in *Theories of Welfare Economics* observes:
Value . . . may be regarded as an inverse index of the physical productivity of labour. Thus a technical development . . . will increase the "riches"; but it will lower the (average) "value" of these products since they now require a smaller quantity of labour "embodied" per unit in their production [p. 27].

[39] See Blaug, "Malthus' Heresy on Gluts," *Ricardian Economics*, Chap. 5; Blaug, "Say's Law and Classical Monetary Theory," *Economic Theory in Retrospect*, Chap. 5; William Fellner, "Say's Law and the Question of Full Employment," *Emergence and Content of Modern Economic Analysis*, Chap. 8; B. A. Corry, *Money, Saving and Investment in English Economics 1800–1850* (London: Macmillan & Co., 1962), pp. 114–153.

[40] See Blaug, *Economic Theory in Retrospect*, p. 14.

As to the question of technological unemployment, Ricardo originally followed the optimistic Smith-Say view of the impossibility of chronic technological unemployment. After the publication (in 1817) of John Barton's *Observations on the Circumstances which Influence the Condition of the Labouring Class of Society*, Ricardo's complacency was shaken.[41]

In the third edition of his *Principles*, Ricardo conceded:

> I am convinced that the substitution of machinery for human labour is often very injurious to the interests of the class of labourers.
>
> My mistake arose from the supposition that whenever the net income of a society increased, its gross income would also increase; I now, however, see reason to be satisfied that one fund, from which landlords and capitalists derive their revenue, may increase, while the other, that upon which the labouring mainly depend, may diminish, and therefore it follows, if I am right, that the same cause which may increase the net revenue of a country may at the same time render the population redundant, and deteriorate the condition of the labourer.[42]

In other words, Ricardo recognized that with the introduction of fixed capital his original basic model was undermined. That model was built upon two simplifications, namely, (1) the confinement of capital to circulating capital only (wages fund), and (2) homogeneity of capital goods (corn). The conversion of part of the wages fund into fixed capital means that the wages fund (the demand for labor) is diminished. Hence the introduction of labor-saving machinery tends to displace labor with consequent adverse effects on wages.

However, Ricardo pointed out:

> The statements which I have made will not, I hope, lead to the inference that machinery should not be encouraged. To elucidate the principle, I have been supposing that improved machinery is suddenly discovered and extensively used; but the truth is that these discoveries are gradual, and rather operate in determining the employment of capital which is saved and accumulated than in diverting capital from its actual employment.[43]

---

[41] See G. Sotiroff, "John Barton (1789–1852)," *The Economic Journal*, Vol. LXII (March, 1952); Mark Blaug, *Ricardian Economics*, pp. 64–74; B. A. Corry, *Money, Saving and Investment in English Economics 1800–1850*, pp. 30–32; and Knut Wicksell, *Lectures on Political Economy*, E. Classen, trans. and L. Robbins, ed. (New York: The Macmillan Company, 1953), I, 133–144.

[42] Ricardo, *op. cit.*, p. 264.

[43] Ricardo, pp. 269–270.

Furthermore, Ricardo emphasized that "he would not tolerate any law to prevent the use of machinery," because "if they gave up a system which enabled them to undersell in the foreign market, would other nations refrain from pursuing it? Certainly not. They were therefore bound, for their own interest, to continue it."[44] Ricardo then reasserted the practical maxim of classical economics. He pointed out that "if the supply of labour were greater than could be employed, then the people must be miserable. But the people had the remedy in their own hands. A little forethought, a little prudence (which probably they would exert, if they were not made such machines of by the poor-laws), a little of that caution which the better educated felt it necessary to use, would enable them to improve their situation."[45]

In spite of these consoling thoughts, Ricardo left the question in "this unsatisfactory position" until the problem was much later reconsidered by the marginalists.[46]

It is interesting to note that Ricardo was mainly responsible for changing the course of economics from what Professor Baumol has called the "magnificent dynamics"[47] to a tight system of static-equilibrium analysis.[48] In a letter to Malthus (October 9, 1820), Ricardo pointed out:

> Political Economy you think is an enquiry into the nature and causes of wealth—I think it should be called an enquiry into the laws which determine the division of the produce of industry amongst the classes which occur in its formation. No law can be laid down respecting quantity, but a tolerably correct one can be laid down respecting proportions. Every day I am more satisfied that the former enquiry is vain and delusive, but the latter only the true objects of the science.[49]

---

[44] Piero Sraffa, ed., *The Works and Correspondence of David Ricardo* (London: Cambridge University Press, 1952), V, 303.

[45] *Ibid.*

[46] Knut Wicksell, *Lectures on Political Economy*, I, 135.

[47] See William J. Baumol, *Economic Dynamics* (New York: The Macmillan Company, 1951), Part I.

[48] Keynes in *The General Theory* points out:
Most treatises on the theory of Value and Production are primarily concerned with the distribution of a *given* volume of employed resources between different uses and with the conditions which, assuming the employment of this quantity of resources, determine their relative rewards and the relative values of their products.
This is the Ricardian tradition. Reprinted from *The General Theory of Employment, Interest, and Money* by John Maynard Keynes, by permission of Harcourt, Brace & World, Inc., p. 4.

[49] Sraffa, ed., *Works and Correspondence of David Ricardo*, VIII, 278–279.

Yet, Ricardo himself (except in the field of international trade) did not develop the theory of value and distribution in the neoclassical sense. This gap in economic theory was to be filled later by the marginalists.[50] Ricardo's view of the problem of distribution was "the belief that the theory of distribution holds the key to an understanding of the whole mechanism of the economic system—of the forces governing the rate of progress, of the ultimate incidence of taxation, of the effects of protection, and so on."[51] Accordingly, Ricardo set the stage for the further development of static equilibrium analysis.[52]

### John Stuart Mill (1806–1878)

Keynes believed that "from the time of Say and Ricardo the classical economists have taught that supply creates its own demand."[53] He quoted the standard passage from John Stuart Mill's *Principles of Political Economy* (1848) as evidence of his claim that Mill upheld Say's Identity.[54] Did Mill actually maintain Say's Law as an "identity"

---

[50] See Hla Myint, *Theories of Welfare Economics*, pp. 62–65. Professor Myint observes that there are two elements in the Ricardian system which complicate the formulation of the theory of optimum allocation of given resources in the modern sense. The first one is the "quantity of labour embodied" theory of value. In adopting such a theory, Ricardo pushed back the whole equilibrating process of the market to the background. In trying to determine price without quantity, he mistook the essence of the allocative process as consisting of commodities produced to suit the relative demand for them. The second is his assumption of constant returns in every industry except in agriculture. This assumption places the emphasis on a relentless tendency of the economic system towards a stationary equilibrium and reduces the static considerations of allocative efficiency to comparative insignificance.

[51] This is the view expressed by Professor Nicholas Kaldor in his "Alternative Theories of Distribution," reprinted from *Review of Economic Studies*, XXIII (1955–56), 84, in *Essays in Economic Thought*, Spengler and Allen, eds. (Chicago: Rand-McNally & Co., 1960), p. 742.

[52] See John H. Williams, "An Economist's Confession," *The American Economic Review*, XLII (March, 1952), 4–5.

[53] See Keynes, *The General Theory*, p. 18.

[54] In *The General Theory*, p. 18, Keynes quoted the following passage:
What constitutes the means of payment for commodities is simply commodities. . . . All sellers are inevitably, and by the meaning of the word, buyers. Could we suddenly double the productive powers of the country, we should double the supply of commodities in every market; but we should, by the same stroke, double the purchasing power. Everybody would bring a double demand as well as supply; everybody would be able to buy twice as much, because every one would have twice as much to offer in exchange.
See John Stuart Mill, *Principles of Political Economy*, abr. and ed. by J. Laurence Laughlin (New York: D. Appleton & Co., 1885), Book III, Chap. xiv, Sec. 2, pp. 557–558.

or as an "equality"? Opinions of contemporary interpreters have been divided. In contrast to Keynes' interpretation, Professors Schumpeter, Becker, and Baumol, as well as M. Blaug have given more sympathetic discussions of Mill's treatment of Say's Law.[55]

Schumpeter argued that Mill did not interpret Say's Law "as implying denial of actual occurrence of 'general glut.' "[56] What Mill had in mind was that general overproduction was not possible in the long run.

Professors Becker and Baumol have observed that Mill had no truck with "the homogeneity postulate." According to them, Mill maintained Say's Equality and rejected Say's Identity. The clearest statement on this point is that in Mill's second essay in his *Unsettled Questions.*[57] The passages they cite are on pages 67 and 74 of Mill's *Essays on Some Unsettled Questions of Political Economy* (1844).

Professor Patinkin, however, observes: "In these pages Mill does clearly provide a vivid picture of the temporary stagnation that would be generated if, for some reason, people 'liked better to possess money than any other commodity' (p. 72). But he does not explain why the stagnation is only temporary, and he certainly does not say—or even imply—that the positive real-balance effect of a declining price level plays any role in the recovery." Thus Professor Patinkin is of the opinion that none of the passages cited (by Ricardo and Mill) "would justify the attempt to associate them with the 'Equality.' "[58]

Professor Blaug, on the other hand, follows the Schumpeter-Becker-Baumol view by stressing the fact that, even though "the classical economists never spelled out Say's Equality . . . their writings are re-

---

[55] See J. A. Schumpeter, *History of Economic Analysis* (New York: Oxford University Press, Inc., 1954), pp. 615–625; Becker and Baumol, "The Classical Monetary Theory," in *Essays in Economic Thought;* Blaug, *Ricardian Economics*, pp. 100–101; and Blaug, *Economic Theory in Retrospect*, pp. 138–149.

[56] See J. A. Schumpeter, *History of Economic Analysis*, p. 622.
Professor Schumpeter further observed that Mill recognized the importance of the effect of hoarding on crises and depressions.

The only difference there is on this point between Mill and Keynes is this: the former confined this excess demand for money to situations of this kind, of which it is one of the consequences and which therefore cannot be explained by it; whereas the latter considered the excess demand for money in depressions only as the most spectacular form of a phenomenon that, in less spectacular forms, is well-nigh ubiquitous or is well-nigh ubiquitous at least in certain phases of capitalist evolution, so that it may become the cause of either cyclical downturns or "secular stagnation". Malthus seems to have taken the latter view [p. 622].

[57] See Becker and Baumol, "The Classical Monetary Theory," in *Essays in Economic Thought*, p. 765.

[58] From *Money, Interest and Prices*, 2nd Edition by Don Patinkin, pp. 649–650, n. Copyright © 1965 by Don Patinkin. Reprinted by permission of Harper & Row, Publishers.

plete with references to a vaguely stated process of adjustment by which deviations from full employment tend to be self-corrective."[59] Professor Blaug further asserts that Mill, in the *Essays*, clearly distinguished Say's Identity from Say's Equality. "Mill does not state the real-balance effect in so many words. . . . Still, an automatic equilibrating mechanism is contemplated."[60] This mechanism is attested to in the following passages from Mill's *Essays:*

> There can never, it is said, be want of buyers for all commodities. . . . This argument is evidently founded on the supposition of a state of barter. . . . If, however, we suppose that money is used, these propositions cease to be exactly true. . . . The buying and selling being now separated, it may very well occur, that there may be, at some given time, a very general inclination to sell with as little delay as possible, accompanied with an equally general inclination to defer all purchases as long as possible. This is always actually the case, in those periods which are described as periods of general excess. And no one, after sufficient explanation, will contest the possibility of general excess, in this sense of the word. . . . It is true that this state can be only temporary, and must even be succeeded by a reaction of corresponding violence, since those who have sold without buying will certainly buy at last, and there will then be more buyers than sellers. . . . An overstocked state of the market is always temporary, and is generally followed by a more than common briskness of demand.

> In order to render the argument for the impossibility of an excess of all commodities applicable to the case in which a circulating medium is employed, money must itself be considered as a commodity. It must, undoubtedly, be admitted that there cannot be an excess of all other commodities, and an excess of money at the same time.[61]

It is evident from the preceding passages that Mill made the distinction between two separate "proofs" of the proposition that general overproduction (or lack of aggregate demand) was impossible, in the long run. The first proof was "founded on the supposition of a state of barter" (Say's Identity). The second proof was based on two related propositions, namely, (1) "that no person desires money for its own sake,"

[59] Reprinted with permission from Mark Blaug, *Economic Theory in Retrospect* (Homewood, Ill.: Richard D. Irwin, Inc.), p. 138.

[60] Reprinted with permission from Mark Blaug, *Economic Theory in Retrospect* (Homewood, Ill.: Richard D. Irwin, Inc.), p. 139.

[61] John Stuart Mill, *Essays on Some Unsettled Questions of Political Economy*, reprinted by The London School of Economics and Political Science, 1948, pp. 69–71.

(unless some very rare cases of misers be an exception),[62] and (2) the Turgot-Smith theory that saving is spending. Both of these propositions are employed by the classical writers as a secular application of Say's Law. Mill's short-run qualification of the neutrality-of-money proposition has been cited in the preceding passages. His defense of the saving-is-spending theorem is as follows:

> A fundamental theorem respecting capital . . . is, that although saved, and the result of saving, it is nevertheless consumed. The word saving does not imply that what is saved is not consumed, nor even necessarily that its consumption is deferred; but only that, if consumed immediately, it is not consumed by the persons who saves it.[63]

It is interesting to note that the Mill of the *Principles* becomes more orthodox in his views than the Mill of the *Essays*. As observed by Professor Corry, "the prolonged depression of the post-war years must have made the simple equilibrium analysis of James Mill's *Elements* appear more than somewhat unrealistic. Then presumably with the relatively increased prosperity of the thirties and early forties—although interspersed with periodic financial crises—the qualifications so necessary to the statement of all economic principles were gradually dropped from the younger Mill's analysis. We must also recall that the idea of the monetary dissenters were coming to be associated with the political extremism of Chartism and similar movements; this doubtless confirmed J. S. Mill's condemnation of such ideas."[64]

Mill's *Principles* includes discussion of the machinery question (technological unemployment) and the wages-fund doctrine.

---

[62] Mill, *Essays*, p. 69.

[63] Mill, *Principles of Political Economy*, pp. 79–80.

A good summary of Mill's theory of capital is given by Blaug in his *Economic Theory in Retrospect*, pp. 166–172. Professor Blaug observes:

> This is of course Adam Smith's saving-is-spending theorem, which underlies Say's Law of Markets. Taken strictly, it implies Say's Identity. But Say's Identity denies the possibility of excess capacity, which has already been admitted under the first proposition. [The first proposition is that capital formation is employment creating. Mill admitted that when there is excess capacity, governments can create capital, an idea that Ricardo had strenuously denied.] It should be evident now that, however much the saving-is-spending theorem encouraged thinkers to ignore "hoarding," its essential meaning was that saving and investment created effective demand just as surely as did consumption expenditures.

Reprinted with permission from Mark Blaug, *Economic Theory in Retrospect* (Homewood, Ill.: Richard D. Irwin, Inc.), p. 166.

[64] Corry, *Money, Saving and Investment in English Economics 1800–1850*, p. 106.

On the issue of technological unemployment, Mill questioned the Ricardian view:

> The argument relied on by most of those who contend that machinery can never be injurious to the laboring-class is, that by cheapening production it creates such an increased demand for the commodity as enables, ere long, a greater number of persons than ever to find employment in producing it. The argument does not seem to me to have the weight commonly ascribed to it.[65]

> All attempts to make out that the laboring-classes as a collective body cannot suffer temporarily by the introduction of machinery, or by sinking of capital in permanent improvements, are, I conceive, necessarily fallacious. . . . It is often said that, though employment is withdrawn from labor in one department, an exactly equivalent employment is opened for it in others, because what the consumers save in the increased cheapness of the particular article enables them to augment their consumption of others, thereby increasing the demand for other kinds of labor. This is plausible, but . . . involves a fallacy; demand for commodities being a totally different thing from demand for labor.[66]

Mill, however, injected an optimistic note:

> Nevertheless, I do not believe that, as things are actually transacted, improvements in production are often, if ever, injurious, even temporarily, to the laboring-classes in the aggregate. They would be so if they took place suddenly to a great amount, because much of the capital sunk must necessarily in that case be provided from funds already employed as circulating capital. But improvements are always introduced very gradually, and are seldom or never made by withdrawing circulating capital from actual production, but are made by the employment of the annual increase. I doubt if there would be found a single example of a great increase of fixed capital, at a time and place where circulating capital was not rapidly increasing likewise.[67]

With regard to Mill's view on the wages-fund doctrine, the most controversial proposition was that the demand for commodities was not demand for labor.[68] Mill's argument was that the volume of employment depended upon the wages fund (savings), which is that part of

---

[65] John Stuart Mill, *Principles*, Laughlin, ed., p. 95.

[66] *Ibid.*, p. 96.

[67] *Ibid.*, p. 97.

[68] For more detailed discussion of the subject see Alfred Marshall, *Principles of Economics* (New York: The Macmillan Company, 1953), Appendix J; A. C. Pigou, "Mill and the Wages Fund," *The Economic Journal* (June, 1949); Blaug, *Economic Theory in Retrospect*, pp. 167–172; and Fellner, *Emergence and Content of Modern Economic Analysis*, pp. 56–59.

total capital that is destined to employ labor.[69] Since the decision to allocate total capital among its various components rests with the capitalist, and since the demand for labor depends only on the part of circulating capital destined for wage payments, a change in consumer demand merely modifies the direction of this already existing wages fund. Thus, a demand for commodities could not be considered as increasing the demand for labor.[70] It should be noted that Mill made use of this dictum to combat the underconsumptionist doctrines of Malthus, Chalmers, and Sismondi. He intended to show that the increase in unproductive expenditures would not necessarily remove unemployment.[71]

Mill's position was untenable. As pointed out by Professor Pigou, "we encounter at once the objection that non-wage-earners, employers or others, when the wages fund is given, may, if they choose, make the wages flow larger or smaller by varying the amounts of their own consumption; by, for example, in any year cutting down their consumption and handing over what they would have consumed in extra real wages to work people." In other words, the wages in any year are not a fixed predetermined amount. Mill himself eventually renounced his wages-fund doctrine altogether in 1869.[72]

---

[69] A concise statement of the evolution of this concept is given by Eduard Heimann in his *History of Economic Doctrines* (New York: Oxford University Press, Inc., 1964), p. 120. Professor Heimann observes:

> Smith had taken this wage fund to be identical with the total capital. Malthus had identified it with the subsistence fund, which tends to lag behind the rising numbers of the population. Ricardo had narrowed the fund down to the circulating capital only, since the fixed capital invested in machines and equipment obviously is not used for wage payments; and Mill finally defined the fund as "only circulating capital, and not even the whole of that, but the part which is expended in the direct purchase of labor," thus anticipating Marx's concept of variable capital, although without the connotation that Marx attached to it.

[70] See Pigou, "Mill and the Wages Fund." Professor Pigou comments: "This entails that, if I spent £100 on the direct hire of labour, I benefit labour in a way that I do not if I spend the same sum on a commodity. . . . This is clearly wrong." Also see Blaug, *Economic Theory in Retrospect*, pp. 167–171.

[71] See Blaug, *Ricardian Economics*, pp. 178–179.

[72] The controversy has been succinctly summarized by Edmund Whittaker in his *Schools and Streams of Economic Thought* (Chicago: Rand McNally & Co., 1960), pp. 166–167. Professor Whittaker observes:

> Pointing out the weakness of the theory, Nassau Senior said that the size of the wages fund was not independent of the productivity of labor. . . . Francis Davy Longe, William Thomas Thornton, Francis Amasa Walker . . . argued that wages did not come from a predetermined amount of capital but were really paid out of the product of labor itself. Convinced by their arguments, Mill formally abandoned the wages fund theory in a review he wrote of Thornton's book.

## The Dissenters

Since the publication of Keynes' *General Theory*, writers have shown renewed interest in the "underworld" economics of the classical and neoclassical period.[73] Among the heretics of the classical period, Lauderdale and Malthus are the best known.[74] Keynes claimed that not until late in life did Malthus accept the notion of the insufficiency of effective demand as a scientific explanation for unemployment.[75] Keynes once stated: "If only Malthus, instead of Ricardo, had been the parent stem from which nineteenth century economics proceeded, what a much wiser and richer place the world would be today!"[76] On the other hand, Professor Blaug, reflecting the views of some contemporary writers, has asserted that "it is fortunate for the history of economics that good logic triumphed over bad. A victory for Malthus would have made economics the happy hunting-ground of every quack with panaceas designed to shore up the allegedly defective market economy."[77]

The foregoing review of current literature on the classical theory of income and employment leads us to the following conclusions:

1. None of the dissenters of this period succeeded in challenging Say's Law effectively, probably because none of them fully understood the logic behind it. The saving-is-spending theorem and the neutrality proposition employed by the orthodox classical writers implied that there was some automatic process of adjustment that would assure full-employment equilibrium. But the classical economists failed to spell out explicitly that the conclusions of Say's Law could be derived from the assump-

---

[73] See Lawrence R. Klein, *The Keynesian Revolution* (New York: The Macmillan Company, 1954), Chap. 5; Alvin H. Hansen, *Business Cycles and National Income* (New York: W. W. Norton & Company, Inc., 1951), Chap. 14; Blaug, *Economic Theory in Retrospect*, pp. 149–159; Harlan L. McCracken, *Keynesian Economics in the Stream of Economic Thought* (Louisiana State University Press, 1961), Chaps. 2 and 3; Corry, *Money, Saving & Investment in English Economics 1800–1850*, Chaps. 7 and 8; and Fellner, *Emergence and Content of Modern Economic Analysis*, pp. 154–159.

[74] The dissenters during the period (1800–1850) are Lauderdale, Malthus, William Spence, Thomas Chalmers, John Rooke, John Barton, John Lalor, and many others. A good summary of their theories is given by Corry in *Money, Saving and Investment in English Economics 1800–1850*, Chapters 7 and 8.

[75] Keynes, *The General Theory*, p. 362.

[76] Keynes, *Essays in Biography* (London: Macmillan & Co., 1933), p. 144.

[77] Blaug, *Economic Theory in Retrospect*, p. 159.

tion of unlimited wage-price flexibility.[78] In order to attack
Say's Law, the dissenters could have invoked the proposition
that *ex ante* saving and *ex ante* investment would not necessarily be equal. But neither Malthus nor Lauderdale had any
such notion. Instead, they followed the orthodox view and assumed the *ex ante* equality of saving and investment. As observed by Professor Corry, "it is difficult to regard savings as a
leakage from the community income stream when at the same
time it is *explicitly* acknowledged that it calls forth an equal
amount of investment."[79]

2. Both Malthus and Lauderdale were concerned with the problem of secular stagnation and not with the short-run problem
   of income determination. By retaining the assumption of the
   equality of *ex ante* saving and investment, they failed to
   analyze the motives behind saving and investment and
   consequently blocked the way to the subsequent Keynesian
   conclusion. Instead, they concentrated on the problem of the
   capacity-creating effect of investment dealt with subsequently
   by post-Keynesian writers.[80]

3. Both Lauderdale and Malthus lacked the Keynesian theoretical
   tools to present a precise theory of income determination.[81] In
   particular, they did not have any notion of a consumption function, nor did they give an adequate analysis of the investment
   demand function. Furthermore, since they assumed the *ex ante*
   equality of saving and investment, they also neglected to provide an adequate analysis of hoarding.

---

[78] See Franco Modigliani, "Liquidity Preference and the Theory of Interest and
Money," reprinted from *Econometrica* (1944), in *Readings in Monetary Theory*
(Homewood, Ill.: Richard D. Irwin, Inc., 1951); Patinkin, *Money, Interest and
Prices*, pp. 649–650; also Fellner, *Emergence and Content of Modern Economic
Analysis*, pp. 80–85.

[79] See Corry, *Money, Saving and Investment in English Economics 1800–1850*,
p. 118.

[80] See Corry, pp. 114–121 and pp. 125–132; and Blaug, *Economic Theory in
Retrospect*, pp. 150–159.

[81] See Klein, *The Keynesian Revolution*, pp. 124–130; also Hansen, *Business
Cycles and the National Income*, pp. 229–258.

# 3

# Neoclassical Theory of Income and Employment

## PRICE FLEXIBILITY AND AUTOMATIC FULL EMPLOYMENT

The main body of neoclassical economics is value and distribution theory—the area in which a major gap was left by classical economic analysis.[1] As mentioned in Chapter 2, the classical economists concentrated their attention on the problem of economic growth. Consequently, the problem of efficient allocation of given resources became in effect a subsidiary theme of classical economics. Only in the theory of foreign trade was the theory of allocative efficiency developed.[2]

Our concern, however, is not with neoclassical theory of value and distribution, but neoclassical theory of income and employment. What is in essence the neoclassical theory on this subject? Unfortunately,

---

[1] The first generation of classical economists was mainly concerned with long-run equilibrium value. Under constant cost assumptions, they maintained that the long-run equilibrium price of a commodity is determined by the costs of production. The second generation of classical writers, notably Nassau Senior and others, recognized the role played by utility in the determination of value. However, the focal point of Senior's value theory is on the supply side of the picture. In effect, it amounts to an extension of the Ricardian labor theory of value by redefining real cost as consisting of two components, namely, labor and abstinence. Consequently, classical theory of value and distribution was very much in need of revision, and this became the major task of neoclassical writers.

[2] See Hla Myint, *Theories of Welfare Economics* (New York: Augustus M. Kelley, Publishers, Reprint of Economics Classics, 1962), Chaps. 4 and 5. Professor Myint observes that, to the classical writers, free competition did not primarily mean a "tightening" process of allocative efficiency within a static framework, rather it meant a "widening" process to extend the division of labor and to facilitate economic growth through productivity increases. Only in the theory of comparative advantage was the theory of allocative efficiency properly developed.

standard textbooks on the history of economic thought do not provide an explicit answer to this question. To extract an answer from neoclassical economics, one must examine the reasons for the attention to the problem of efficient allocation of given resources. In fact, the neoclassical writers themselves provided the clue to this answer by their stress on the assumption of full employment.

The full-employment assumption of neoclassical economics implies the acceptance of the general conclusions of Say's Law. To put it another way, the English neoclassical writers and the continental Lausanne-School economists implicitly assumed that wage and price flexibility would automatically assure full employment.[3] This optimistic assumption followed from their marginal productivity theory of production and distribution. They believed that the short-run problem of output and employment would be settled within the confines of the labor market. In other words, the supply of and demand for labor determine not only the real-wage rate but also the level of employment.[4]

Given the level of output and employment as determined by the aggregate demand and supply functions of labor, and assuming price flexibility, total spending would be adequate to clear the markets of what had been produced. More specifically, a flexible rate of interest would equate investment with saving at full employment. Thus wage and price flexibility would solve the problem of insufficient aggregate demand. Hence, the neoclassical writers did not develop a theory of aggregate demand as an explanation for income determination in the short run. This is also the reason why Keynes made his frontal attack on classical economics by starting from the neoclassical supply curve of labor.[5]

Now, what is the explanation for the absolute levels of money-wages and prices in the neoclassical system? The explanation is the quantity theory of money. Here the so-called neoclassical dichotomy appears. The dichotomy is that in the neoclassical system, the real variables

---

[3] See William Fellner, *Emergence and Content of Modern Economic Analysis* (New York: McGraw-Hill Book Company, 1960), pp. 149–152. Professor Fellner observes that the continuous clearing of all markets in the Walrasian general equilibrium system implies the absence of any wage or price rigidities.

[4] See L. R. Klein, "Theories of Effective Demand and Employment," *Journal of Political Economy*, LV (April, 1947), 108–131.

[5] As pointed out by Professor R. J. Ball in his *Inflation and the Theory of Money* (Chicago: Aldine Publishing Company, 1964), p. 49, Keynes' repeated references to the classical writers in *The General Theory* do not refer to the English classical school from Adam Smith to J. S. Mill. Rather, Keynes was referring to neoclassical writers, particularly Professor Pigou.

(namely, output, employment, and the real-wage rate) are determined entirely in the real sector, and the monetary elements (namely, the absolute-price level and the money-wage level) are determined by the quantity of money. Inadvertently, the neoclassical writers separated monetary theory from value theory, in spite of the intentions of Marshall and his followers to integrate value theory and monetary theory. (This matter is further pursued in Part II, Chapters 8, 9, and 10.) The neoclassical theory of employment and the price level may be succinctly stated by means of the following reconstructed neoclassical model.[6] This is the model found in most current textbooks on macroeconomics.[7]

## A Reconstructed Neoclassical Model

The reconstructed neoclassical model is based on the following assumptions:

1. A closed private economy (i.e., no foreign trade).
2. Given capital stock and technological and organizational knowledge in the short run.
3. A given quantity of money.
4. National output divided between consumption and investment expenditures.
5. Labor a homogenous factor.
6. Perfect competition in all markets.

A generalized functional representation of the model consists of the seven equations at the top of the following page.

---

[6] Professor Ball in *Inflation and the Theory of Money* cogently observes:
It would perhaps be best to add the word *type* after the adjective neoclassical or Keynesian. The object of this is to preclude the rather futile disputes that arise periodically as to the parentage of a theory or whether Keynes himself would subscribe to something described as Keynesian. The word type can best be understood as indicating something in sympathy with the underlying principles of a particular intellectual milieu [p. 49].

[7] For illustrations see Gardner Ackley, *Macroeconomic Theory* (New York: The Macmillan Company, 1961), Part II; Joseph P. McKenna, *Aggregate Economic Analysis* (2nd ed.; New York: Holt, Rinehart & Winston, Inc., 1965), Chap. 14; Franklin V. Walker, *Growth, Employment and the Price Level* (Englewood Cliffs, N.J.: Prentice-Hall, Inc., 1963), Chap. 5; Wallace C. Peterson, *Income, Employment and Economic Growth* (New York: W. W. Norton & Company, Inc., 1962), Chap. 4; Thomas F. Dernburg & Duncan M. McDougall, *Macroeconomics* (New York: McGraw-Hill Book Company, 1960), Chap. 10; Myron H. Ross, *Income: Analysis and Policy* (New York: McGraw-Hill Book Company, 1964), Chap. 9.

$$Y = Y(N) \qquad\qquad \text{Eq. (3-1)}$$

$$N_d = N_d\left(\frac{w}{P}\right) \qquad\qquad \text{Eq. (3-2)}$$

$$N_s = N_s\left(\frac{w}{P}\right) \qquad\qquad \text{Eq. (3-3)}$$

$$M = kPY \qquad\qquad \text{Eq. (3-4)}$$

$$S = S(r) \qquad\qquad \text{Eq. (3-5)}$$

$$I = I(r) \qquad\qquad \text{Eq. (3-6)}$$

$$S = I \qquad\qquad \text{Eq. (3-7)}$$

where $(Y)$ stands for real output; $(N)$ symbolizes employment; $(N_d)$ is the demand for labor and $(N_s)$ represents the supply of labor; $(w/P)$ is the real-wage rate; $(S)$ and $(I)$ stand for saving and investment, respectively; $(r)$ is the rate of interest; $(M)$ is the quantity of money; and $(PY)$ the money income.

The "real" sector is summarized by the first three equations. Equation (3-1) is the aggregate production function in the short run. It states that, in the short run—with given capital stock, technological and organizational knowledge, and given resources—total real output $(Y)$ is an increasing function of the variable input, labor $(N)$. Figure 3-1 is the graphical representation of this function. The shape of the function indicates that beyond a certain point, diminishing marginal returns set in as more and more of the variable factor is added to the fixed factor(s).

Equation (3-2) is the demand-for-labor function, which states that the demand for labor $(N_d)$ is a decreasing function of the real-wage rate $(w/P)$. Any point on the $N_d$ curve represents the optimum factor-hiring position of the firm in neoclassical distribution theory. The equilibrium position of the firm as a buyer of factor inputs is $MP_L \cdot P = w$, where $(MP_L)$ is the marginal physical productivity of labor; $(P)$ is the price of the output produced (the product of the two is sometimes

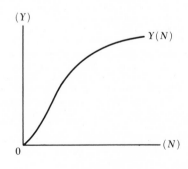

Figure 3-1

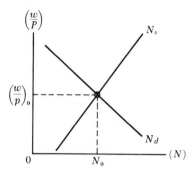

Figure 3-2

called the marginal value product of labor, which constitutes the firm's demand for labor); and $(w)$ is the money-wage rate determined in the labor services market. The maximizing position of the firm may alternatively be written as $MP_L = w/P$. Figure 3-2 is the graphic representation of this function. The real-wage rate $(w/P)$ is plotted on the vertical axis; $(N)$ is plotted on the horizontal axis. The negatively inclined function is the demand for labor function in the aggregate sense, which reflects the slope of the aggregate production function $(\partial Y/\partial N)$.

Equation (3-3) is the supply-of-labor function, which has its origin in the theory of Stanley Jevons, the English marginal-utility theorist. It states that the supply of labor $(N_s)$ is an increasing function of the real-wage rate. This assertion is based on the general principle of the increasing marginal disutility of work, another standard theory of neoclassical economics. The graphic representation of this function is the positively inclined curve $(N_s)$ in Figure 3-2. The intersection of the two curves determines the equilibrium level of employment $(N_0)$ and the equilibrium level of the real-wage rate $(w/P)_0$ simultaneously. Once we know the equilibrium $(N_0)$, from the aggregate production function, we can derive the equilibrium level of output $(Y_0)$.

It should be noted that the equilibrium values $(N_0)$ and $(Y_0)$, derived in this way, necessarily are the full-employment equilibrium levels of output and of employment, for the intersection point of the $(N_d)$ and $(N_s)$ curves means that the market for labor services is cleared. This is so, because any point on the $(N_d)$ curve is an optimal position for the firms; and any point on the $(N_s)$ curve defines an employment situation that is optimal for the households. The point of intersection indicates that both parties are completely satisfied, i.e., have attained market-equilibrium. By Walras' Law, applied to a "labor and final output" economy, the point of intersection also implies equilibrium in the final-

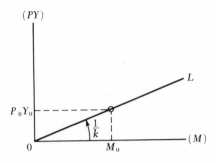

**Figure 3-3**

output market. The classical and neoclassical economists generally concentrated their analyses on this single, full-employment equilibrium position.

The three equations mentioned above determine the full-employment of labor, the full-employment level of output and the level of the real-wage rate corresponding to full-employment equilibrium. This, in essence, is the simplest short-run employment model of the neoclassical school, which is usually not described explicitly in the standard textbooks on the history of economic thought. This simple model shows that the approach used places major emphasis on the supply side. The conclusions of Say's Law implicit in this model will be dealt with when we describe the working of the whole system.

Equilibrium in the money market is represented by Eq. (3-4). The supply of nominal money is represented by the symbol $(M)$ on the left-hand side of the equation; and the demand for nominal money balances $(kPY)$ is on the right-hand side. (This is basically the equilibrium equation of the Marshallian cash-balances version of the quantity theory of money. The implications of this approach for monetary theory are discussed in Part II, Chapter 8.) The equation states that people hold cash balances only because there is imperfect synchronization between their receipts and payments. In Keynesian terminology, the demand for money is composed of the transactions and precautionary demand $(L_1)$ with no recognition of the speculative demand $(L_2)$ for money. Hence, the quantity theory is compatible with Say's Law.[8]

Figure 3-3 represents the money-market equilibrium equation. The vector $(0L)$, the slope of which is $(1/k)$, shows the amount of $(M)$ re-

---

[8] For a good discussion of the relationship between Say's Law and the quantity theory of money, see Gardner Ackley, *Macroeconomic Theory*, Chap. 5.

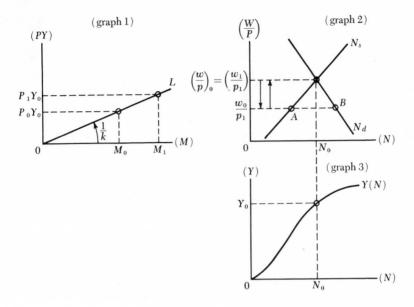

**Figure 3-4**

quired for each level of $(PY)$, or alternatively, the levels of $(PY)$ that can be supported by each possible quantity of $(M)$. The exogenously determined quantity of money is $(M_0)$. Given $(M_0)$ and $(1/k)$, the equation indicates that the money income would be $(PY)_0$. Since $(Y_0)$, the full-employment output, is determined entirely by "real" factors, and since $(1/k)$, which is the income velocity of circulation $(V)$, is assumed to be stable in the short run, $(M_0)$ determines $(P_0)$, which is the unique price level compatible with general equilibrium. Once we obtain $(P_0)$, from the equilibrium level of $(w/P)_0$ we derive the corresponding $(w_0)$.

The conclusion from the quantity theory that, in equilibrium, money is neutral under a system of wage-price flexibility, can be illustrated by the interaction of the three markets. Suppose that we start with an initial full-employment equilibrium position, with $(N_0)$, $(Y_0)$, $(w/P)_0$, $(M_0)$, $(P_0)$ and $(w_0)$, as illustrated by the three graphs in Figure 3-4. The initial equilibrium will be disturbed when the quantity of money is increased from $(M_0)$ to $(M_1)$. The excess quantity of money will increase aggregate demand for the full-employment output. The result will be inflation, i.e., the fixed $(Y_0)$ will be sold at a higher price level $(P_1)$. In graph 1, this phenomenon is indicated by the higher money income $(P_1Y_0)$ associated with $(M_1)$. If there is a lag in the increase in the

money-wage rate, the higher monetary demand will raise the profitability of the firms. This would induce the producers to increase their
demand for labor. An alternative statement of the outcome is that, with
the increase in the general price level $(P)$, the real-wage rate tends to
decrease $(w_0/P_1)$. This phenomenon is depicted by the decrease in the
real-wage rate in graph 2 of Figure 3-4. The decrease in the real-wage
rate creates a situation in which the demand for labor would be greater
than the supply of labor. The excess demand for labor is indicated by
the distance $(AB)$ in graph 2 of Figure 3-4. The competitive bidding
for labor will eventually drive up the money-wage rate from the original $(w_0)$ to $(w_1)$. Labor market equilibrium will be restored when the
excess demand is eliminated by the rising real-wage rate $(w_1/P_1 =
w_0/P_0)$. The real variables (namely, $Y$, $N$, and the real-wage rate) in the
new equilibrium remain unchanged. It is in this sense that neoclassical
monetary theorists drew their neutral-money conclusions. Changes on
the monetary side affect only absolute prices and money-wage rates,
both of which will increase proportionately to the increase in the quantity of money.[9]

Figure 3-4 also illustrates the basic neoclassical tenet that wage-price
flexibility automatically assures full-employment equilibrium in the
labor market. This basic tenet was reiterated by Professor A. C. Pigou
in his *Industrial Fluctuations* (1927) and again in his *Theory of Unemployment* (1933), which became the main target of Keynes' attack.
Professor Pigou reaffirmed the neoclassical tradition by stating:

> With perfectly free competition . . . there will always be at work
> a strong tendency for wage-rates to be so related to demand that
> everybody is employed. . . . The implication is that such unem-
> ployment as exists at any time is due wholly to the fact that
> changes in demand conditions are continually taking place and that
> frictional resistances prevent the appropriate wage adjustments
> from being made instantaneously.[10]

> If the wage-rate is perfectly plastic, the alteration in the quantity
> of labour at work will be nill.[11]

The last three equations convey the basic idea that a flexible rate of
interest (which is part and parcel of the price mechanism) will assure
the equality of saving and investment at any level of output set by the
interaction of the demand and supply of labor functions in the real

---

[9] See Ackley, *Macroeconomic Theory*, Chap. 6.

[10] A. C. Pigou, *Theory of Unemployment* (London: Macmillan & Co., 1933),
p. 252, cited by A. H. Hansen, *A Guide to Keynes* (New York: McGraw-Hill Book
Company, 1953), p. 16.

[11] Pigou, *Industrial Fluctuations* (London: Macmillan & Co., 1927), cited in
*A Guide to Keynes.*

sector of the neoclassical system. Equation (3-5) states that saving is, other things being equal, an increasing function of the rate of interest. Equation (3-6) states that, other things being equal, investment demand is inversely related to the rate of interest. Equation (3-7) is the capital-market-equilibrium condition, i.e., that the supply of savings is matched by the demand for savings. This is the classical as well as neoclassical saving-investment theory of interest, which is rejected by *The Keynesian Revolution*.[12] Figure 3-5 represents these three equations. The rate

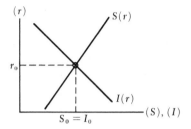

**Figure 3-5**

of interest $(r)$ is plotted on the vertical axis; savings and investment $(S)$ $(I)$, on the horizontal axis. Equilibrium in the capital market is indicated by the intersection of the two functions. The equilibrium rate of interest is $(r_0)$.

The assumption of full-employment equilibrium rendered the classical and neoclassical theories of interest *real* theories and not *monetary* ones. The logical sequence involved is as follows. At full employment, the economy may be depicted as operating at a point on the production-possibilities curve (Figure 3-6). At full employment, consumption and investment become mutually exclusive alternatives. An increase in investment $(I)$ in a full-employment economy requires a reduction in consumption $(C)$, which frees resources for additional investment. The inducement to increase savings (reduce consumption) is the rise in the rate of interest that results from investors bidding for the available supply of savings out of the full-employment level of income $(Y_0)$. It is for this reason that additional investment could be made under full-employment conditions without creating inflation. Stated differently, this idea explains the interest rate as an equilibrating mechanism.

[12] See Lawrence R. Klein, *The Keynesian Revolution* (New York: The Macmillan Company, 1954), pp. 84–86.

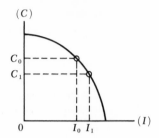

**Figure 3-6**

This mechanism is illustrated in Figure 3-7. Assume an innovation that causes the investment-demand schedule to shift upward to $I(r)_1$. The rate of interest will rise to $(r_1)$. The interest-rate induced increase in savings is indicated by the upward movement along the given saving function. By the same token, consumption expenditure is simultaneously reduced.

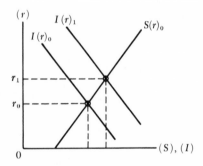

**Figure 3-7**

Thus, the equilibrium rate of interest, which is the rate that maintains full-employment equilibrium, is determined entirely by real factors. Under full-employment and price-flexibility assumptions, an increase in the quantity of money results only in proportional changes in the absolute price level and the money-wage rate. The full-employment-equilibrium level of output $(Y_0)$ and the equilibrium rate of interest $(r)$ are both independent of monetary factors.[13] The implications of this neoclassical dichotomy are discussed in Part II.

---

[13] See J. M. Keynes, *The General Theory of Employment, Interest, and Money* (New York: Harcourt, Brace & World, Inc., 1936), Chap. 14; and Joseph W. Conard, *Introduction to the Theory of Interest* (Berkeley: University of California Press, 1959), Chap. 4.

# 4

# The Keynesian
# Revolution

## The Fundamental Issues Raised By Keynes

In *The General Theory* (1936) Keynes rejected the neoclassical theory of employment that price flexibility would automatically assure full-employment equilibrium.[1] He attacked Pigou for attributing the cause of unemployment to labor's insistence on a high real-wage rate. Instead, he advanced the new theory that, at less than full employment, the equilibrium levels of output and employment were determined by aggregate demand.[2] Thus, Keynes opened his first volley at the neoclassical supply function of labor.[3]

---

[1] Professor Don Patinkin observes:
At the core of the Keynesian polemics of the past ten years and more is the relationship between price flexibility and full employment. The fundamental argument of Keynes is directed against the belief that price flexibility can be depended upon to generate full employment automatically.
See his "Price Flexibility and Full Employment," reprinted from *The American Economic Review* (1948), in *Readings in Monetary Theory*, Friedrich A. Lutz and Lloyd W. Mints, eds. (Homewood, Ill.: Richard D. Irwin, Inc., 1951), p. 252.

[2] Professor D. C. Champernowne points out:
The main object of writing *The General Theory* may be regarded as that of refuting the thesis that the cause of heavy unemployment is the insistence by wage earners on high real wages. In place of that thesis a correct theory of employment is to be provided.
See his "Expectations and Links Between the Economic Future and the Present" in *Keynes' General Theory: Reports of Three Decades*, Robert Lekachman, ed. (New York: St. Martin's Press, Inc., 1964), p. 175.

[3] For a lucid discussion on this point, see R. J. Ball, *Inflation and the Theory of Money* (Chicago: Aldine Publishing Company, 1964), pp. 53–56; also see A. H. Hansen, *A Guide to Keynes* (New York: McGraw-Hill Book Company, 1953), pp. 19–25; Hansen, *Monetary Theory and Fiscal Policy* (New York: McGraw-Hill Book Company, 1949), Chap. 8; and Dudley Dillard, *The Economics of John Maynard Keynes* (New York: Prentice-Hall, Inc., 1948), pp. 24–27.

To summarize the highlights of the "Keynesian Revolution," the reconstructed neoclassical model and the Keynesian system are compared in mathematical form in the chart at the top of page 63.[4]

Only three differences are revealed in the formal structures of the two systems: (1) Keynes rejected the neoclassical supply-of-labor function and assumed rigid wages ($w = w_0$) for situations of less than full employment; (2) Keynes added the speculative demand for money $L(r)$ to the neoclassical transactions and precautionary demand for money ($kPY$); and (3) Keynes assumed that income would be a far more important determinant of saving (consumption) than the neoclassical rate

---

[4] The Keynesian system has been summarized in many ways. The skeleton outlines made by Professor Hansen and Professor Dillard are widely used. See Hansen, *A Guide to Keynes*, Chap. 9; and Dillard, *The Economics of John Maynard Keynes*, pp. 48–50.

Anatol Murad summarizes the Keynesian system in the following diagram. See Anatol Murad, *What Keynes Means* (New Haven: College & University Press, 1962), Chap. 14.

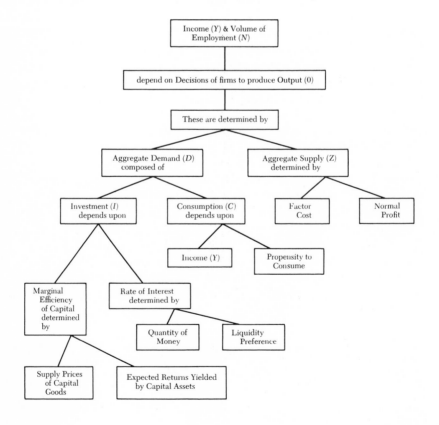

| The Neoclassical System | | The Keynesian System | |
|---|---|---|---|
| $Y = Y(N)$ | Eq. (3-1) | $Y = Y(N)$ | Eq. (4-1) |
| $N_d = N_d\left(\dfrac{w}{P}\right)$ | Eq. (3-2) | $N_d = N_d\left(\dfrac{w}{P}\right)$ | Eq. (4-2) |
| $N_s = N_s\left(\dfrac{w}{P}\right)$ | Eq. (3-3) | $w = w_0$ | Eq. (4-3) |
| $M = kPY$ | Eq. (3-4) | $M = kPY + L(r)$ | Eq. (4-4) |
| $S = S(r)$ | Eq. (3-5) | $S = S(Y)$ | Eq. (4-5) |
| $I = I(r)$ | Eq. (3-6) | $I = I(r)$ | Eq. (4-6) |
| $S = I$ | Eq. (3-7) | $S = I$ | Eq. (4-7) |

of interest, $S = S(Y)$. These three theoretical innovations constitute Keynes' denial of the neoclassical automatic mechanism generating full employment.[5] They also symbolize some of the fundamental issues raised by Keynes. For instance, the first point represents Keynes' rejection of the neoclassical postulate that workers would not offer labor services if the real wage rate were cut below the prevailing real wage rate.[6] The rejection of the neoclassical supply-of-labor function not only undermines the basic neoclassical theory of income and employment, but also destroys the validity of the neoclassical remedy for unemployment. By assuming wage rigidity under conditions of less than full employment, we can no longer count on the mechanism of price flexibility to generate full employment automatically. Therefore, the neoclassical theory is no longer adequate as a general theory of income and employment. A new theory that accords major consideration to the role of aggregate demand must be installed in its place.

Keynes rejected the efficacy of the neoclassical remedy for unemployment by recognizing that the money income of wage earners represents the bulk of total consumption expenditures. A cut in the money-wage rate would mean a fall in aggregate demand. Thus, the neoclassical remedy is self-defeating. Keynes suggested that manipulation of aggregate demand is a far more effective remedy. The argument involves the following reasoning: (1) Under conditions of short-run increasing marginal cost, measures to increase aggregate demand will eventually push up prices; (2) with the current money-wage rate remaining unchanged, the rise in the general price level means a re-

---

[5] Professor Gardner Ackley calls these innovations "obstacles to full employment." See his *Macroeconomic Theory* (New York: The Macmillan Company, 1961), Chap. 9.

[6] Professor Hansen points out that this neoclassical postulate contains a bundle of "two very plain and simple propositions: (1) workers will refuse the proffer of employment if the *real* wage rate is cut below the current real wage; (2) a cut in *money* wage rates is an effective means to reduce real wage rates." See *A Guide to Keynes*, p. 22.

duction in the real-wage rate; (3) since the demand for labor is inversely related to the real-wage rate, the decrease in the real-wage
rate following the increase in aggregate demand will remove the unemployment.[7] In other words, at the given money-wage rate, any
change in the general price level consequent to a change in aggregate
demand would lead to a shift in the demand function of labor and
cause a change in the volume of employment. This means that "the
general level of prices and the level of employment are no longer independent of each other as they were in our neoclassical world. The neoclassical dichotomy is broken and monetary theory and value theory
come closer together, for given the level of money wages, the general
price level would now vary with the level of employment."[8] This is one
of the fundamental issues raised by Keynes in *The General Theory*.

The second fundamental issue raised by Keynes concerns the monetary sphere. This issue is epitomized in his liquidity-preference theory
of interest. The schedule of liquidity preference has been said to be
the "crucial concept by which money is introduced into the theory of
output."[9] In other words, the liquidity-preference concept is a denial
of the neutral-money implications of Say's law of markets. It will be
recalled that neoclassical economics excluded the theory of output
and employment, as well as the theory of interest, from the subject
matter of monetary theory. Both the level of output (and hence employment) and the equilibrium rate of interest were thought to be
determined by real forces only. As aptly put by Professor Harry G.
Johnson, "the essence of the Keynesian revolution was to shift the
subject-matter of monetary theory, placing the emphasis on the level
of employment as the central subject of monetary theory and posing
the determination of the rate of interest as a specifically monetary
problem."[10] This issue is discussed further in Part II, Chapter 9.

A third issue—closely related to the second—is symbolized by the
introduction of the saving function. Professor Gardner Ackley describes
this issue as "an 'inconsistency' between saving and investment. If this
situation prevails, then the classical correctives fail (even though

---

[7] For a more detailed exposition of this argument, see Hansen, *Monetary Theory and Fiscal Policy* (New York: McGraw-Hill Book Company, 1949), Chap. 8.

[8] Ball, *Inflation and the Theory of Money*, p. 53.

[9] See Dillard, "The Theory of a Monetary Economy," in *Post-Keynesian Economics*, K. K. Kurihara, ed. (New Brunswick: Rutgers University Press, 1954), p. 9.

[10] Harry G. Johnson, "Monetary Theory and Keynesian Economics," *Pakistan Economic Journal*, VIII (June, 1958), 56–70. Reprinted in *Money, National Income, and Stabilization Policy*, Warren L. Smith and Ronald L. Teigen, eds. (Homewood, Ill.: Richard D. Irwin, Inc., 1965).

wages are perfectly flexible), and full employment may become impossible."[11] On the same point Professor Lawrence R. Klein observes that "the Keynesian Revolution rejected the classical theory of interest."[12] There is no assurance that the equation ($S = I$) has a positive solution for the rate of interest ($r$) at full employment. "In fact, if savings and investment are both interest-inelastic, the chances are very great that there will be no solution to this equation."[13] If the rate of interest fails to bring saving and investment into equilibrium, changes in income ($Y$) will perform the function of equating saving with investment. This, of course, is the familiar multiplier analysis in modern income theory.

A fourth fundamental issue raised by Keynes—the stability of the dynamic system—is not apparent in the formal structure of the model. This issue has been clearly defined, however, by Professors Patinkin and Klein. Professor Patinkin points out: "For the real significance of the Keynesian contribution can be realized only within the framework of dynamic economics. . . . The fundamental issue raised by Keynesian economics is the stability of the dynamic system: its ability to return automatically to a full-employment equilibrium within a reasonable time (say a year) if it is subjected to the customary shocks and disturbances of a peacetime economy."[14] Professor Patinkin further observes: "In the absence of sufficient interest- and price-elasticity, the adjustment process becomes a long, drawn-out one." Even under perfect competition and wage-price flexibility, "it cannot then realistically be assumed that firms will continue producing at an unchanged level, for this would require them to accumulate inventories at ever increasing levels. Hence they must eventually take some step to bring current output—and consequently current input—into line with current sales.

---

[11] Ackley, *Macroeconomic Theory*, p. 171.

[12] Klein, *The Keynesian Revolution* (New York: The Macmillan Company, 1954), p. 84.

Professor Klein further observes:
The principal difference, then, between Keynes and the classics centers around their theories of savings and investment. The multiplier theory, or the theory of the determination of effective demand, is the Keynesian savings-investment theory. The theory of the determination of the rate of interest is the classical savings-investment theory. The money equation merely serves the purpose of determining the level of wages and prices, and does not play an essential part in showing the differences between the new and old economics. [p. 86.]

[13] Klein, "Theories of Effective Demand and Employment," reprinted from *Journal of Political Economy*, April, 1947, p. 111, in *Readings in Economic Analysis*, R. V. Clemence, ed. (Cambridge, Mass.: Addison-Wesley Publishing Co., Inc., 1950), I, 263.

[14] Patinkin, "Price Flexibility and Full Employment," in *Readings in Monetary Theory*, pp. 279–280.

And this is the beginning of involuntary unemployment."[15] Conveying the same idea, Professor Klein writes:

> Unemployment is extremely likely even under perfect competition. It shows clearly that the discussion of the new results of Keynesian economics should not be centered in the price sphere of the economy; rather in the probability, psychological, and expectational sphere of the economy. One should investigate the determinants of the shapes of the Keynesian functions. These are the strategic economic variables. They tell whether or not a full employment solution is possible. The long-familiar observation about the stickiness of wages supplements the results of Keynesian economics and brings the student into contact with actuality.[16]

### ALTERNATIVE STATEMENT

Perhaps we may obtain a better perspective of the "Keynesian Revolution" by assessing the important differences between the neoclassical and Keynesian systems from another standpoint.[17]

As we compare the two systems, the question is: Which of the Keynesian theoretical innovations constitutes the crucial difference between the systems? Several competing views have been advanced in the literature. As observed by Professor Ackley, these views "are matters of emphasis, and of degree."[18] Professor Modigliani's view has received substantial support from many writers.[19] According to this view, the explanation of Keynesian under-employment equilibrium in a static framework depends upon either wage rigidity or the "liquidity trap." Adding the speculative demand for money, $L(r)$, to the neoclassical demand-for-money function, but without the further assumption of the liquidity trap, will not change the neoclassical conclusions, so long as wage flexibility exists.[20] Graphs 1–5 in Figure 4-1 represent this view.

---

[15] From *Money, Interest and Prices*, 2nd Edition, p. 318, by Don Patinkin. Copyright © 1965 by Don Patinkin. Reprinted by permission of Harper & Row, Publishers.

[16] Klein, *The Keynesian Revolution*, p. 90.

[17] For a lucid discussion of this topic see Ackley, *Macroeconomic Theory*, Chap. 15; and Ball, *Inflation and the Theory of Money*, pp. 56–59.

[18] Ackley, *Macroeconomic Theory*, p. 406.

[19] See Franco Modigliani, "Liquidity Preference and the Theory of Interest and Money," reprinted from *Econometrica* (1944), in *Readings in Monetary Theory*.

[20] In Professor Modigliani's words:
The liquidity-preference theory is not necessary to explain underemployment equilibrium; it is sufficient only in a limiting case: the "Keynesian case." In the

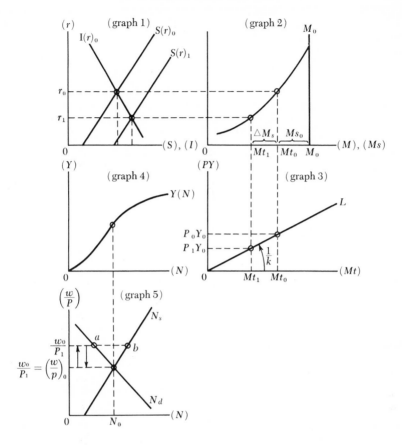

**Figure 4-1**

The second graph in the figure represents the total supply of money with the speculative cash balances $(M_s)$ abstracted from it. The rate of interest is plotted on the vertical axis; and the total money stock, as well as the quantity of money demanded for speculative balances $(Ms)$, is plotted on the horizontal axis. The full-employment equilibrium values of $(Y_0)$, $(N_0)$ and $(w/P)_0$ are determined in graphs 4 and 5; the equilibrium rate of interest $(r_0)$, which equates investment with savings at the full-employment level of real income, is determined in graph 1.

---

general case it is neither necessary nor sufficient; it can explain this phenomenon only with the additional assumption of rigid wages.
See "Liquidity Preference and the Theory of Interest and Money," *Econometrica*, XII, 1944, reprinted in *Readings in Monetary Theory*, p. 223.

Knowing $(r_0)$ from graph 2, we can subtract the speculative balances from the given $(M_0)$ and obtain the transactions balances $(Mt_0)$. Knowing $(Mt_0)$, the equilibrium price level $(P_0)$ is determined (see graph 3). Lastly, from the equilibrium $(w/P)_0$, given $(P_0)$, we obtain $(w_0)$. This is our initial full-employment equilibrium position.

The graphs in Figures 4-1 and 4-2 may be used to illustrate Modigliani's point that liquidity preference by itself is neither necessary nor sufficient to explain Keynesian underemployment equilibrium. Suppose a shift of a parameter occurs in the form of an increase in saving. This is represented in graph 1 in Figure 4-1 by the shift of the saving schedule from $S(r)_0$ to $S(r)_1$. In terms of comparative statics, the equilibrium rate of interest will be lowered from $(r_0)$ to $(r_1)$. The lowering of the rate of interest will induce an increase in speculative holdings. This is represented in graph 2 by moving down the liquidity preference function, with the result that the amount available for transactions balances is reduced. The reduction of $(Mt_0)$ to $(Mt_1)$ means a reduction of total spending. Since output remains at $(Y_0)$, the reduction of aggregate demand will cause the price level that clears the market (the equilibrium price level) to decrease from $(P_0)$ to $(P_1)$. This is illustrated in graph 3 by the decrease in money income from $(P_0 Y_0)$ to $(P_1 Y_0)$. Assuming that there is a lag in money-wage rate adjustment, the decrease in the price level will cause the real-wage rate to increase. This is indicated by the increase of $(w/P)$ from $(w/P)_0$ to $(w_0/P_1)$ in graph 5. The result will be an excess supply of labor, measured by the distance $(ab)$ in graph 5. Here is the crucial point. If wages are flexible, competition among laborers will reduce the money-wage rate, which will, in turn, induce an increase in the demand for labor. Full-employment equilibrium in the labor market will eventually be restored when the money-wage rate falls porportionally to $(w_1)$, resulting in $(w_1/P_1 = w_0/P_0)$.

The net result of an increase in saving as described in the preceding paragraph is: (1) a lowering of the equilibrium rate of interest, (2) a decrease in the equilibrium price level and money income, and (3) a decrease in the money-wage rate. The real variables, namely, employment, output, and the real-wage rate, remain unchanged in the new equilibrium situation. The result proves that a change on the monetary side (in this case, the change originates on the real side) could only affect the monetary magnitudes in this modified neoclassical system. The conclusions are exactly the same as those derived from the previous model without liquidity preference. There is, however, one essential difference between the two models, namely, the explanation of the determination of the price level. In this modified system that includes liquidity preference, the equilibrium price level is no longer determined by the quantity of money alone. The price level is now jointly determined by the rate of interest and the quantity of money.

Professor Modigliani's argument that in the absence of the liquidity trap, underemployment equilibrium requires the assumption of rigid wages, may be illustrated as follows:

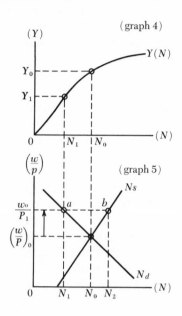

**Figure 4-2**

Under a system of rigid wages, an increase in the real-wage rate following an increase in saving (as described in Figure 4-1) will be permanent. Thus, the labor market will continuously be in a disequilibrium situation. The demand for labor will remain at point (*a*) in graph 5 of Figure 4-1. The net result is the Keynesian underemployment equilibrium. This phenomenon is illustrated in Figure 4-2, which reproduces graphs 4 and 5 of Figure 4-1. Graph 5 of Figure 4-2 shows that the real-wage rate is too high for full-employment equilibrium in the labor market. The excessively high real-wage rate is due to the downward rigidity of the money-wage rate ($w_0$), and actual employment under this condition is ($N_1$) and not ($N_0$). But at this higher real-wage rate, the intended labor supply would be ($N_2$). The result will be involuntary unemployment measured by the distance ($N_2 - N_1$). The actual employment ($N_1$) is the equilibrium employment from the standpoint of producers, because any point on the (*Nd*) schedule is an optimal position for the firms. Knowing the underemployment equilibrium (*N*₁), from the production function we obtain the underemployment-equilibrium output (*Y*₁). This is shown in graph 4. It should be noted that, under a system with downward rigidity of money-wage rates, the equilibrium values of the real variables, such as (*N*₁) and (*Y*₁), are jointly determined by monetary conditions.[21]

However, within a dynamic framework, involuntary unemployment is possible even in a neoclassical world of perfect competition and wage-price flexibility. This has been demonstrated by Professors Klein and Patinkin.[22]

Professor Patinkin approaches the problem from the standpoint of the stability of an equilibrium system. The analysis centers around the rapidity of adjustment of the relevant factors in the system. Thus, an equilibrium may be defined as stable if a departure from it will be rapidly and automatically eliminated or become negligible.[23] The orthodox writers before *The General Theory* usually assumed the reaction of the relevant factors to be prompt. They wrote under the assumptions of what Professor G. L. S. Shackle calls "the theory of pure choice."[24] "A subject facing pure choice"—this presumes "the available alternatives to be perfectly known" to him—"has no motive for not dealing at once with every question that arises concerning the details of the action he shall adopt. For he knows everything about the consequences of every available act." "There is thus room for money only as a unit of account and none for money as a store of value, an asset." Hence, "theories of pure choice are 'nonmonetary' theories."[25] Obviously, the smooth working of the model described in Chapter 3

---

[21] Hence, Professor Modigliani says,

Systems with rigid wages share the common property that the equilibrium value of the 'real' variables is determined essentially by monetary conditions rather than by 'real' factors. . . . The monetary conditions are sufficient to determine money income and, under fixed wages and given technical conditions, to each money income there corresponds a definite equilibrium level of employment. This equilibrium level does not tend to coincide with full employment except by mere chance.

See *Readings in Monetary Theory*, p. 211.

[22] This is another way of stating the Klein and Patinkin views described in the preceding section on the fundamental issues raised by Keynes.

[23] This is the definition given by William J. Baumol in *Economic Dynamics* (New York: The Macmillan Company, 1951), pp. 113–116.

[24] See G. L. S. Shackle, "Recent Theories Concerning the Nature and Role of Interest," reprinted in *Surveys of Economic Theory* prepared for the American Economic Association and the Royal Economic Society, Vol. I (London: Macmillan & Co., 1965).

[25] *Ibid.*, p. 109.

depends upon the assumption of promptness of adjustment. Once this assumption is dropped, the adjustment process becomes a long drawn-out affair. Thus, underemployment equilibrium is highly likely even with perfect competition and wage-price flexibility. This contention

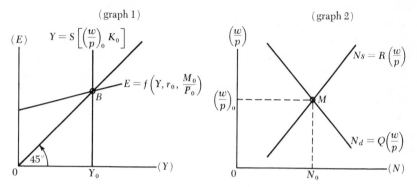

**Figure 4-3**

is described in Figure 4-3.[26] Graph 1 of Figure 4-3 depicts the commodities market. The system is initially at full-employment with the aggregate demand function intersecting the aggregate supply function at point $(B)$. The aggregate demand function is $E = f(Y, r, M/P)$, where $(E)$ is aggregate demand; $(Y)$ is output or real income; $(r)$ is the rate of interest; and $(M/P)$ is "real balances."[27] The inclusion of real balances as one of the determinants of aggregate demand makes the function price-elastic. This is the non-Keynesian element introduced by Professor Patinkin into the familiar Keynesian diagram with a view to highlighting the essential theoretical differences. The aggregate supply function is $Y = S[(w/P)_0, K_0]$. This is another non-Keynesian element introduced by Professor Patinkin. For in the familiar Keynesian cross model, the 45° line represents a suppressed aggregate-supply function.[28] The Patinkin aggregate-supply function means that aggregate supply or output $(Y)$ is a function of the real-wage rate and the given total capital stock $(K_0)$. It summarizes the technical production function and the demand-for-and supply-of-labor functions. Graph 2 of

---

[26] From Figures XIII-1 and XIII-2, *Money, Interest and Prices*, 2nd Edition, pp. 316–317, by Don Patinkin. Copyright © 1965 by Don Patinkin. Reprinted by permission of Harper & Row, Publishers.

[27] The Patinkin model and the implications of the "real-balance effect" are discussed in detail in Chapter 5.

[28] See the algebraic formulation of the truncated Keynesian model in Chapter 5.

Figure 4-3 is the same diagram depicting the labor market as in the preceding reconstructed neoclassical model. The initial full-employment equilibrium values of the relevant variables are: $(Y_0)$, $(N_0)$, $(w/P)_0$, $(M_0)$, $(P_0)$, $(w_0)$, and $(r_0)$. Thus, $(E)$ can be stated as $E = f(Y_0, r_0, M_0/P_0)$. The equilibrating mechanism via the real-balance effect is discussed in Chapter 5 and in Part II. Here it is sufficient to note that with a constant supply of nominal money, a decrease in the general price level would increase the purchasing power of the given quantity of money. Holders of cash balances will be inclined to increase their spending (assuming that their optimal cash balances remain unchanged) either directly, or indirectly via the bond market and the interest-rate mechanism. An increase in the price level will have the opposite effect.

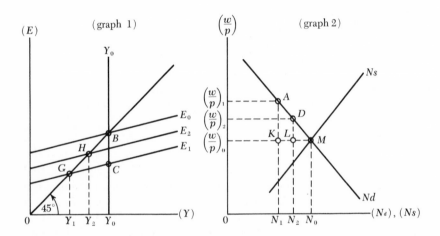

**Figure 4-4**

Assume that the position of full-employment equilibrium described in Figure 4-3 is disturbed by a downward shift in the consumption function or the investment function. This is represented in Figure 4-4, graph 1, by a downward shift of the aggregate demand function from $(E_0)$ to $(E_1)$. This shift creates a deflationary gap in the commodity market equal to $(BC)$. Professor Patinkin's task is to examine the nature of the automatic equilibrating mechanism which this initial disturbance sets into operation. If all relevant factors in the system react promptly, full-employment equilibrium will soon be restored via the real-balance effect. Producers, with promptness in the adjustment process, "will react to their temporary inability to sell by simply permitting their inventories to build up. That is, they will leave their level of production unchanged at $Y_0$."[29] However, "once this assumption is dropped, the whole argument must be drastically modified."[30] The long, drawn-out deflationary process involuntarily forces firms and producers to cut down current output and input. "And this is the beginning of involuntary unemployment."[31] Aggregate supply now decreases to $(Y_1)$ in graph 1 of Figure 4-4; the volume of employment decreases to $(N_1)$ in graph 2 of the same figure. Thus, as Professor Patinkin points out: "First we see that involuntary unemployment can exist even in a system of perfect competition and wage and price flexibility." And, "Second, we see that a deficiency in commodity demand can generate a decrease in labor input without requiring a prior increase in the real-wage rate."[32] The explanation for this point is as follows: When firms are involuntarily forced to depart from their optimum commodity-supply curve (symbolized by $Y = S [(w/p)_0, K_0]$), they are simultaneously forced to depart from their optimum demand for labor curve. Point $(K)$, in graph 2 of Figure 4-4, is a position of disequilibrium. For the existence of excess capacity represented by the distance $(Y_0 - Y_1)$ in graph 1 will continue to exert downward pressure on the price level; and the existence of an excess supply of labor at the same real-wage rate depicted by the distance $(N_0 - N_1)$ in graph 2 will continue to press down the money-wage rate. The real-balance effect created by the continuous price decline will exert both a direct and an indirect upward pressure on $(E)$. If the aggregate demand curve is pushed up to $(E_2)$, the firm will adjust their output to $(Y_2)$. Simultaneously, employment will tend to increase to $(N_2)$. If the aggregate demand function fails to increase further, disequilibrium will persist. Professor Patinkin calls attention to the fact that "the involuntary un-

---

29 From *Money, Interest and Prices*, 2nd Edition, p. 318, by Don Patinkin. Copyright © 1965 by Don Patinkin. Reprinted by permission of Harper & Row, Publishers.

30 From *Money, Interest and Prices*, 2nd Edition, p. 318, by Don Patinkin. Copyright © 1965 by Don Patinkin. Reprinted by permission of Harper & Row, Publishers.

31 From *Money, Interest and Prices*, 2nd Edition, p. 318, by Don Patinkin. Copyright © 1965 by Don Patinkin. Reprinted by permission of Harper & Row, Publishers.

32 From *Money, Interest and Prices*, 2nd Edition, pp. 323–324, by Don Patinkin. Copyright © 1965 by Don Patinkin. Reprinted by permission of Harper & Row, Publishers.

employment of *The General Theory* need *not* have its origin in wage rigidities."[33] The failure of the economy to restore full-employment equilibrium within a reasonable time is attributed to the influences of interest-inelasticities, and distribution and expectation effects. In other words, involuntary unemployment should be discussed in what Professor Klein calls "the probability, psychological, and expectational sphere."[34] Professor Shackle's theory of "impure choice"[35] expresses the same idea. "A subject facing impure choice may elect a 'simple' immediate act designed to secure freedom of deferred choice among more specialized alternatives. In fact, rather than decide what to buy, he may elect to retain money."[36] This is Keynesian economics.

## EVALUATION OF THE GENERAL THEORY

*The General Theory* is both a theory of the determination of income and employment and a monetary theory. The familiar Hicks-Hansen restatement of Keynes' theory succinctly highlights this point. Figure 4-5 represents the Hicks-Hansen model found in most current textbooks on macroeconomics. This diagram contains three important theoretical propositions. First, it indicates that the equilibrium level of real income $(Y)$ and the equilibrium rate of interest $(r)$ are simultaneously determined by four functional relations: the saving function, the investment function, the demand-for-money function, and the quantity of money, exogenously determined by the monetary system. Second, the diagram points to the integration of monetary theory (indicated by the *LM* function), the theory of determination of income and employment (indicated by the determination of equilibrium $Y$), and the theory of interest (indicated by the determination of $r$). Third, the diagram

---

[33] From *Money, Interest and Prices*, p. 340, 2nd Edition by Don Patinkin. Copyright © 1965 by Don Patinkin. Reprinted by permission of Harper & Row, Publishers.

Prof. Patinkin further observes:
Nevertheless, our theory does depend on rigidities. For, by definition, any system which fails to respond quickly and smoothly to equilibrating market forces is suffering from rigidities. But the offending rigidities are not those of extraneous monopolistic elements . . . but those inherent in the very fact that the level of aggregate commodity demand . . . is the resultant of individual decisions to consume and to invest, and that these decisions respond only "stickily" to market changes in interest and prices. They are the rigidities of sovereign consumers and investors unwilling to modify their expenditure habits on short notice [p. 343].

[34] See preceding section on fundamental issues raised by Keynes.

[35] See Shackle, *op. cit.*

[36] Shackle, p. 109.

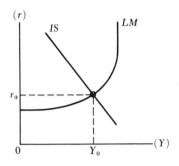

**Figure 4-5**

explains that the equilibrium rate of interest is determined by both real *(IS)* and monetary *(LM)* forces. *The General Theory* as a monetary theory is discussed and evaluated in Chapter 9. *The General Theory* as a theory of income determination and employment is evaluated in the remainder of this chapter. No attempt is made here to survey the voluminous literature on this subject.[37] The reader simply is reminded of a few salient ideas which have received wide support among the majority of writers.

## Major Contributions

One of the major contributions of *The General Theory* "lies in the general nature of Keynes' approach to the problem of income and employment."[38] As a theory for dealing with problems of unemployment and economic planning, it constitutes a great advance. Concentrating on the analysis of the determinants of spending decisions instead of treating aggregate demand as a global quantity (such as *MV* in the equation of exchange), Keynes provided a useful general equilibrium

---

[37] For representative works, see William Fellner, "What is Surviving?" *American Economic Review*, Vol. XLVII (May, 1957); Dudley Dillard, "The Influence of Keynesian Economics on Contemporary Thought," *American Economic Review*, Vol. XLVII (May, 1957); James R. Schlesinger, "After Twenty Years: The General Theory," *Quarterly Journal of Economics*, Vol. LXX (November, 1956); Harry G. Johnson, "The General Theory After Twenty-Five Years," *American Economic Review*, Vol. LI (May, 1961); *The New Economics*, Seymour E. Harris, ed. (New York: Alfred A. Knopf, 1947); and *Keynes' General Theory: Reports of Three Decades*, Robert Lekachman, ed.

[38] Johnson, "The General Theory after Twenty-Five Years," *American Economic Review*, p. 13.

model, which is "much easier to understand and to apply than the quantity theory relationships."[39] In economic terminology, we are practically all Keynesians now.

Another major contribution of *The General Theory* is its dynamic orientation and implications.[40] In spite of the static nature of the formal model, the Keynesian system may best be described as a disequilibrium system. This is the view advanced by Professors Patinkin, Clower, Klein, and Johnson.[41]

## Major Criticisms

*Supply considerations.*—The General Theory is not without theoretical weaknesses. In the first place, Keynes inverted Say's Law by placing the focal point of his analysis on the determinants of aggregate demand. Instead of saying "supply creates its own demand," Keynes' theory implies that "demand creates its own supply."[42] This implication is apparent in the familiar Keynesian analysis which represents the suppressed aggregate-supply function by the 45° line.[43] Many writers—including Professors Don Patinkin, James R. Schlesinger, Sidney Weintraub, Paul Davidson, Eugene Smolensky—have found Keynes' treatment of supply considerations relatively inadequate.[44] In fact, many post-Keynesian economists have supplemented Keynes'

---

[39] *Ibid.*, p. 16.

[40] Professor J. A. Schumpeter pointed out that the model, not the book, was essentially static. See his *History of Economic Analysis* (New York: Oxford University Press, Inc., 1965), pp. 1174–1179. Mrs. Joan Robinson observes: "Keynes brought back time into economic theory." See her *Economic Philosophy* (Chicago: Aldine Publishing Company, 1962), p. 74.

[41] See Don Patinkin, "Price Flexibility and Full Employment," in *Readings in Monetary Theory;* Robert Clower, "Keynes and the Classics: A Dynamic Perspective," *Quarterly Journal of Economics*, Vol. LXXIV (May, 1960); L. R. Klein, "The Keynesian Revolution" and "The Empirical Foundations of Keynesian Economics" in *Post-Keynesian Economics*, K. K. Kurihara, ed. (New Brunswick, N.J., Rutgers University Press, 1954); and Harry G. Johnson, "The General Theory After Twenty-Five Years."

[42] The caricature of Say's Law is the slogan: "Supply creates its own demand." The real meaning of Say's Law is price flexibility and automatic full employment. See Chap. 2.

[43] It will be recalled that in the familiar Keynesian-cross diagram the intersection of the aggregate demand function and the 45° line conveys the meaning that in the short-run, aggregate supply is governed by aggregate demand.

[44] See Patinkin, *Money, Interest, and Prices;* Schlesinger, "After Twenty Years: The General Theory"; Sidney Weintraub, *A General Theory of the Price Level, Output, Income, Distribution, and Economic Growth* (Philadelphia: Chilton Book Company, 1959); Paul Davidson and Eugene Smolensky, *Aggregate Supply and Demand Analysis* (New York: Harper & Row, Publishers, 1964).

treatment of income determination with additional supply considerations.[45] The following excerpts illustrate this point.

Professor Patinkin writes:

> The usual macroeconomic interpretation of Say's identity "is that, regardless of the rate of interest and the level of prices, the total demand of household and firms for commodities is always equal to the total income of the economy. Graphically this means that the aggregate demand curve must coincide with the 45° line. . . . This is a statement of the classical position—as seen with Keynesian eyes.[46]
>
> It can readily be shown that this line of reasoning is yet another fallacious by-product of the usual Keynesian neglect of the supply side of the commodity market.[47]

Professor Schlesinger comments:

> Over-all demand is, of course, to some extent affected by relations on the supply side; Keynes's treatment of demand was therefore over-simple in that it neglected the possibility that the relative prices prevailing in the different sectors determine, in part, the total amount of outlays.[48]

Professor John H. Williams observes:

> One over-all criticism of Keynesian economics that seems to me justified is that Keynes' emphasis on the demand side—his principle of effective demand—sins quite as much in its taking for granted the adaptibility of supply as the classical economists did in their reverse emphasis.[49]

*Aggregate demand.*—Another important criticism of *The General Theory* concerns the principle of aggregate demand itself. Professor Sumner H. Slichter remarked:

> Keynes, who twenty years ago performed the invaluable service of demonstrating that economics was suffering from the lack of

---

[45] See Chapter 5 of this volume.

[46] From *Money, Interest and Prices*, 2nd Edition, pp. 355–357, by Don Patinkin. Copyright © 1965 by Don Patinkin. Reprinted by permission of Harper & Row, Publishers.

[47] From *Money, Interest and Prices*, 2nd Edition, p. 358, by Don Patinkin. Copyright © 1965 by Don Patinkin. Reprinted by permission of Harper & Row, Publishers.

[48] Schlesinger, "After Twenty Years: The General Theory," *Quarterly Journal of Economics*, p. 592.

[49] See John H. Williams, "An Economist's Confession," *American Economic Review*, XLII (March, 1952), 8.

an adequate theory of demand, constructed a theory which gave little hint of the great and growing capacity of advanced industrial countries to increase the demand for goods. His theory of consumption . . . assigned a far too passive role to industrial consumers, and his theory of investment exaggerated the disposition to hoard and gratuitously assumed that the economy possesses only a meager capacity to discover or to create investment opportunities.[50]

Professor Slichter maintained that consumption is a dynamic influence on the economy—"The level of consumption is determined to a significant extent by conditions other than the level of real income."[51] The other determinants of consumption emphasized by Professor Slichter— all of which contribute to the development of a highly dynamic concept of consumption—are the total volume of consumer resources (income, accumulated assets, credit) and conditions and institutions affecting consumption (such as the strength or weakness of class lines, the rapidity of expansion, and technological change).[52] Professor Slichter held that investment is also dynamic. "As a matter of fact, a large proportion of technological discoveries aid in the making of additional technological progress and, thus, the creation of additional investment opportunities."[53] Hence, Keynes' theory of aggregate demand should be revised to include these institutional developments.

This view is supported by Professor Arthur F. Burns.[54] His criticism is best summarized in a sentence: "viz, the consumption function and the volume of intended investment, which are impounded in *ceteris paribus* by the Keynesian theory, cannot (except by accident) remain constant, since the very process of adjusting to the data (the consumption function and the volume of intended investment) will, quite apart from independent influences that may operate on these data, induce changes in them."[55] Professor Burns is of the opinion that the determinacy of Keynes' theory "reflects a pleasant but dangerous illusion."[56]

Other criticisms of the theory of aggregate demand are represented by the post-Keynesian emphasis on the effects of financial wealth on

---

[50] See Sumner H. Slichter, *Economic Growth in the United States* (Baton Rouge: Louisiana State University Press, 1961), p. 84.

[51] Slichter, p. 88.

[52] Slichter, pp. 135–141.

[53] Slichter, p. 101.

[54] Arthur F. Burns, *The Frontiers of Economic Knowledge* (First Science ed.; New York: John Wiley & Sons, Inc., 1965).

[55] Burns, p. 217.

[56] Burns, p. 5.

the propensity to consume.[57] Professor A. C. Pigou in his *Employment and Equilibrium* (1941) gave the first formulation of the effect of wealth on consumer expenditure, although he had been anticipated by Professor Gottfried Haberler in his *Prosperity and Depression*.[58] The "wealth effect" has been further pursued by Professors Modigliani and Brumberg, James Tobin, and other post-Keynesian writers.[59]

Keynesian investment theory has also been undergoing fundamental changes.[60] The post-Keynesian emphasis on "stock" variables, as distinct from "flow" variables and their interrelationships, is manifested both in the theory of consumption and in the theory of investment. The relationship between capital stock and investment has been made explicit in the various formulations of the "capital stock adjustment principle" in post-Keynesian business cycle theory. Furthermore, in the theory of economic growth, the question of technological progress versus investment as a source of growth has received a great deal of attention in recent years.[61]

*The General Theory as a monetary theory.*—A third group of criticisms centers around *The General Theory* as a monetary theory. These criticisms are reviewed in Chapters 9 and 10.

*Treatment of expectations.*—A fourth group of criticisms is directed toward Keynes's treatment of expectations. For instance, Professor Albert G. Hart has pointed out two major deficiencies in Keynes's analysis: (1) Keynes failed "to confront *ex-ante* and *ex-post* reasoning";

---

[57] See Chap. 5 for further discussions of this subject.

[58] For a lucid summary of this development, see Patinkin, *Price Flexibility and Full Employment;* also Ackley, *Macroeconomic Theory,* pp. 269–273, and Klein, "Empirical Foundations of Keynesian Economics," in *Post-Keynesian Economics,* pp. 288–295.

[59] See Franco Modigliani and Richard Brumberg, "Utility Analysis and the Consumption Function: An Interpretation of Cross-Section Data," in *Post-Keynesian Economics;* James Tobin, *Relative Income, Absolute Income and Saving* in *Money, Trade, and Economic Growth* (New York: The Macmillan Company, 1951); Milton Friedman, *A Theory of Consumption Function* (New York: National Bureau of Economic Research, 1955).

[60] See Chapter 5.

[61] See Edmund S. Phelps, "The New View of Investment: a Neoclassical Analysis," *The Quarterly Journal of Economics,* LXXVI (November, 1962), 548–567; Robert Solow, "Investment and Technical Progress" in *Mathematical Methods in the Social Sciences,* Arrow, Karlin and Suppes, eds. (Stanford: Stanford University Press, 1960); Edward F. Denison, *The Sources of Economic Growth in the United States and the Alternatives Before Us,* Supplementary Paper No. 13 (New York: the Committee for Economic Development, 1962); Donald Dewey, *Modern Capital Theory* (New York: Columbia University Press, 1965), pp. 143–148; and H. A. J. Green, "Embodied Progress, Investment, and Growth," *American Economic Review,* Vol. LVI (March, 1966).

and (2) Keynes transformed the theory of uncertainty into a search for 'certainty equivalents'."[62] The certainty equivalents of long-term expectations of returns on investment are formalized in the concept of marginal efficiency of capital. Keynes wrote:

> In practice we have tacitly agreed, as a rule, to fall back on what is, in truth, a *convention*. The essence of this convention—though it does not, of course, work out quite so simply—lies in assuming that the existing state of affairs will continue indefinitely, except in so far as we have specific reasons to expect a change . . . . If we can rely on the maintenance of the convention, an investor can legitimately encourage himself with the idea that the only risk he runs is that of a genuine change in the news over the near future, as to the likelihood of which he can attempt to form his own judgement, and which is unlikely to be very large.[63]

The hypothesis of convention thus renders the concept of expectations and uncertainty redundant. As stated by Professor Ozga, "No expectations need to be taken into account. The businessmen are supposed to behave as if they were adjusting their positions not to their expectations but to these observable data."[64]

*Policy implications.*—The policy implications of *The General Theory* have also been under criticism. As pointed out by Professor Klein, "Keynesian economics gives us a set of tools with which to work on the unemployment problem, but it does not deal at all with many other socio-economic questions that also deserve a large share of our attention and study."[65] The other questions listed by Professor Klein are: (1) fair employment, (2) a highly skewed income distribution, and (3) the problem of resource allocation.[66] The last problem has been given increased attention by post-Keynesian writers.[67] This point is further discussed in Chapter 5.

---

[62] Albert G. Hart, "Keynes's Analysis of Expectations and Uncertainty," in *The New Economics*, Seymour E. Harris, ed., p. 419.

[63] Reprinted from *The General Theory of Employment, Interest, and Money*, pp. 152–153, by John Maynard Keynes, by permission of Harcourt, Brace & World, Inc.

[64] See S. A. Ozga, *Expectations in Economic Theory* (Chicago: Aldine Publishing Company, 1965), p. 155.

[65] Klein, *The Keynesian Revolution*, p. 186.

[66] See Klein, *The Keynesian Revolution*, pp. 186–187.

[67] For instance, Professor John Kenneth Galbraith in *The Affluent Society* (Boston: Houghton Mifflin Company, 1958) discusses the problem of "social balance"; see also *Private Wants Public Needs*, Edmund S. Phelps, ed. (New York: W. W. Norton & Company, Inc., 1965), which is a collection of essays on the problem of resource allocation.

*Other limitations.*—Professor Joan Robinson has made another criticism of Keynesian economics. Professor Robinson writes: "Keynes' theory has little to say, directly, to the underdeveloped countries, for it was framed entirely in the context of an advanced industrial economy, with highly developed financial institutions and a sophisticated business class. The unemployment that concerned Keynes was accompanied by under-utilization of capacity already in existence. It had resulted from a fall in effective demand. The unemployment of underdeveloped economies arises because capacity and effective demand never have been great enough."[68]

Furthermore, Keynes, like his English predecessors, had nothing to say about the impact of technology on the economic system. In fact, as pointed out by Professor Slichter, "Keynes was extraordinarily pessimistic about the supply of investment opportunities—probably because he so completely ignored technology in his thinking and lacked an appreciation of the potentialities of technological discoveries."[69] Consequently, Keynesian economic policy is no longer sufficient to cope with the problem of automation and technological unemployment.

---

[68] Joan Robinson, *Economic Philosophy*, p. 119.

[69] Slichter, *Economic Growth in the United States*, p. 30.

# 5

# Post-Keynesian Developments in the Theory of Income and Employment

The criticisms of the theoretical shortcomings of *The General Theory* mentioned in the preceding chapter provide us with clues to some major trends in post-Keynesian theories of income determination. We proceed to discuss this subject under the following seven topics: (1) algebraic formulations of the truncated Keynesian model; (2) a linear version of the Hicks-Hansen model; (3) the aggregate-supply function; (4) the "real-balance effect"; (5) theory of consumer behavior; (6) theory of investment; (7) technological and structural unemployment.

Although this chapter is not explicitly devoted to a consideration of post-Keynesian theories of economic fluctuation and growth, the reader will find some of the essential ingredients of these theories carefully discussed in the section on the theory of investment. Specifically, we refer to the discussions of Duesenberry's basic model of dynamic income determination, the disembodied technical progress and neoclassical growth model, and Solow's model of embodied technical progress.[1]

---

[1] For an excellent survey of post-Keynesian theories of economic growth, see F. H. Hahn and R. C. O. Matthews, "The Theory of Economic Growth: A Survey," *Surveys of Economic Theory*, prepared for The American Economic Association and The Royal Economic Society (New York: St. Martin's Press, Inc., 1965), II, pp. 1–124. Also see Stanley Bober, *The Economics of Cycles and Growth* (New York: John Wiley & Sons, Inc., 1968); and Matthews, "Capital Stock Adjustment Theories of the Trade Cycle and the Problem of Policy," in *Post-Keynesian Economics*, K. K. Kurihara, ed. (New Brunswick, N.J.: Rutgers University Press, 1954), pp. 170–191.

## Algebraic Formulations of the Truncated Keynesian Model

One of the major trends in post-Keynesian macroeconomics is to state and extend Keynesian ideas in mathematical form.[2] Most of the algebraic formulations of the basic idea of income determination found in modern textbooks start with the truncated Keynesian model. The truncated model is the basic Keynesian idea depicted by the Keynesian diagonal-cross diagram.[3] It will be recalled that the truncated model may be represented by a system of three equations in three unknowns:

$$Y = C + I \qquad \text{Eq. (5-1)}$$
$$C = a + bY \qquad \text{Eq. (5-2)}$$
$$I = I_0 \qquad \text{Eq. (5-3)}$$

where $(Y)$ represents output (real income); $(C)$ is consumption expenditure; $(I)$ is investment expenditure; $(a)$ is the intercept of the consumption function; and $(b)$ symbolizes the slope of the consumption function, or the marginal propensity to consume. Eq. (5-1) depicts the equilibrium condition in the commodity market. It is the equation of the 45° line. Eq. (5-2) is the only behavioral equation in this truncated basic model. It denotes that consumption is a linear function of $(Y)$. Eq. (5-3) states that investment is a known constant. Thus, investment becomes an exogenous variable in this basic model. Consequently, the number of unknowns has been reduced to two. The problem here is to find the equilibrium values of the two endogenous variables: $(Y)$ and $(C)$. Analytically, finding the equilibrium value of $(Y)$ amounts to finding the point of intersection of the $(C + I)$ function and the 45° line. Once the equilibrium condition is defined as $(Y = C + I)$, the problem is reduced to solving the system of simultaneous equations for $(Y)$. First, we substitute Eqs. (5-2) and (5-3) in Eq. (5-1) and then proceed to solve the equation in one unknown $(Y)$:

$$Y = (a + bY) + (I_0)$$
$$Y - bY = a + I_0$$
$$Y(1 - b) = a + I_0$$
$$Y = \frac{1}{1 - b}(a + I_0)$$

---

[2] It is ironical that Keynes himself was not in favor of mathematical models. See *The General Theory of Employment, Interest, and Money* (New York: Harcourt, Brace & World, Inc., 1936), pp. 297–298.

[3] So far as we know, the term "truncated model" was first introduced by Professor Richard A. Musgrave in *The Theory of Public Finance* (New York: McGraw-Hill Book Company, 1959).

The equilibrium value of $(Y)$ is given by the solution: $Y = (1/1 - b)$ $(a + I_0)$. Once the equilibrium value of $(Y)$ is known, we can substitute it in the linear consumption function to find the equilibrium value of $(C)$. The economic significance of the solution may be stated as follows: First, we see that $(Y)$ is now expressed in terms of the parameters, namely, $(a)$, $(b)$ and $(I_0)$. From this reduced form of the system we can

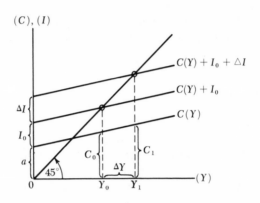

**Figure 5-1**

easily perceive that changes in $(Y)$ will be caused by changes in the parameters. Second, the total effects on $(Y)$ of a change in the exogenous variable $(I_0)$ can be measured only when all the interrelations of the model are taken into account. The interrelations of this simple basic model are as follows: When $(I)$ increases, $(Y)$ will also increase. Since $C = F(Y)$, $(C)$ will also increase. As has been observed, "this is a case of interdependence which nonmathematical theory has difficulties in handling."[4]

The interrelationships stated above lead us to an analysis of the "instantaneous" multiplier.[5] The instantaneous multiplier shows the total effect of a change in $(I)$ on $(Y)$. It can be derived from the solu-

---

[4] E. F. Beach, *Economic Models* (New York: John Wiley & Sons, Inc., 1957), p. 33.

[5] The "instantaneous" multiplier is used in "Comparative Statics." "Comparative statics" is succinctly defined by Michael J. Brennan in his *Preface to Econometrics* (Cincinnati: South-Western Publishing Company, 1960) as follows: "Comparative statics deals with changes from one equilibrium to another equilibrium, and this change is assumed to be timeless" [p. 200]. In other words, all adjustments are assumed to be instantaneous because we are in this particular case interested only in the end result.

tion or the reduced form of the model. The original equilibrium $(Y)$ is $(Y_0)$ in Fig. 5-1. The equilibrium value of $(C)$ is $(C_0)$. When investment expenditure is increased from $(I_0)$ to $(I_0 + \Delta I)$, $(Y_0)$ will increase by $(\Delta Y)$ *to* $(Y_1)$. The magnitude of the $(\Delta Y)$ in the new equilibrium is given by the equation $\Delta Y = (1/1 - b) \, \Delta I$, which shows the total $(\Delta Y)$ induced by $(\Delta I)$ after taking into consideration of income-induced $(\Delta C)$ via the marginal propensity to consume $(b)$. The equation $\Delta Y = (1/1 - b) \, \Delta I$ is derived as follows:

The original equilibrium income:

$$Y = \frac{1}{1-b}(a + I_0) \qquad \text{Eq. (5-4)}$$

The new equilibrium income after $(\Delta I)$:

$$Y + \Delta Y = \frac{1}{1-b}(a + I_0) + \frac{1}{1-b}(\Delta I) \qquad \text{Eq. (5-5)}$$

Subtracting Eq. (5-4) from Eq. (5-5) will give us the difference between $(Y_0)$ and $(Y_1)$, which is $(\Delta Y)$. From the subtraction we obtain $\Delta Y = (1/1 - b) \, \Delta I$, or $\Delta Y / \Delta I = 1/(1 - b)$. This equation shows that $(b)$, or the marginal propensity to consume $(\Delta C / \Delta Y)$ is the crucial determinant of the size of the multiplier. It is so because the total effect of a change in $(I)$ on $(Y)$ must take into consideration the interdependence within the system. In other words, we must take into consideration all the income-induced changes in the system. In this simple basic model, only one important income-induced change is explicitly stated, namely, the marginal propensity to consume $(b)$.[6] Other income-induced changes could be introduced into the multiplier analysis in more generalized models.

Without changing its basic logic, the truncated model could be expanded to include other induced changes in the system.[7] The basic model could be expanded to a system of seven equations (page 86).

[6] For a detailed discussion on the relationship between the marginal propensity to consume and the multiplier, see Alvin H. Hansen, *A Guide to Keynes* (New York: McGraw-Hill Book Company, 1953), Chap. 4. For a discussion of the "period multiplier," see Robert Aaron Gordon, *Business Fluctuations* (New York: Harper & Row, Publishers, 1961), pp. 111–117.

Alternatively, the multiplier can be derived from the saving function. A lucid exposition on this subject is given by Joseph P. McKenna, *Aggregate Economic Analysis* (New York: Holt, Rinehart & Winston, Inc., 1965), Chap. 4.

[7] For a more detailed discussion of the generalized model, see Barry N. Siegel, *Aggregate Economics and Economic Policy* (Homewood, Ill.: Richard D. Irwin, Inc., 1960), pp. 125–129.

$$Y = C + I + G + X - M \qquad \text{Eq. (5-6)}$$
$$C = a + b\ (Y - T) \qquad \text{Eq. (5-7)}$$
$$I = I_0 + iY \qquad \text{Eq. (5-8)}$$
$$M = c + mY \qquad \text{Eq. (5-9)}$$
$$T = T_0 + tY \qquad \text{Eq. (5-10)}$$
$$G = G_0 \qquad \text{Eq. (5-11)}$$
$$X = X_0 \qquad \text{Eq. (5-12)}$$

Eq. (5-6) is both a statement of the definition that real national income is equal to actual total real expenditures, and an equilibrium condition. The component parts of aggregate demand are expanded to include government expenditures $(G)$, exports $(X)$, and imports $(M)$. Eq. (5-7) is the consumption function with a slight modification. $(C)$ is now related to disposable income, which by definition is equal to national income $(Y)$ minus net tax receipts of the government $(T)$. [Net tax receipts $(T)$ by definition are equal to total gross tax revenues minus transfer payments.] The purpose of introducing the variable $(T)$ into the model is to take into consideration the "built-in stabilizers" in the government budget.[8] Eq. (5-8) is the investment function, which states that, other things being equal, the level of national income is an important determinant of business-investment expenditures. $(I_0)$ is the intercept of the function, which represents the autonomous, or non-income-induced investment expenditures, analogous to $(a)$ of the consumption function. $(i)$ is the slope of the linear investment function, or the marginal propensity to invest $(\Delta I/\Delta Y)$, which indicates the income-induced part of investment.[9] Eq. (5-9) is the import function, which states that, other things being equal, imports $(M)$ is a linear function of the level of $(Y)$; $(c)$ is the intercept, or the non-income-induced imports, and $(m)$ is the marginal propensity to import $(\Delta M/\Delta Y)$. The purpose of introducing the variables $(X - M)$ into the model is to show the relationship between national income and foreign trade.[10] Eq. (5-10) is the net tax receipts function which states that, other things being equal, net tax revenue is a linear function of national income. $(T_0)$ is the intercept

---

[8] See Siegel, Chap. 6; also Davidson and Smolensky, *Aggregate Supply and Demand Analysis* (New York: Harper & Row, Publishers, 1964), Chap. 7.

[9] For a more detailed discussion of level-induced investment see Kenneth K. Kurihara, *National Income and Economic Growth* (Chicago: Rand McNally & Co., 1961), Chap. 6; also E. S. Brooman, *Macroeconomics* (London: George Allen & Unwin, 1962), pp. 156–160. It should be noted that the analysis of income-level-induced investment is a static analysis. In dynamic analysis the acceleration principle replaces the marginal propensity to invest.

[10] See Davidson and Smolensky, Chap. 8.

and $(t)$ is the marginal propensity to tax $(\Delta T / \Delta Y)$. Eq. (5-11) states that government expenditures $(G)$ is a known constant; and Eq. (5-12) states that total exports $(X)$ is also a known constant.

The problem here again is one of finding the equilibrium values of the unknowns of the model. To find the equilibrium level of $(Y)$ is to solve the system of equations for $(Y)$. Following the same procedure, we substitute Eqs. (5-7), (5-8), (5-9), (5-10), (5-11) and (5-12) in equation (5-6) and obtain:

$$Y = \frac{1}{1 - b - i + bt + m}(a + c + I_0 + G_0 + X_0 - bT_0)$$

This is the solution or the reduced form of the system of simultaneous equations. A change in any of the parameters or the exogenous variables will lead to a change in $(Y)$. The total effects of such a change on $(Y)$ can be measured by the multiplier which is the expression $1/(1 - b - i + bt + m)$. In this generalized form, we see that the multiplier includes the four induced changes in the system. More elaborate models could incorporate other induced changes into the analysis. However, the rationale would still be the same.

The truncated model, whether in its basic simple form or in the more generalized form, deals mainly with the commodity-market equilibrium. It says nothing about the roles of money or the rate of interest in the determination of equilibrium income. In order to show that income equilibrium requires both commodity- and money-market equilibria, it is necessary to expand the model to include an analysis of money-market equilibrium.

The truncated model can also be formulated more compactly in matrix terms. The three simultaneous equations of the basic model may be condensed into the following two simultaneous equations:

$$(1) \quad Y = C + I_0$$
$$(2) \quad C = a + bY$$

These can be rearranged in the form

$$(1) \quad Y - C = I_0$$
$$(2) \quad -bY + C = a$$

so that the endogenous variables $(Y)$ and $(C)$ appear only on the left-hand side of the equations, and the exogenous variable $(I_0)$, together with the parametric constant $(a)$, appear only on the right. Using matrix notation, this system of two simultaneous equations can be written as shown at the top of the next page.

$$\begin{bmatrix} 1 & -1 \\ -b & 1 \end{bmatrix} \begin{bmatrix} Y \\ C \end{bmatrix} = \begin{bmatrix} I_0 \\ a \end{bmatrix}$$

where the coefficient matrix is $\begin{bmatrix} 1 & -1 \\ -b & 1 \end{bmatrix}$; the column vector of endogenous variables is $\begin{bmatrix} Y \\ C \end{bmatrix}$; and the column vector of parameters is $\begin{bmatrix} I_0 \\ a \end{bmatrix}$.

Following Cramer's rule, the solutions for the endogenous variables are:

$$Y = \frac{\begin{bmatrix} I_0 & -1 \\ a & 1 \end{bmatrix}}{\begin{bmatrix} 1 & -1 \\ -b & 1 \end{bmatrix}} = \frac{I_0 + a}{1 - b}$$

$$C = \frac{\begin{bmatrix} 1 & I_0 \\ -b & a \end{bmatrix}}{\begin{bmatrix} 1 & -1 \\ -b & 1 \end{bmatrix}} = \frac{a + bI_0}{1 - b}$$

These, of course, are the same solutions as obtained before.


## A LINEAR VERSION OF THE HICKS-HANSEN MODEL

The truncated model may be extended to include the quantity of money and the rate of interest. The following is a linear version of the Hicks-Hansen model.[11] The Hicksian (*IS*) curve is derived from the commodity sector of the model, which consists of a system of three equations:

$$Y = C + I \qquad\qquad \text{Eq. (5-13)}$$
$$C = a + bY \qquad\qquad \text{Eq. (5-14)}$$
$$I = I_0 - vr \qquad\qquad \text{Eq. (5-15)}$$

where $(r)$ is the rate of interest and $(v)$ the slope of the investment demand function $(\Delta I/\Delta r)$. Eq. (5-13) is the equilibrium condition (alternatively, $S = I$). Eq. (5-15) is the investment demand function, which states that, given the marginal efficiency of capital, investment is a

---

11 For a more complicated version of the Hicks-Hansen model see *Readings in Money, National Income and Stabilization Policy*, W. L. Smith and R. L. Teigen, eds. (Homewood, Ill.: Richard D. Irwin, Inc., 1965), pp. 6–18.

function of the rate of interest. The negative sign in front of $(v)$ indicates that investment and the rate of interest are inversely related.

To derive the $(IS)$ curve, we solve for $(r)$:

$$Y = (a + bY) + (I_0 - vr)$$
$$vr = a + I_0 - (1 - b)Y$$
$$r = \frac{a + I_0}{v} - \frac{1 - b}{v}(Y)$$

The last expression is the $(IS)$ curve, which states that a high level of $(Y)$ is associated with a low $(r)$ and vice versa.

The monetary sector consists of the following equations:

$$M_d = kY - mr \qquad \text{Eq. (5-16)}$$
$$M_s = M_0 \qquad \text{Eq. (5-17)}$$
$$M_d = Ms \qquad \text{Eq. (5-18)}$$

where $(M_d)$ denotes the demand for money; $(k)$ is the slope of the money demand function with respect to income; $(m)$ is the slope of the demand-for-money function with respect to the rate of interest. The negative sign in front of $(m)$ indicates that the lower the $(r)$, the more money the public will want to hold at a given income. This, of course, is another way of stating the liquidity-preference theory. $(M_s)$ is the supply of money, which is assumed to be a known constant. Eq. (5-18) is the equilibrium condition for the monetary sector, which means that the demand for money must be equal to the supply of money.

The $(LM)$ curve is derived by solving for $(r)$:

$$kY - mr = M_0$$
$$mr = kY - M_0$$
$$r = \frac{-M_0}{m} + \frac{k}{m}(Y)$$

The last expression is the $(LM)$ curve, indicating that a rise in $(Y)$ is associated with a higher $(r)$ at a given $(Ms = M_0)$.

The intersection point of the $(IS)$ and $(LM)$ schedules signifies the simultaneous determination of the equilibrium level of $(Y)$ and the corresponding equilibrium $(r)$. To find the equilibrium level of $(Y)$, we can use the equilibrium condition $(IS = LM)$ to eliminate $(r)$ and solve explicitly for $(Y)$ as follows:

$$IS = LM$$
$$\frac{a + I_0}{v} - \frac{1 - b}{v}(Y) = \frac{-M_0}{m} + \frac{k}{m}(Y)$$
$$Y = \frac{1}{1 - b + \dfrac{vk}{m}}\left[a + I_0 + \left(\frac{v}{m}\right)M_0\right]$$

The last expression states the equilibrium value of $(Y)$. The multipliers for changes in $(I)$ and in the stock of money can be derived from the same reduced form of the model. For instance, the level of $(I)$ is increased from $(I_0)$ to $(I_0 + \Delta I)$. The new level of $(Y)$ is given by

$$Y + \Delta Y = \frac{1}{1 - b + \dfrac{vk}{m}} \left[ \left(\frac{v}{m}\right) M_0 + a + I_0 + \Delta I \right]$$

Subtracting the original equilibrium level of $(Y)$ given by the expression $Y = 1/1 - b + vk/m[(v/m)M_0 + a + I_0]$ from this new level and dividing through by $(\Delta I)$, we have

$$\frac{\Delta Y}{\Delta I} = \frac{1}{1 - b + \dfrac{vk}{m}}$$

By a similar procedure, the multiplier for a change in the stock of money can be derived:

$$\frac{\Delta Y}{\Delta M} = \frac{1}{(1 - b)\dfrac{m}{v} + k}$$

It should be noted that the multiplier for a change in $(I)$ with a constant stock of money is smaller than the multiplier for a change in the stock of money. The reason is that the increase in $(Y)$ following the increase in $(I)$ will cause the rate of interest to rise, if the stock of money remains constant. The increase in the rate of interest will choke off further investment. The multiplier effect in this case is therefore smaller than in the case in which the rate of interest is prevented from rising by an increase in the money supply. Figure 5-2 illustrates this

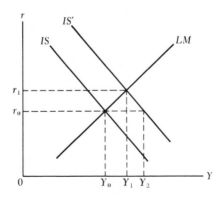

**Figure 5-2**

point. The figure shows that the actual income change from $(Y_0)$ to $(Y_1)$ following a shift in the $(IS)$ curve is dampened by the rise in the rate of interest from $(r_0)$ to $(r_1)$. The dampening effect of $(\Delta r)$ is indicated by the distance $(Y_1$ to $Y_2)$.

## THE AGGREGATE-SUPPLY FUNCTION

In discussing money and prices, Keynes wrote:

> The general price-level depends partly on the rate of remuneration of the factors of production which enter into marginal cost and partly on the scale of output as a whole, i.e. (taking equipment and technique as given) on the volume of employment.[12]

Although this quotation conveys the general tenor of the Keynesian theory of money and prices as distinct from the traditional quantity theory of money, *The General Theory* as a theory of income and employment ignores the problem of a changing price level. The various algebraic models constructed by post-Keynesian writers also adopt the simplifying assumption of constant supply prices. Thus, one of the challenging tasks in post-Keynesian economics is to incorporate price-level changes into the Keynesian system. The theoretical framework was laid down by Professor Sidney Weintraub in 1956.[13] This approach has been extended in recent years by Professors Paul Davidson, Eugene Smolensky, and others.[14]

The basic idea underlying the development in this direction may be summarized as follows. When aggregate spending rises, employment and prices are also expected to increase. The relative magnitudes of the price and employment changes will depend upon the aggregate-supply function, which summarizes the cost and productivity conditions in the economy. When prices start rising, there will be a redistribution of income away from the fixed-income groups. This redistribution-of-income effect will in turn affect the second round of aggregate spending. This process will be repeated until the economy reaches a new equilibrium.

---

[12] Reprinted from *The General Theory of Employment, Interest, and Money*, p. 294, by John Maynard Keynes, by permission of Harcourt, Brace & World, Inc.

[13] See Sidney Weintraub, "A Macroeconomic Approach to the Theory of Wages," *American Economic Review*, Vol. XLVI (December, 1956); and Weintraub, *An Approach to the Theory of Income Distribution* (Philadelphia; Chilton Book Company, 1958).

[14] See Davidson and Smolensky, *Aggregate Supply and Demand Analysis*.

The task implied in the basic idea is to link value and distribution theory to Keynesian macroeconomics. The bridge here is the aggregate-supply function. In order to build income distribution into the function, the following equation has been adopted by Professors Weintraub, Davidson, and Smolensky to depict the aggregate supply function:

$$Z = wN + F + R$$

where $(Z)$ denotes aggregate supply $(GNP)$; $(w)$ is the money wage rate; $(N)$ represents the volume of employment; $(F)$ is fixed income; and $(R)$ stands for gross profits. The implications of inter-relations among aggregate supply, employment, and the distribution of income are illustrated in Table 5-1—a hypothetical numerical example given by Professors Davidson and Smolensky in their *Aggregate Supply and Demand Analysis.*[15]

**Table 5-1**

**A Hypothetical Example of Aggregate Supply
and the Distribution of Income**

| $(Z)$<br><br>GNP<br>(billions) | $(N)$<br><br>Employment<br>(millions) | $(wN)$<br>Total<br>Wage Bill<br>(billions) | $(F)$<br>Fixed Incomes<br>or Costs<br>(billions) | $(R)$<br><br>Gross Profits<br>(billions) |
|---|---|---|---|---|
| $ 0 | 0 | $ 0 | $5 | $ −5 |
| 20 | 2 | 10 | 5 | 5 |
| 40 | 3 | 15 | 5 | 20 |
| 65 | 4 | 20 | 5 | 40 |
| 95 | 5 | 25 | 5 | 65 |

Assume the given money wage rate $(w)$ is $5,000 per year.

Table 5-1 shows that, if entrepreneurs in the aggregate expected GNP to be zero, they would not hire any workers. (This is the explanation for the aggregate-supply function $(Z)$ starting from the origin.) If GNP were expected to be $20 billions, then 2 million workers would be employed and the total wage bill $(wN)$ would be $10 billions. If a GNP of $40 billions were expected, 3 million workers would be employed. By using the data in columns $(Z)$ and $(N)$ of Table 5-1, we can plot the aggregate-supply function $(Z)$ (Fig. 5-3). From the data in

---

[15] From Table 9.1, p. 123 in *Aggregate Supply and Demand Analysis* by Paul Davidson and Eugene Smolensky (Harper & Row, 1964). Reprinted by permission of Harper & Row, Publishers.

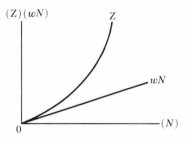

**Figure 5-3**

columns $(N)$ and $(wN)$, a total wage bill line $(wN)$ can be plotted. At any level of employment, the position of the aggregate supply function relative to the wage-bill line determines the relative wage share. The vertical difference between the aggregate-supply function and the wage-bill line at any employment level represents $(Z - wN = F + R)$. It is clear that profits $(R)$ are the residual share $(Z - wN - F = R)$.

The price level is implicit at each point on the aggregate-supply function. This is so because in a static framework, the conditions of diminishing marginal returns and fixed money rates mean increasing costs as output expands. Prices, therefore, would rise as the volume of employment increases. Simultaneously, the rise in prices would redistribute income in favor of the recipients of profits and at the expense of wage earners and fixed-income groups (as long as wages remain constant). This is shown in Fig. 5-3 by the increasing gap between the aggregate-supply function and the total wage bill line. Table 5-1 conveys the same implication.

The aggregate-demand function is not independent of the distribution of income. A twofold relationship between aggregate demand and distribution of income is envisaged by Professors Weintraub, Davidson, and Smolensky. On the one hand, the increase in aggregate demand will lead to a redistribution of income in favor of profit recipients via increases in prices. On the other hand, the redistribution of income will, in turn, affect aggregate demand via the consumption patterns of the three major groups of income recipients, namely, wage earners, rentiers, and profits recipients. Figure 5-4 represents the derivation of such an aggregate demand function.[16]

Graph 1 of Fig. 5-4 shows the relationship between total rentier income and employment. Rentier incomes are equivalent to the fixed

---

[16] The discussion in this section is based on Davidson and Smolensky, *Aggregate Supply and Demand Analysis*, Chap. 9.

cost of firms. The relationship between rentier income and employment is represented by the horizontal line ($FF'$). It is assumed that real
consumption of the rentiers is basically determined by their real income, and that their marginal propensity to consume is less than unity.
As employment and prices increase, the real income of the rentiers
declines. Although their money consumption expenditures remain unchanged, their real consumption decreases. The horizontal line ($C'$)
represents the relationship between rentiers' money outlays on consumption and employment. It lies below ($FF'$), because the marginal
propensity to consume is less than unity. It should be noted that the
positive intercept of the aggregate consumption function is attributable
to the ($C'$) line.

Graph 2 of Fig. 5-4 shows the total wage bill line ($wN$), and the
($C^w$) line represents the wage earners' money outlays on consumption.
The ($C^w$) line lies below the ($wN$) line because the wage earners' marginal propensity to consume is assumed to be less than unity. The slope
of the ($C^w$) line is positive because the wage earners' total money outlays on consumption is the summation of constant money outlays by

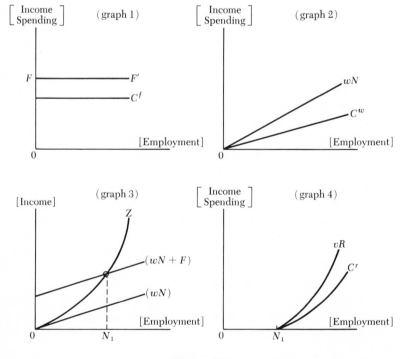

**Figure 5-4**

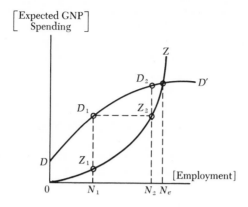

**Figure 5-5**

the previously employed and the increased money expenditures of the newly employed.

Graph 3 shows that the total cost curve is $(wN + F)$ and profit $(R)$ is the residual share $(R = Z - wN - F)$. The total revenue curve is the aggregate-supply function $(0Z)$. Assuming that dividends are equal to some fraction $(v)$ of total profits $(R)$, dividends will be equal to zero at the level $(N_1)$. Since dividends are assumed to be related to profits, and since only the part of gross profits that is distributed as dividends is available for consumption, the money outlay on consumption by profit recipients is an increasing function of the level of employment. This relationship is represented by the upward sloping $(C^r)$ line. This line lies below the $(vR)$ line because the profit recipients' marginal propensity to consume is also assumed to be less than one.

The aggregate-consumption function is the vertical sum of the consumption functions of rentiers, wage earners and profit recipients. The aggregate-demand function $(DD^1)$ is the sum of the aggregate-consumption function and the exogenously given investment expenditure $(I = I_0)$.

The equilibrium level of employment is determined by the intersection of the aggregate-supply and the aggregate-demand functions. This is shown in Fig. 5-5. The aggregate-demand function has an upward rising slope but increases at a much slower rate than the positively sloped aggregate-supply function. This is explained by (1) the fall in real consumption of rentiers in the face of rising prices and (2) the rise in savings (because the marginal propensities to consume are assumed to be less than one).

The Weintraub-Davidson-Smolensky analysis has extended the Keynesian theory of income determination by incorporating into the system the roles played by the price level and the functional distribution of income. It follows that the Keynesian multiplier analysis can be extended in the same direction.

## THE REAL-BALANCE EFFECT

The real-balance effect has been one of the important theoretical innovations since the publication of *The General Theory*. As mentioned earlier, it was originated by Professor Haberler, but it was Professor Patinkin who subsequently employed it to validate the basic conclusions of classical and neoclassical theory. By explicitly introducing the real balance as one of the determinants of the demand and supply functions of the system, he succeeded in demonstrating three important theoretical points: (1) that the "real-balance effect" could eliminate the classical and neoclassical dichotomy between value and monetary theory; (2) that the quantity-theory's conclusions (i.e., in equilibrium, money is neutral, and the rate of interest is independent of the quantity of money) could be validated by using the real-balance effect as an equilibrating mechanism; and (3) that the Keynesian underemployment equilibrium could only be interpreted as a disequilibrium situation in which the dynamic adjustment is slow. The first two points are problems of monetary theory. They will be discussed in Part II. The last point, however, falls within the confines of the theory of income and employment.

In the preceding chapter, we touched upon Professor Patinkin's evaluation of *The General Theory*. To recapitulate, Patinkin criticized Keynes for overlooking two important points: (1) "the direct influence of the real-balance effect on" aggregate demand, and (2) "the supply side of the commodity market which, by its excess over the demand, generates this effect."[17] In other words, the Keynesian position is oversimplified because it completely denies the possibility of an automatic decrease in the extent of involuntary unemployment following a downward shift of the aggregate-demand function. This point is illustrated by contrasting the familiar Keynesian diagonal-cross diagram and Professor Patinkin's modified diagonal-cross diagram.

---

[17] From *Money, Interest and Prices*, 2nd Edition, p. 325, by Don Patinkin. Copyright © 1965 by Don Patinkin. Reprinted by permission of Harper & Row, Publishers.

Keynesian Diagonal-cross Diagram

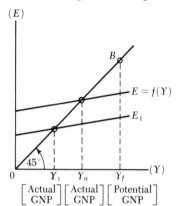

Patinkin's Diagonal-cross Diagram

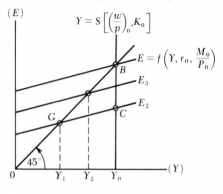

**Figure 5-6**                    **Figure 5-7**

Figure 5-6 is the Keynesian diagonal-cross diagram. Notice that it has no explicit aggregate-supply function. The 45° line represents a suppressed aggregate-supply function, as well as a statement of the equilibrium condition in the commodity market. It indicates that the total cost of production of any level of output, say $(Y_0)$, must be matched by an equal amount of actual sales proceeds, if the producers are to be expected to continue to produce at the same level of output. The idea that aggregate supply in the short run (with given capacity) is governed by aggregate demand is symbolized by the intersection of the aggregate-demand function $(E)$ and the 45° line. It is in this sense that Say's Law is being inverted. In this diagram, a downward shift of the $(E)$ function gives no indication of any possibility of an automatic decrease in the extent of involuntary unemployment. For instance, if the $(E)$ function shifts downward from the full-employment level indicated by point $(B)$ on the 45° line, the extent of involuntary unemployment will be represented by the distance $(Y_0Y_f)$. This is the underemployment equilibrium position, because the 45° line diagram overlooks the real-balance effect on the demand side, and neglects the supply side of the commodity market, whereby the excess of supply over demand generates the real-balance effect.

Now, let us examine Fig. 5-7, which is the modified diagonal-cross diagram of Professor Patinkin. (This is the same figure as Fig. 4-3.) The important differences are: (1) there is an explicitly stated aggregate-supply function, $Y = S[(w/P_0), K_0]$, which is no longer subsumed under the 45° line; and (2) the real-balance effect is explicitly introduced into the aggregate-demand function, $E = F(Y, r_0, M_0/P_0)$. Once these two important points are brought out explicitly, the Keynesians are compelled "to concede that the intersection of the aggregate-demand curve $E_2$ with the 45° diagonal at $G$ does not imply that there exist no automatic market forces to push real income up from the less-than-full-employment level $(Y_1)$."[18]

The upshot of this debate is that "in a static world with a constant stock of money, price flexibility assures full employment. But in the real dynamic world in which we live, price flexibility with a constant stock of money might generate full employment only after a long period; or might even lead to a deflationary spiral with continuous unemployment."[19] In other words, Keynesian underemployment equilibrium in a static world necessitates the assumption of downward wage rigidity. Under the assumption of wage and price flexibility, involuntary unemployment can only be interpreted as a disequilibrium situation in which the dynamic adjustment is slow. This narrows the analytical gap between Keynesian and traditional economics. As pointed out by Professor Patinkin, "In brief, our interpretation takes the debate on the degree of government intervention necessary for a practicable full-employment policy out of the realm of those questions that can be decided by *a priori* considerations of internal consistency and logical validity, and into the realm of those questions that can be decided only by empirical consideration of the actual magnitudes of the relevant economic parameters."[20]

The essential differences between the alternative macrostatic systems are highlighted by comparing the reconstructed neoclassical system, the Keynesian system, and the Patinkin system in mathematical form (p. 99).

The modified neoclassical system constructed by Professor Patinkin consists of four markets—those for finished goods, labor services, bonds, and money, respectively. In each of these markets we have a demand function, a supply function, and a statement of the equilibrium condi-

---

18 *Ibid.,* p. 339.

19 Patinkin, "Price Flexibility and Full Employment," in *Readings in Monetary Theory,* reprinted from *The American Economic Review* (1948), (Homewood, Ill.: Richard D. Irwin, Inc., 1951), pp. 277–278.

20 From *Money, Interest and Prices,* 2nd Edition, p. 340, by Don Patinkin. Copyright © 1965 by Don Patinkin. Reprinted by permission of Harper & Row, Publishers.
Patinkin points out:
   For a survey of relevant empirical studies, see Johnson, "Monetary Theory and Policy" [*American Economic Review,* Vol. LII (June, 1962)], pp. 365–377. See also Michio Morishima and Mitsuo Saito, "A Dynamic Analysis of the American Economy, 1902–1952," *International Economic Review,* V [1964]. . . .

| Neoclassical System | | Keynesian System | |
|---|---|---|---|
| $Y = Y(N)$ | Eq. (3-1) | $Y = Y(N)$ | Eq. (4-1) |
| $N_d = N_d\left(\dfrac{w}{p}\right)$ | Eq. (3-2) | $N_d = N_d\left(\dfrac{w}{p}\right)$ | Eq. (4-2) |
| $N_s = N_s\left(\dfrac{w}{p}\right)$ | Eq. (3-3) | $w = w_0$ | Eq. (4-3) |
| $M = kPY$ | Eq. (3-4) | $M = kPY + L(r)$ | Eq. (4-4) |
| $S = S(r)$ | Eq. (3-5) | $S = S(Y)$ | Eq. (4-5) |
| $I = I(r)$ | Eq. (3-6) | $I = I(r)$ | Eq. (4-6) |
| $S = I$ | Eq. (3-7) | $S = I$ | Eq. (4-7) |

## Patinkin System

$$E = F\left(Y, r_0, \frac{M_0}{P_0}\right) \qquad \text{Eq. (5-19)}$$

$$Y = S\left[\left(\frac{w}{p}\right)_0, K_0\right] \qquad \text{Eq. (5-20)}$$

$$E = Y \qquad \text{Eq. (5-21)}$$

$$N_d = Q\left(\frac{w}{p}, K_0\right) \qquad \text{Eq. (5-22)}$$

$$N_s = R\left(\frac{w}{p}\right) \qquad \text{Eq. (5-23)}$$

$$N_d = N_s \qquad \text{Eq. (5-24)}$$

$$B_d = rPF\left(Y_0, \frac{1}{r}, \frac{M_0{}^F}{P}\right) \qquad \text{Eq. (5-25)}$$

$$B_s = rPF\left(Y, \frac{1}{r}, \frac{M_0{}^H}{P}\right) \qquad \text{Eq. (5-26)}$$

$$B_d = B_s \qquad \text{Eq. (5-27)}$$

$$M_d = PL\left(Y_0, r, \frac{M_0}{p}\right) \qquad \text{Eq. (5-28)}$$

$$M_s = M_0 \qquad \text{Eq. (5-29)}$$

$$M_d = M_s \qquad \text{Eq. (5-30)}$$

tion. By virtue of what has come to be called Walras' Law, we know that if equilibrium exists in any three of these markets, it must also exist in the fourth. In examining the equilibrium of the system as a whole, then, it is sufficient to concentrate on any three markets, and omit the fourth from explicit consideration.

The commodity market consists of Eqs. (5-19), (5-20), and (5-21). Equation (5-19) is the aggregate-demand function including real balances as one of the determinants of total spending. Equation (5-20) is the explicit aggregate-supply function, which is suppressed in the oversimplified Keynesian position. Equation (5-21) is the equilibrium condition.

It should be noted that the real-balance effect is the price-induced part of the wealth effect. Another part of the wealth effect is the interest-induced effect, which was first described by Professor Lloyd A. Metzler in 1951.[21] The Metzler analysis is discussed in Chapter 10. Here it is sufficient to say that, in a state of recession, the rate of interest will decrease. If the value of real wealth is simply the capitalized value of the income streams derived from real wealth, the decrease in the rate of interest (the discount rate) will cause the discounted value of the streams of income to increase. Thus the individual will be wealthier and his propensity to consume will tend to rise (the propensity to save will tend to fall). Symbolically, the value of real wealth may be written as: $W = Y/r$; where $(W)$ is the value of real wealth, $(Y)$ denotes the stream of income derived from real wealth, and $(r)$ represents the rate of interest.[22]

## THEORY OF CONSUMER BEHAVIOR

The consumption function is one of the analytical tools forged by Keynes to attack Say's Law.[23] Keynes wrote in *The General Theory:*

---

[21] See Lloyd A. Metzler, "Wealth, Saving, and the Rate of Interest," *Journal of Political Economy*, Vol. LIX (April, 1951).

[22] In 1967, Professors Boris P. Pesek and Thomas R. Saving made a comprehensive study of the wealth effect and monetary theory. See their *Money, Wealth, and Economic Theory* (New York: The Macmillan Company, 1967). They observe at the outset that

> The history of wealth effect is one of the most ironic ones in economics. Keynes stated both parts of the wealth effect, emphasized their importance, and then let wealth slip through his fingers by his failure to build it into his analysis. His critics rediscovered one effect but, except for Gottfried Haberler, minimized its empirical relevance. His supporters admitted that Keynes did not consider it—which he did—but excused his alleged failure by arguing that he must have considered it unimportant—which he did not. Both sides, in general, ignored the problems connected with the wealth effect for more than a decade: twelve years after the appearance of the *General Theory* a memorial to Keynes was published and in the whole volume there is but one passage mentioning the wealth effect and that passage rejects it out of hand simply as ". . . a modern recrudescence of an excessive pre-occupation with the mere quantity of money—a preoccupation no less defensible than the old." Don Patinkin in his Second Edition compiled a whole list of postwar writings in which the price-induced wealth effect is being ignored; we may merely add some spice to it by pointing out that Don Patinkin himself, even now, keeps ignoring the interest-induced wealth effect [pp. 21–22].

[23] Ruth P. Mack made the following observation:
Keynes emphasized the part played by income in determining consumption. Certainly this was not a new idea. Ernst Engle had described how expenditures related to the level of family living in the middle of the nineteenth

The fundamental psychological law, upon which we are entitled to depend with great confidence both *a priori* from our knowledge of human nature and from the detailed facts of experience, is that men are disposed, as a rule and on the average, to increase their consumption as their income increases, but not by as much as the increase in their income.[24]

Keynes postulated two basic ideas concerning the relationship between income and consumption: (1) Real consumption expenditures are a stable function of real income. (2) The marginal propensity to consume is positive, but less than unity. These propositions lead to important questions about the consumption function: namely, (1) whether consumption is proportional to income, so that the average and marginal propensities to consume coincide; and (2) whether income should be regarded as past, current, or expected, or some combination of the three. Since publication of *The General Theory*, various efforts have been made to investigate these problems. Surveys of these empirical and theoretical studies have found their way into most current textbooks on macroeconomics.[25]

To indicate major trends in post-Keynesian development, the follow-

---

century. Henry L. Moore, in the early twentieth century, had considered the level of economic activity in empirical studies of demand, and E. E. Slutsky in 1915 had introduced apparatus in theoretical demand analysis for dealing with alterations in income. But the great depression and Lord Keynes assigned a stellar role to Income instead of to Price, which had been traditionally given top billing.

See "Economics of Consumption," in *A Survey of Contemporary Economics*, Bernard F. Haley, ed. (Homewood, Ill.: Richard D. Irwin, Inc., 1952), II, 40.

Professor Ackley has remarked:

Whether we emphasize that unemployment is caused by wage rigidity, by speculation, or by inconsistency, the primary determinant of the *extent* of unemployment, and therefore of the level of national income and output, is the slope of the consumption function. . . . Thus the consumption function, insufficient by itself to explain anything, becomes the kingpin of the Keynesian structure after all. This is what justifies Hansen in calling it 'the heart of Keynesian analysis', and which supports the extensive and continuing efforts to define, refine, and to measure statistically the nature and stability of the relationship of income and consumption.

See Gardner Ackley, *Macroeconomic Theory* (New York: The Macmillan Company, 1961), p. 406.

[24] Reprinted from *The General Theory of Employment, Interest, and Money* by John Maynard Keynes, p. 96, by permission of Harcourt, Brace & World, Inc.

[25] For instances, see: Ackley, *Macroeconomic Theory*, Chaps. 10, 11, and 12; Thomas F. Dernberg and Duncan M. McDougall, *Macro-economics* (2nd ed.; New York: McGraw-Hill Book Company, 1963), pp. 76–81; Barry N. Siegel, *Aggregate Economics and Public Policy* (Homewood, Ill.: Richard D. Irwin, Inc., 1960), Chaps. 8 and 9; Wallace C. Peterson, *Income, Employment, and Economic Growth* (New York: W. W. Norton & Company, Inc., 1962), Chap. 6; Myron H. Ross, *Income: Analysis and Policy* (New York: McGraw-Hill Book Company, 1964), Chaps. 3 and 4.

ing discussion presents two aspects of these studies:[26] (1) theories of the consumption function; and (2) studies on the influence of variables other than income on consumption.[27]

## Theories of the Consumption Function

The consumption function derived from family budget surveys seemed to bear out Keynes' postulate of disproportionality, namely, the average and marginal propensities to consume do not coincide. However, estimates of national saving, and other aggregates, made by Professor Simon Kuznets in 1946, and Professor Raymond Goldsmith in 1955, indicate that the long-run average propensity to save (or to consume) has remained virtually constant since the 1870's.[28] These apparently contradictory findings require reconciliation. As pointed out by Professor Houthakker, "the proposed solutions to this contradiction have all taken the form of reinterpretation of the independent variable in the consumption function.[29] The three current hypotheses are: (1) the "absolute income" hypothesis associated with Professor James Tobin; (2) the "relative income" hypothesis associated with Professors Duesenberry and Modigliani; and (3) Professor Friedman's "permanent income" hypothesis.

*The absolute income hypothesis.*—Keynes related consumption to absolute income. Professor James Tobin subsequently tested this hypothesis with three kinds of budget data: (1) budgets of the same families over three successive years, (2) budgets of Negro and white families in the same cities in the same year, and (3) budgets of families in different cities in the same year. "In all three tests, the 'absolute income' interpretation proved to explain the observations better than the alternative theories."[30] However, testing the hypothesis on budgets

---

[26] Professor Robert Ferber in his "Research on Household Behavior," *American Economic Review*, Vol. LII (March, 1962), points out: "The great bulk of studies of household behavior in the past fifteen years have dealt with one or more of the following aspects of the subject: (1) Theories of spending, or saving, behavior; (2) Influence of variables other than income on spending and saving; (3) Determinants of asset holdings; (4) Determinants of specific expenditures; (5) Decision process" (p. 19).

[27] For a comprehensive survey of the material discussed in this section see Ferber's "Research on Household Behavior."

[28] See Simon Kuznets, *National Product Since 1869* (New York: National Bureau of Economic Research, 1946); and Raymond Goldsmith, *A Study of Saving in the United States* (Princeton, N.J.: Princeton University Press, 1955).

[29] H. S. Houthakker, "The Permanent Income Hypothesis," *American Economic Review*, XLVIII (June, 1958), 396.

[30] James Tobin, "Relative Income, Absolute Income, and Saving," in *Money, Trade, and Economic Growth: Essays in Honor of John H. Williams* (New York: The Macmillan Company, 1951), p. 156.

of Negro and white families in the same cities in the same year "required the help of the hypothesis that net saving depends on asset holdings as well as on income."[31]

With the introduction of asset holdings as an additional explanatory variable of consumption, Professor Tobin demonstrated that absolute levels of income determine saving rates, but that the existence of asset holdings by consumers tends to depress the propensity to save. Thus, the first factor is offset by the second. The result is a stable, long-run saving function. In Professor Tobin's words, "this invariance could be explained alternatively by the growth of asset holdings."[32]

*The relative income hypothesis.*—An alternative solution to the apparent contradiction is provided by the relative income hypothesis.[33] Professor James S. Duesenberry's *Income, Saving, and the Theory of Consumer Behavior* (1949) "began as a critique of the Keynesian consumption function. This critique is based on a demonstration that two fundamental assumptions of aggregate-demand theory are invalid. These assumptions are (1) that every individual's consumption behavior is independent of that of every other individual, and (2) that consumption relations are reversible in time."[34] By the second assumption, Professor Duesenberry means: "that the change in expenditures resulting from a fall in income is the same in absolute magnitude as that resulting from a rise."[35] In reformulating the theory of consump-

---

[31] Tobin, in *Money, Trade, and Economic Growth*, p. 156.
It should be noted that the emphasis on asset holdings as determinants of consumption is tantamount to a modification of the Keynesian consumption function. As mentioned earlier, the Pigouvian "real-balance effect" was, perhaps, the earliest modification of the Keynesian hypothesis.

[32] Tobin, in *Money, Trade, and Economic Growth*, p. 156.
According to Professor Robert Ferber,
In its empirical applications the absolute income hypothesis has generally followed one or two forms. One form has been to express the level of saving, or of consumption expenditures, as a function of income and other variables, i.e.,: (1) $S = a + bY + cZ + u$, where S represents saving, Y is income, Z is a conglomeration of other variables, $u$ is a stochastic term, and the other letters represent parameters. The second form involves expressing the saving ratio as a function of the same variables, i.e.: (2) $S/Y = a' + b'Y + c'Z + u'$.
Ferber, *op. cit.*, p. 22.

[33] Ferber, p. 23. Professor Ferber observes:
. . . the relative income hypothesis . . . seems to have been first propounded by Dorothy Brady and Rose Friedman. Its underlying assumption is that saving rate depends not on the level of income but on the *relative position* of the individual on the income scale, i.e., $(S/Y) = a + b(Y/\overline{Y})$ where S and Y represent individual saving and income, respectively, and $\overline{Y}$ represents average income. Much additional theoretical and empirical support of this hypothesis was provided by the work of Modigliani and of Duesenberry, carried out at about the same time.

[34] James S. Duesenberry, *Income, Saving, and the Theory of Consumer Behavior* (Cambridge, Mass.: Harvard University Press, 1949), p. 1.

[35] Duesenberry, p. 3.

tion, he points out: "A real understanding of the problem of consumer behavior must begin with a full recognition of the social character of consumption patterns."[36] By the "social character of consumption patterns," he refers to the tendency existing in the American social system of people to strive constantly toward a higher consumption level and to emulate the consumption patterns of the income group one aspires to join. Thus, consumers' preferences are not independent of each other, but rather are interdependent; and the differences in relative incomes are the strategic factors determining consumption expenditures. Once an individual reaches a particular income level and the standard of living associated with it, any subsequent reduction of income (during a period of recession, for example) will lead to efforts to maintain the peak level of consumption at the expense of saving.

In order to use the relative-income hypothesis to explain the long-run constancy of the savings ratio, it is necessary to assume that there has been no change in the distribution of income. For if consumer behavior is emulative, then people's consumption (saving) is linked to what happens to the families that are being emulated. Hence, a more uniform distribution of income would result in a decrease in consumption (rise in saving).

A closely allied hypothesis is the "past-peak-of-income" hypothesis that Professor Duesenberry uses to explain short-run fluctuations in saving and to refute the Keynesian assumption that consumption relations are reversible. The essence of the hypothesis is that during a period of prosperity, consumption will progressively adjust itself to a higher peak than any previously reached; and that once people become accustomed to this higher standard of living, they are reluctant to return to a lower level during a period of recession. In Professor Duesenberry's own words: "We can conclude then that the income or consumption of the last cyclical peak will carry a special and very heavy weight in determining consumption at a given (lower) level of income during a depression."[37] Thus, as income decreases, consumption declines at a rate proportionately less than the decrease in income. Consumption is sustained by the reduction in current saving, so that the saving-to-income ratio declines during a recession. When income rises during the subsequent recovery period, saving rises rapidly, and consumption rises gradually. But when the previous peak of income is exceeded, consumption responds more vigorously to current income, and saving, therefore, rises less rapidly. Here we see that the Keynes-

---

[36] Duesenberry, p. 19.

[37] Duesenberry, p. 89.

ian assumption of the reversibility of consumption relations in time is negated.

In combining the two related hypotheses, Professor Duesenberry proposed a consumption function of the following form:

$$\frac{S_t}{Y_t} = a \frac{Y_t}{Y_0} + b$$

where (S) and (Y) denote saving and income, respectively, the subscript (t) symbolizes the current period and the subscript (o) refers to the previous peak. In this equation the savings ratio is regarded as a function of the ratio of current income to the highest income previously attained $(Y_t/Y_0)$. If this ratio is constant (as in periods of steadily rising income), the savings ratio is constant. During periods of recession when current income falls below the previous peak income $(Y_0)$, the savings ratio will fall.[38]

*The permanent-income hypothesis.*—A third solution of the apparent contradiction between the results of the long-run and short-run empirical studies is Professor Friedman's permanent-income hypothesis.[39] The idea is based on a division of both consumption and income into permanent and transitory components. By permanent income is meant "the product of two factors: the wealth of a consumer unit, estimated as the discounted present value of a stream of future expected receipts, and at the rate *r*, at which these expected receipts

---

[38] Professor Duesenberry's estimated equation, fitted to the data for 1929–1940 is: $S_t/Y_t = 0.25 \ Y_t/Y_0 - 0.196$.
See *Income, Saving, and the Theory of Consumer Behavior*, p. 90.

[39] See Milton Friedman, *A Theory of Consumption Function*, National Bureau of Economic Research, General Series 63 (Princeton: Princeton University Press, 1957). An often quoted passage from the study follows:
Consider a large number of men all earning $100 a week and spending $100 a week on current consumption. Let them receive their pay once a week, the pay days being staggered, so that one-seventh are paid on Sunday, one-seventh on Monday, and so on. Suppose we collect budget data for a sample of these men for one day chosen at random, defined income as cash receipts on that day, and defined consumption as cash expenditures. One-seventh of the men would be recorded as having an income of $100, six-sevenths as having an income of zero. It may well be that the men would spend more on pay day than on other days but they would also make expenditures on other days, so we would record the one-seventh with an income of $100 as having positive savings, the other six-sevenths as having negative savings. Consumption might appear to rise with income, but, if so, not as much as income, so that the fraction of income saved would rise with income. These results tell us nothing meaningful about consumption behavior; they simply reflect the use of inappropriate concepts of income and consumption. Men do not adapt their cash expenditures on consumption to their cash receipts, and their cash expenditures on consumption may not be a good index of the value of services consumed—in our simple example, consumption expenditures might well be zero on Sunday [p. 220].

are discounted."[40] Permanent consumption is assumed to be a multiple $(k)$ of permanent income. This ratio (between permanent consumption and permanent income) is dependent on the rate of interest, the ratio of "nonhuman" wealth to income, and the catch-all variable, of which individuals' ages and tastes are principal components. However, this ratio $(k)$ is independent of permanent income. Transitory consumption is assumed to be uncorrelated with transitory income. "Measured" consumption (the sum of transitory and permanent consumption, which is the magnitude observed from cross-sectional data for a period), therefore, depends only on permanent income, and not on measured income.

In other words, Professor Friedman's hypothesis may be said to rest on three fundamental principles:

1. An individual consumer's observed (measured) income and observed consumption in any period may be divided into two components: a "transitory" component and a "permanent" component. Symbolically,

$$Y = Y_p + Y_t$$
$$C = C_p + C_t$$

where $(Y)$ denotes measured income; $(Y_p)$ represents "permanent income"; and $(Y_t)$ is the "transitory" component. The same meanings apply to $(C)$, $(C_p)$, and $(C_t)$.

2. Permanent consumption is a multiple $(k)$ of "permanent income." Symbolically,

$$C_p = kY_p$$
$$k = f(r, w, u)$$

where $(k)$ is a function of the interest rate $(r)$, the ratio of nonhuman wealth to total wealth (nonhuman plus human wealth) $(w)$, and a catch-all variable reflecting the consumer's propensity to consume $(u)$. The main determinants of the propensity to consume are such factors as age and tastes. Thus, $(k)$ is independent of the level of $(Y_p)$. Furthermore, consumption is defined in the physical sense (the physical consumption of goods and services).

3. The consumer unit is assumed

> to determine its standard of living on the basis of expected returns from its resources over its lifetime. These returns are expected to be constant from year to year, though in actual practice some fluctuation would result over time with changes in

---

[40] Ferber, *op. cit.*, p. 26.

the anticipated amount of capital resources. The expenditures of the consumer unit are set as a constant proportion ($k$) of this permanent level of income, the value of ($k$) varying for consumer units of different types and of different tastes. Actual consumption and actual income deviate from these planned, or permanent, levels to the extent that transitory factors enter in, e.g., a crop failure in the case of farm family income or unexpected medical bills in the case of spending. However, these transitory factors are essentially random and independent of each other, with the primary result of serving to obscure the true underlying relationship between the permanent components of income and consumption.[41]

Hence, if the estimated relationship between income and consumption is a linear one in the form $C = a + bY$, according to the permanent income hypothesis, "the slope of the relation between observed consumption and observed income, namely (assuming linearity) $b$ in: $C = a + bY$ can be shown to be equivalent to $kPy$, where $Py$ is the ratio of the variance of the permanent component of income to the total variance of income, i.e.:[42]

$$P_y = \frac{\Sigma(Y_p - \overline{Y}_p)^2}{\Sigma(Y - \overline{Y})^2}$$

It should be noted that Professor Friedman's hypothesis is an integral part of the logical structure of his restatement of the quantity theory of money.[43] Accordingly, it will be considered again in Chapter 10. Suffice it here to say that Professor Friedman approaches the analysis of the demand for money in terms of the broad concept of wealth. "Total wealth includes all resources of 'income' or consumable services."[44] "Income" is defined as expected yield on wealth, or "permanent income." Since observed consumption depends solely on permanent income (hence, the demand for money—or its reciprocal, the velocity of circulation—also depends on permanent income), and since

---

[41] Ferber, p. 27.

[42] Ferber, p. 28.

[43] Professor Robert W. Clower observes:

. . . the conceptual framework of Friedman and Schwartz's *History* is virtually indistinguishable from that of Friedman's earlier *A Theory of Consumption Function*. Once this analogy is grasped, the whole of Friedman and Schwartz's analytical narrative is seen to follow a purposeful pattern; what at first sight seems a slightly untidy argument is instead discovered to be a masterly mosaic of logic and facts.

"Monetary History and Positive Economics," *The Journal of Economic History*, XXIV, No. 3 (September, 1964), 370.

[44] Milton Friedman, ed., *Studies in the Quantity Theory of Money* (Chicago: University of Chicago Press, 1956), p. 4.

permanent income fluctuates much less than observed income, it follows that the demand for money is highly stable. According to Professor Robert W. Clower, a free translation of the Friedman-Schwartz thesis is as follows:

The "normal" stock of money $(M_p)$ and the permanent income level $(Y_p)$ are related by the equation of the form:

$$M_p = KY_p{}^a \qquad\qquad \text{Eq. (5-31)}$$

where $(K)$ is a constant representing the reciprocal of the permanent income velocity of money, and $(a)$ is a constant $(a > 1)$ representing the permanent income elasticity of demand for money. To connect $(M_p)$ and $(Y_p)$ with the measured stock of money $(M)$ and income $(Y)$, the following equations are introduced:

$$M \equiv M_p + M_t \qquad\qquad \text{Eq. (5-32)}$$
$$Y \equiv Y_p + Y_t, \text{ or, } Y_p \equiv Y - Y_t \qquad\qquad \text{Eq. (5-33)}$$

where $(M_t)$ denotes the transitory component of $(M)$; and $(Y_t)$ is transitory income. These two identities, together with Eq. (5-31) give us the following relationship:[45]

$$M = K(Y - Y_t)^a + M_t \qquad\qquad \text{Eq. (5-34)}$$

*The Modigliani-Brumberg formulation.*—A variation of the permanent income hypothesis has been formulated by Professors Franco Modigliani and Richard Brumberg.[46] The results of their work not only "basically confirm the propositions put forward by Keynes in *The General Theory*," but also succeed in tying "this aspect of his [Keynes'] analysis into the mainstream of economic theory by replacing his mysterious psychological law with the principle that men are disposed, as a rule and on the average, to be forward-looking animals."[47] They depart from Keynes, however, by claiming "that the proportion of income saved is essentially independent of income; and that systematic deviations of the saving ratio from the normal level are largely accounted

---

[45] This equation connects the measured stock of money $(M)$ and measured money income. It is derived in the following way: Substituting Eq. (5-31) into Eq. (5-32), we obtain: Eq. (5-34a) $M = KY_p{}^a + M_t$. Substituting Eq. (5-33) into Eq. (5-34a), we obtain: $M = K(Y - Y_t)^a + M_t$.

For Professor Clower's version, see "Monetary History and Positive Economics," pp. 369–370.

[46] Franco Modigliani and Richard Brumberg, "Utility Analysis and the Consumption Function: An interpretation of Cross-Section Data," in *Post-Keynesian Economics*, K. K. Kurihara, ed. (New Brunswick, N.J.: Rutgers University Press, 1954), pp. 388–436.

[47] *Ibid.*, p. 430.

for by the fact that short-term fluctuations of income around the basic earning capacity of the household, as well as the gradual changes in this earning capacity, may cause accumulated savings to get out of line with current income and age."[48]

Their claim rests largely on the following two propositions:

1. . . . the major purpose of saving is to provide a cushion against the major variations of income that typically occur during the life cycle of the household as well as against less systematic short-term fluctuations in income and needs;

2. . . . the provisions that household would wish to make, and can afford to make, for retirement as well as for emergencies, must be basically proportional, on the average, to its basic earning capacity, while the number of years over which these provisions can be made is largely independent of income levels.[49]

Let us now consider their basic model. In the first place, they call attention to the traditional theory of the household, which asserts that there need not be any close and simple relation between consumption and income in a given period. According to the traditional theory, "the rate of consumption in any given period is a facet of a plan which extends over the balance of the individual's life, while the income accruing within the same period is but one element which contributes to the shaping of such a plan."[50] Following the traditional approach to consumer behavior, Professors Modigliani and Brumberg start their analysis with a utility function, which can be written as

$$U = U(C_t, C_{t+1}, \ldots C_L, A_{L+1}) \qquad \text{Eq. (5-35)}$$

where $(U)$ is utility; $(C)$ denotes consumption; $(L)$ stands for life-span; and $(A)$ indicates assets.[51] The equation states that the consumer's util-

---

[48] *Ibid.*

[49] *Ibid.*

[50] *Ibid.*, p. 392.

[51] Professors Modigliani and Brumberg employ the following variables in their analysis:
*Ibid.*, p. 390.
$(C_t)$ = consumption of the individual during the $t$-th year of his life, where $(t)$ is measured from the beginning of the earning span;
$(Y_t)$ = income in the $t$-th year, $(Y_t)$ and $(C_t)$ denote current income and consumption, while $(Y_\tau)$ and $(C_\tau)$ denote expected income and planned consumption in the $\tau$-th year;
$(A_t)$ = asset at beginning of age period $(t)$;
$(N)$  = the earning span;
$(M)$  = the retirement span;
$(L)$  = the life span, that is, $(N + M)$; and
$(r)$  = the rate of interest.

ity is a function of present and prospective consumption and assets that he will receive over his lifetime. This function is to be maximized subject to a budget constraint, which consists of the total resources available to him.

Secondly, Professors Modigliani and Brumberg introduced the following simplifying assumptions:

ASSUMPTION I: The price level is not expected to change appreciably over time. Furthermore, it is assumed that "the typical household . . . does not inherit assets to any significant extent and in turn does not plan on leaving assets to its heirs. These conditions can be formally stated as: $A_1 = 0$, $\overline{A}_{L+1} = 0$."[52] It follows that "current and future planned consumption must be functions of current and expected (discounted) income plus initial assets."[53] Symbolically, the consumption function may be written as,

$$\overline{C}_\tau = f(V_t, t, \tau), \tau = t, t+1, \ldots, L; \qquad \text{Eq. (5-36)}$$

where $(t)$ denotes the present age of the individual; $(V_t)$ stands for the current total resources which is the sum of current and expected (discounted) income plus initial assets, i.e.,

$$V_t = \sum_{\tau=t}^{N} \frac{Y_\tau}{(1+r)^{\tau+1-t}} + A_t \qquad \text{Eq. (5-37)}$$

The symbol $(\overline{C}_\tau)$ represents the individual's planned consumption pattern based on the expectation that his total resources would amount to $(V_t)$, and a given rate of interest $(r)$.

ASSUMPTION II: "The utility function is such that the proportion of his total resources that an individual plans to devote to consumption in any given year $\tau$ of his remaining life is determined by his tastes and not by the size of his resources."[54] The following equation represents this assumption:

$$\overline{C}_\tau = Y_\tau{}^t V_t \qquad \tau = t, t+1, \ldots, L \qquad \text{Eq. (5-38)}$$

where $(Y_\tau{}^t)$ represents the proportion of the consumer's total resources that he plans to consume in any given year $(\tau)$.

ASSUMPTION III: If interest rate is zero $(r=0)$, the expression [Eq. (5-37)]

$$V_t = \sum_{\tau=t}^{N} \frac{Y_t}{(1+r)^{\tau+1-t}} + A_t$$

[52] *Ibid.*, p. 394.
[53] *Ibid.*, p. 395.
[54] *Ibid.*, pp. 395–396.

can be rewritten as:

$$V_t = Y_t + (N - t)Y_t^e + A_t$$

where $(Y_t^e)$ stands for the average income expected over the balance of the earning span, or, symbolically,

$$Y_t^e = \frac{\sum\limits_{\tau = t+1}^{N} Y_t}{N - t}$$

Eq. (5-36) now can be rewritten as:

$$\overline{C}_\tau = Y_\tau{}^t(V_t) = Y_\tau{}^t[Y_t + (N - t)Y_t^e + A_t]$$

which implies:

$$\sum\limits_{\tau=t}^{L} C^\tau = [Y_t + (N - t)Y_t^e + A_t] \sum\limits_{\tau=t}^{L} Y_\tau{}^t$$

Recalling the assumption that the consumer does not inherit assets to any significant extent and in turn does not plan on leaving assets to his heirs, we also have:

$$\sum\limits_{\tau=t}^{L} C_\tau = Y_t + (N - t)Y_t^e + A_t$$

Thus,

$$Y_t + (N - t)Y_t^e + A_t = [Y_t + (N - t)Y_t^e + A_t] \sum\limits_{\tau=t}^{L} Y_\tau{}^t$$

Dividing both sides of the equation by $[Y_t + (N - t)Y_t^e + A_t]$ we obtain:

$$\sum\limits_{\tau=t}^{L} Y_\tau{}^t = 1 \qquad\qquad \text{Eq. (5-39)}$$

This expression leads us to Assumption IV.

ASSUMPTION IV: "All the $Y_\tau{}^t$ are equal; i.e., our hypothetical prototype plans to consume his income at an even rate throughout the balance of his life. Let $Y_t$ denote the common values of the $Y_\tau{}^t$ for an individual of age $t$."[55] From Eq. (5-39), we then have:

$$\sum\limits_{\tau=t}^{L} Y_\tau{}^t = (L_t)Y_t = 1, \text{ or}$$

$$Y_t = \frac{1}{L_t} \qquad\qquad \text{Eq. (5-40)}$$

where $(Lt \equiv L + 1 - t)$ denotes the remaining life span at age $(t)$. Substituting Eq. (5-40) into Eq. (5-38), we obtain the desired consumption function at the top of page 112.

---

[55] *Ibid.*, p. 397.

$$C_t = \frac{1}{L_t} \left[ Y_t + (N - t)Y_t{}^e + A_t \right] \qquad \text{Eq. (5-41)}$$

The corresponding expression for saving is:

$$S \equiv Y - C = \frac{L - t}{L_t} Y - \frac{N - t}{L_t} Y^e - \frac{1}{L_t} A \qquad \text{Eq. (5-42)}$$

Now we can see why the Modigliani-Brumberg thesis has been called the "life-cycle theory of saving." According to Eq. (5-41), "current consumption is a linear and homogeneous function of current income, expected average income, and initial assets, with coefficients depending on the age of the household."[56] Their departure from Keynes' hypothesis is brought out in bold relief.

### Influence of Variables Other Than Income

Keynes' consumption function is a *ceteris paribus* function, i.e., other things being equal, consumption is a function of income. One further development in post-Keynesian empirical studies of the consumption function has been the attempt to ascertain the effects of those variables entering into the *ceteris paribus* assumption.

One group of such studies is focused on the socioeconomic characteristics of the household. For instance, Harold Watt's study (1958) highlights the role played by occupation and education in the determination of consumption spending.[57] Watts finds that those with more education expect higher incomes and spend more. Studies carried out at the Survey Research Center of the University of Michigan emphasize the role of the age factor in consumer behavior.

Another group of studies centers around the financial characteristics of the household, one of which is the "wealth effect." On the theoretical level, the wealth effect has been stressed in various ways by Professors Pigou, Lerner, Tobin and Friedman.[58] On the empirical side, Morris Cohen, George Katona, L. R. Klein, and others have made extensive studies on the effects of liquid assets on consumption expenditures.[59] "Various students of the problem have suggested that net worth is a more relevant concept than liquid assets. This concept is

---

[56] *Ibid.*, p. 398.

[57] H. W. Watts, *Long-run Income Expenditure and Consumer Savings*, Cowles Foundation Paper No. 123 (New Haven, 1958).

[58] See Abba P. Lerner, "The Burden of National Debt," in *Income, Employment, and Public Policy: Essays in Honor of Alvin H. Hansen* (New York: W. W. Norton & Company, Inc., 1948). The other works have been cited before.

[59] See Morris Cohen, "Liquid Assets and Consumption Function," *Review of Economic Studies* (May, 1964); and Lawrence R. Klein, "Assets, Debts, and Economic Behavior," in *Studies in Income and Wealth*, Vol. 14 (New York: National Bureau of Economic Research, 1951).

also much closer to the definition of wealth in the MBA (Modigliani-Brumberg-Ando) formulation of the permanent income hypothesis, in which wealth plays a basic role. Unfortunately, data on net worth are difficult to collect, and hypotheses based on net worth and total resources have yet to be subjected to direct examination."[60]

A third group of studies stresses the roles played by expectations and attitudes in consumer behavior. George Katona's *Psychological Analysis of Economic Behavior* (1963) is an outstanding work on this subject.[61] Professor Katona writes: "In the Survey of Consumer Finances conducted at the beginning of 1946, consumers were asked about their various plans and expectations for the year 1946—the first postwar year—and about the reasons for those plans and expectations. It developed that many people expected to spend more for regular living expenses in 1946 than they had in 1945, because they were aware of a rising price trend and expected it to continue."[62] With regard to income expectations, Professor Katona advances the following hypothesis: "Income expectations are based on levels of aspiration or, more specifically, they are based on the same considerations that determine the levels of aspiration. Past performance will then be a major consideration. If a person's income has been going up according to his aspirations, he will expect it to go up further; if, however, he has been unsuccessful in increasing his income, or if contrary to his aspirations his income has declined, he will not expect a higher income."[63] On the attitudes toward assets, Professor Katona observes: "Accumulation is limited, for poor as for rich people, by the ever-prevailing conflict between spending and saving. At the same time that larger reserves for 'rainy days' or retirement are needed and desired, many other more immediate needs are pressing toward satisfaction. Because of this ever present conflict, it is possible that large asset holdings may influence some people to spend a greater portion of their income. They may save less, not because they do not desire to save, but because, having substantial assets, they find it harder to say no—to their wives, children, or to their own desires."[64]

---

[60] Ferber, *op. cit.*, p. 38.

[61] George Katona, *Psychological Analysis of Economic Behavior* (New York: McGraw-Hill Book Company, 1963).

[62] From *Psychological Analysis of Economic Behavior* by George Katona. Copyright 1963 by McGraw-Hill Book Company. Used with permission of McGraw-Hill Book Company.

[63] From *Psychological Analysis of Economic Behavior* by George Katona. Copyright 1963 by McGraw-Hill Book Company. Used with permission of McGraw-Hill Book Company.

[64] From *Psychological Analysis of Economic Behavior* by George Katona. Copyright 1963 by McGraw-Hill Book Company. Used with permission of McGraw-Hill Book Company.

## THEORY OF INVESTMENT

Keynes' formulation of the theory of investment in terms of the functional relationship between investment expenditures and the rate of interest has been criticized by a number of post-Keynesian writers.[65] It will be recalled that, like his consumption function, Keynes' investment demand schedule is a *ceteris paribus* function, and is not intended to provide a complete theory of investment. A more complete theory of investment must pull the parametric factors out of the *ceteris paribus* pond and ascertain the effects of each of them on investment. A growing amount of empirical investigation has been devoted to this broad area of investment decisions. Surveys of these studies may be found in current textbooks on macroeconomics.[66] The following sections discuss some of the important landmarks in post-Keynesian investment theory.

### Integration of the Financial and Acceleration Theories

One of the landmarks appears to be the tendency to integrate the "financial" and "acceleration" theories of investment. The role of profits in the determination of investment has been emphasized by empirical studies.[67] As pointed out by Professor Edwin Kuh, "The main propositions that emerge are quite simply these: first, the greater are the profits, the greater will be the level of internally generated funds,

[65] See, for instance, Alvin H. Hansen, *Business Cycles and National Income* (New York: W. W. Norton & Company, Inc., 1951), pp. 133–136; W. H. White, "Interest Inelasticity of Investment Demand—The Case from Business Attitude Surveys Re-examined," *American Economic Review*, Vol. XLVI (September, 1956); M. D. Brockie and A. L. Grey, "The Marginal Efficiency of Capital and Investment Programming," *The Economic Journal* (December, 1956); John R. Meyer and Edward Kuh, *The Investment Decision: An Empirical Study* (Cambridge, Mass.: Harvard University Press, 1957); James S. Duesenberry, *Business Cycles and Economic Growth* (New York: McGraw-Hill Book Company, 1958), Chaps. 5 and 6.

For studies in the 1930's, see H. D. Henderson, *The Significance of the Rate of Interest*, Oxford Economic Papers, No. 1 (January, 1938), reprinted in *Oxford Studies in the Price Mechanism*, T. Wilson and P. W. S. Andrews, eds. (New York: Oxford University Press, 1951).

[66] See, for instance, Myron H. Ross, *Income: Analysis and Policy*, Chap. 6; Wallace C. Peterson, *Income, Employment and Economic Growth*, Chap. 7; Barry N. Siegel, *Aggregate Economics and Public Policy*, Chap. 11; Gerald Sirkin, *Introduction to Macroeconomic Theory* (Homewood, Ill.: Richard D. Irwin, Inc., 1961), Chap. 5; Franklin V. Walker, *Growth, Employment and the Price Level* (Englewood Cliffs, New Jersey: Prentice-Hall, Inc., 1963), Chap. 11.

[67] See James S. Duesenberry, *Business Cycles and Economic Growth*, Chaps. 5 and 6; Edgar M. Hoover, "Some Institutional Factors in Business Investment Decisions," *American Economic Review* (May, 1954); and Meyer and Kuh, *The Investment Decision: An Empirical Study*.

given normal dividend behavior and, second, the greater are internal funds, the greater will be the rate of investment."[68]

It is interesting to note that this hypothesis is the culmination of several trends of thought. In the first place, it reflects the economists' increasing awareness of the changing institutional framework. Keynes and the multiplier-accelerator theories did not take the existence of modern corporations into consideration. Once the investment decision process of modern corporations is included in the theory of investment, the role played by profits and internal funds in the determination of investment can no longer be ignored.

Secondly, on the theoretical level, Professors S. C. Tsiang, Duesenberry, and others have criticized the acceleration principle in its pure form.[69] As pointed out by Professor Tsiang, "The greatest weakness of the acceleration principle . . . is its complete disregard of the supply of capital to individual firms as a determinant of the rate of their investment activities. An implicit assumption behind the acceleration principle seems to be that the supply of capital of each individual firm is almost infinitely elastic and consequently plays no part in the determination of the rate of investment. . . ."[70]

Thirdly, the "financial" theory of investment is derived in part from the theory of uncertainty.[71] Traditional theory of investment has been developed under the assumption of certainty.[72] As pointed out by Professor J. Hirschleifer, "Among the phenomena left unexplained under

---

[68] Edwin Kuh, "Theory and Institutions in the Study of Investment Behavior," *American Economic Review*, LIII (May, 1963), 263.

[69] See S. C. Tsiang, "Accelerator, Theory of the Firm, and the Business Cycle," *Quarterly Journal of Economics*, Vol. LXV (August, 1951); Duesenberry, *Business Cycles and Economic Growth*, pp. 38–45; A. D. Knox, "The Acceleration Principle and the Theory of Investment: A Survey," *Economica*, Vol. XIX, 1952.

[70] See S. C. Tsiang, "Accelerator, Theory of the Firm, and the Business Cycle," Professor Duesenberry also observes:
The acceleration-principle theory of investment is a special and rigid application of the more general relation between capital stock, income, and returns on investment. Numerous assumptions are required to justify the transition. In particular, it is necessary to assume (1) that the amount of real capital per unit of output which a firm desires is effectively independent of the cost of raising funds for investment or (2) that the cost of raising funds is invariant with respect to the amount raised [pp. 38–39].
From *Business Cycles and Economic Growth* by James S. Duesenberry. Copyright 1958 by McGraw-Hill Book Company. Used with permission of McGraw-Hill Book Company.

[71] See J. Hirschleifer, "Investment Decision Under Uncertainty—Choice-Theoretic Approaches," *Quarterly Journal of Economics*, Vol. LXXIX (November, 1965) and Vol. LXXX (May, 1966); also Myron J. Gordon, "Security and a Financial Theory of Investment," *Quarterly Journal of Economics*, Vol. LXXIV (August, 1960).

[72] See Irving Fisher, *The Theory of Interest* (New York: The Macmillan Company, 1930).

the certainty assumption are: the value attached to 'liquidity,' the willingness to buy insurance, the existence of debt and equity financing, and the bewildering variety of returns or yields on various forms of investment simultaneously ruling in the market."[73] It will be recalled that Keynes had placed a great deal of emphasis on expectations. He wrote: "The schedule of the marginal efficiency of capital is of fundamental importance because it is mainly through this factor (much more than through the rate of interest) that the expectation of the future influences the present."[74] However, he did not formulate a precise theory under the assumption of uncertainty. Subsequently, Professor Kalecki and others have shown that there is an increasing subjective risk accompanying increased indebtedness relative to the firm's own capital. "One way of putting it is that profitability dominates the selection among alternative investment opportunities, while risk governs the *scale* of investment."[75] The theory of investment decision under uncertainty has been further developed in recent years by Professors Kenneth J. Arrow, G. Debreu, James Tobin, J. Hirschleifer, and others.[76]

The "acceleration" theory of investment has been a central feature of post-Keynesian business cycle theory. This dynamic theory of saving and investment was first stated by Sir Roy Harrod in 1936 and subsequently expanded by Professors Hicks and Samuelson in 1939.[77] Defi-

---

[73] Hirshleifer, *op cit.*, LXXIX, 509.

[74] Reprinted from *The General Theory of Employment, Interest, and Money*, p. 145, by John Maynard Keynes, by permission of Harcourt, Brace & World, Inc.

[75] Gordon, *op. cit.*, p. 479.

[76] See Kenneth J. Arrow, "The Role of Securities in the Optimal Allocation of Risk-bearing," *Review of Economic Studies*, Vol. XXXI (April, 1964); G. Debreu, *Theory of Value* (New York: John Wiley & Sons, Inc., 1959), Chap. 7; James Tobin, "Liquidity Preference as Behavior Towards Risk," *Review of Economic Studies*, Vol. XXV (February, 1958); Hirshleifer, "Risk, the Discount Rate, and Investment Decisions," *American Economic Review*, Vol. LI (May, 1961); and Hirshleifer, "Efficient Allocation of Capital in an Uncertain World," *American Economic Review*, Vol. LVI (May, 1964).

[77] See Roy Harrod, *The Trade Cycle* (London: 1963); Paul A. Samuelson "Interaction Between the Multiplier Analysis and the Principle of Acceleration," reprinted from *Review of Economics and Statistics*, 1939, in *Readings in Business Cycle Theory* (Philadelphia: Blakiston, 1951).

A simple multiplier-acceleration-principle interaction model follows.

Eq. (1) is a definition of income:

$$Y_t = C_t + I_t \qquad\qquad \text{Eq. (1)}$$

Eq. (2) is a lagged consumption function:

$$C_t = a + bY_{t-1} \qquad\qquad \text{Eq. (2)}$$

ciencies in the dynamic adjustment process of the original formulation have been successfully remedied by Professors Hicks, Kaldor, Goodwin, and others.[78]

Our concern here is to illustrate the integration of the financial and acceleration theories of investment. This integration has been ably demonstrated by Professor Duesenberry in *Business Cycles and Economic Growth* (1958). In his basic income-generation model, Duesenberry presents a generalized version of a multiplier-accelerator process, which is derived from the following equation system:[79]

$$I_t = \alpha Y_{t-1} + \beta K_{t-1} \qquad \text{Eq. (5-43)}$$
$$C_t = a Y_{t-1} + b K_{t-1} \qquad \text{Eq. (5-44)}$$
$$K_t = (1 - k)K_{t-1} + I_t \qquad \text{Eq. (5-45)}$$
$$Y_t = I_t + C_t \qquad \text{Eq. (5-46)}$$

Eq. (5-43) represents the integration of the financial and acceleration theories of investment. The symbol $(I)$ denotes investment; $(Y)$ and $(K)$ represent income and capital stock, respectively; the subscript $(t)$ refers to the current period and $(t-1)$ refers to the previous period. $(\alpha)$ and $(\beta)$ are parameters. The former "represents the effect of changes in income on investment, which is felt in two ways. A change in income changes the marginal efficiency of investment, and it also changes the marginal cost of funds by changing profits."[80] The latter

---

Eq. (3) is the acceleration theory of investment. $(\beta)$ is the technologically determined capital-output ratio; and $(Y_{t-1} - Y_{t-2})$ means the rate of change of income in the previous period. In other words, it is a lagged function.

$$I_t = \beta (Y_{t-1} - Y_{t-2}) \qquad \text{Eq. (3)}$$

Substituting Eqs. (2) and (3) into (1), we obtain a recursive equation relating income at time $(t)$ to income in the two preceding periods:

$$Y_t = (b + \beta)Y_{t-1} - (\beta)Y_{t-2} + a \qquad \text{Eq. (4)}$$

If at time $(t)$, there is an increase in autonomous expenditure, say $(\Delta G)$, then Eq. (4) can be written as

$$Y_t = (b + \beta)Y_{t-1} - (\beta)Y_{t-2} + [a + \Delta G] \qquad \text{Eq. (5)}$$

We can now trace the movement of $(Y)$ through successive periods.

[78] John R. Hicks, *A Contribution to the Trade Cycle* (London: Oxford University Press, 1950); Nicholas Kaldor, "A Model of the Trade Cycle," reprinted from *Economic Journal*, 1940, in *Readings in Business Cycles and National Income*, A. H. Hansen and R. V. Clemence, eds. (New York: W. W. Norton & Company, Inc., 1953).

[79] Duesenberry, *Business Cycles and Economic Growth*, Chap. 9.

[80] From *Business Cycles and Economic Growth* by James S. Duesenberry. Copyright 1958 by McGraw-Hill Book Company. Used with permission of McGraw-Hill Book Company.

"reflects the influence of capital stock on investment working through both marginal efficiency and profits."[81]

The financial theory is subsumed under the independent variables of the investment function via the following route. Investment may be regarded as a function of income $(Y)$, capital stock $(K)$, profits $(\Pi)$, and capital-consumption allowances $(R)$. This functional relationship may be written as:

$$I_t = f(Y_{t-1}, K_{t-1}, \Pi_{t-1}, R_t)$$

Since profits depend positively on aggregate demand and negatively on capital stock, we have:

$$\Pi_t = \Pi(Y_t, K_t)$$

Capital-consumption allowances may be treated as a fraction of capital stock. This relation may be expressed as:

$$R_t = kK_{t-1}$$

where $(k)$ is the fraction.

Now, we have seen that both $(\Pi)$ and $(R)$ can be expressed in terms of $(Y)$ and $(K)$. Hence, they could be subsumed under $(Y)$ and $(K)$. In this way the investment function is derived.

It should be noted that the Duesenberry investment function represents a substantial modification of the acceleration theory of investment. The investment function in the original formulation of the acceleration principle is in the lagged form:

$$I_t = \beta(Y_{t-1} - Y_{t-2})$$

where $(\beta)$ is the technologically given accelerator, or the capital-output ratio $(K/Y)$. It states that investment occurs in proportion to the rate of increase in income. This proposition is based upon a number of strong assumptions. As mentioned earlier, one of the implicit assumptions is that the supply of capital is infinitely elastic and consequently plays no part in the determination of the rate of investment. Another implicit assumption is that the accelerator is not an economic relationship, but a technically given datum. All these restrictive assumptions have been removed in this new formulation. Professor Duesenberry points out:

> The $(\beta)$ in our equation will be much less than the average ratio of capital to output (which is the accelerator in multiplier-accel-

---

erator interaction models). A $1 increase in income (capital-stock constant) will increase the rate of business investment by an amount which is not much larger than the increase in business savings resulting from a $1 increase in income. . . . As a consequence of those considerations, an increase in income will have a much smaller immediate effect on expenditure than would occur in a simple multiplier-accelerator model. That conclusion will be reinforced when we take the lags in dividend payments, construction, and housing demand into account.[82]

Turning now to Eq. (5-44), the consumption function, we see that the determinants of investment also influence consumption. The parameter ($a$) "is the marginal propensity to consume out of GNP. An increase in the marginal propensity to consume out of disposable income increases ($a$). But $a$ also reflects the increase in profits which results (*cet. par.*) from an increase in income. An increase in the sensitivity of profits to changes in income therefore reduces $a$. That influence is partly offset by the effects of profits on dividends and the effect of changes in dividends on consumption. The influence of changes in capital stock on consumption is reflected by $b$. That influence results from the influence of capital stock on profits through the influence of profits on dividends and dividends on consumption."[83] More specifically, the consumption function may be written as:

$$C_t = f(Y_{t-1} - \Pi_{t-1} - R_{t-1} + d_t)$$

where ($d$) stands for dividend payments. Since $\Pi = \Pi(Y, K)$, $R = kK$, and $d = f(\Pi)$, these independent variables can also be subsumed under ($Y$) and ($K$). Hence,

$$C_t = aY_{t-1} + bK_{t-1}$$

It should be noted that "the $a$ in our equation will be much smaller than the marginal propensity to consume out of disposable income because it reflects the influence of income changes on profits and business savings."[84]

With both ($a$) and ($\beta$) much smaller than those in multiplier-accelerator interaction models, the possibility of either explosive or anti-

[82] From *Business Cycles and Economic Growth* by James S. Duesenberry. Copyright 1958 by McGraw-Hill Book Company. Used with permission of McGraw-Hill Book Company.

[83] From *Business Cycles and Economic Growth* by James S. Duesenberry. Copyright 1958 by McGraw-Hill Book Company. Used with permission of McGraw-Hill Book Company.

[84] From *Business Cycles and Economic Growth* by James S. Duesenberry. Copyright 1958 by McGraw-Hill Book Company. Used with permission of McGraw-Hill Book Company.

damped situations will be reduced. "As a result, the system has more stability than a multiplier-accelerator model. The stability of the system is also increased by the fact that both saving and investment depend on profits, so that both tend to move in the same direction. It is also shown that lags in the reaction of consumption to changes in income tend to increase the stability of the system."[85]

Equation (5-45) is an identity. It is derived in the following way:

$$K_t \equiv K_{t-1} + (I_t - R_t)$$
$$R_t = kK_{t-1}$$
$$K_t \equiv K_{t-1} + I_t - kK_{t-1}$$
$$\therefore K_t \equiv (1-k)K_{t-1} + I_t$$

Equation (5-46) is, of course, the definition of income.
If we substitute Eqs. (5-43) and (5-44) in Eq. (5-46), we obtain:

$$Y_t = (\alpha + a)Y_{t-1} + (\beta + b)K_{t-1} \qquad \text{Eq. (5-47)}$$

If we substitute Eq. (5-43) in Eq. (5-45), we have:

$$K_t = \alpha Y_{t-1} + [\beta + (1-k)]K_{t-1} \qquad \text{Eq. (5-48)}$$

From the last two equations we can derive a recursive equation relating income at time $(t)$ to income in the two preceding periods:

$$Y_t = [(\alpha + a) + (\beta + 1 - k)]Y_{t-1} +$$
$$[\alpha(\beta + b) - (\alpha + a)(\beta + 1 - k)]Y_{t-2}$$

"This is a generalized version of a multiplier-accelerator process. In the simple multiplier-accelerator process the investment equation is written as $I_t = \alpha Y_{t-1} - K_{t-1}$, so that $\beta = -1$. Depreciation is usually neglected and investment treated as net investment, so that $k = 0$. The connection between the capital stock and consumption is neglected, so that $b = 0$. If we substitute those values in the equation for $Y_t$, $(\beta + 1 - k) = 0$, $\alpha(\beta + b) = 0$,

$$Y_t = (\alpha + a)Y_{t-1} + \alpha(-1)Y_{t-2}$$

we obtain the usual form of the equation for the multiplier-accelerator process."[86]

In a broader context, the Duesenberry model represents a unifying theory explaining three related problems: (1) investment behavior,

---

[85] From *Business Cycles and Economic Growth* by James S. Duesenberry. Copyright 1958 by McGraw-Hill Book Company. Used with permission of McGraw-Hill Book Company.

[86] From *Business Cycles and Economic Growth* by James S. Duesenberry. Copyright 1958 by McGraw-Hill Book Company. Used with permission of McGraw-Hill Book Company.

(2) business cycles, and (3) the adjustment of secular growth in demand to secular growth in potential output. Thus, it is also a theory of economic growth. Like the Harrod-Domar analysis, the equilibrium growth rate in the Duesenberry model is determined from the demand side.[87] The demand-dominated growth model is explicitly stated by Professor Duesenberry as follows:

From Eq. (5-47), $Y_t = (\alpha + a)Y_{t-1} + (\beta + b)K_{t-1}$, the rate of growth of income $(r_y)$ is derived:

$$r_y = \frac{Y_t - Y_{t-1}}{Y_{t-1}} = (\alpha + a - 1) + (\beta + b)\frac{K_{t-1}}{Y_{t-1}} \qquad \text{Eq. (5-49)}$$

The rate of growth of capital $(r_k)$, in terms of Eq. (5-48), is given by:

$$r_k = \frac{K_t - K_{t-1}}{K_{t-1}} = \frac{\alpha Y_{t-1}}{K_{t-1}} + (\beta - 1) \qquad \text{Eq. (5-50)}$$

It is clear that "the two rates of growth are determined entirely by the ratio of capital stock to income. That being the case, the two rates of growth will remain constant if the ratio $(k/y)$ $[K_t/Y_t]$ remains constant. The ratio of capital to income will remain constant if the rate of growth of capital equals the rate of growth of income."[88] This, of course, is the condition for steady-state growth.[89] Fig. 5-8 represents the steady-state or equilibrium rate of growth.

In Fig. 5-8, the growth rates are measured vertically and the capital-output ratio horizontally. Equation (5-49) is a straight line of negative slope, and Eq. (5-50) is a rectangular hyperbola. The two curves intersect at points $(P)$ and $(Q)$.

> Of the two intersections, one corresponds to a stable equilibrium position, the other to an unstable one. . . . The intersection of $r_k$ and $r_y$ at $P$ is stable. If $k/y$ lies to the left of $P$, $r_k$ exceeds $r_y$. $k$ therefore grows faster than $y$, and $k/y$ rises until it reaches $P$. Similarly, if $k/y$ lies between $P$ and $Q$, $r_y$ exceeds $r_k$, and the ratio of

---

[87] Professors Hahn and Matthews observe:
The equilibrium rate of growth in such models is determined by the parameters of the system—the saving ratio, the capital-output ratio, or whatever other parameters may be involved in more complicated formulations of the underlying functions. . . . Such demand-dominated models have much in common with cycle models, and indeed, as is well known, identical models may in some cases lead to either growth or cycle according to the values of the parameters in the investment function, the saving function and so on.
See Hahn and Matthews, *op. cit.*, pp. 8–9.

[88] From *Business Cycles and Economic Growth* by James S. Duesenberry. Copyright 1958 by McGraw-Hill Book Company. Used with permission of McGraw-Hill Book Company.

[89] A steady-state growth means that all variables grow at the same constant rate.

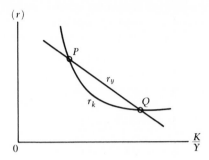

**Figure 5-8**

$k$ to $y$ will fall until $P$ is reached. If $k/y$ lies to the right of $Q$, $r_k$ again exceeds $r_y$, and $k/y$ rises, $r_y$ and $r_k$ fall until $r_k$ attains the maximum negative value permitted by the constraints on capital decumulation. We might call the range of values to the left of $Q$ the "stability range" of the system.[90]

Point $(Q)$, on the other hand, represents an unstable equilibrium position. "If, however, the value of $k/y$ after the shock lies to right of $Q$, income will continue to decline even after the behavior equations snap back to their old position. Eventually income will stop falling because there is a limit to the speed with which capital can be decumulated. Income can begin to rise again after a long period of capital decumulation."[91]

The essential argument of Professor Duesenberry is "that all depressions prior to 1929 were caused by shocks of a variety of types and that income never fell below the critical value mentioned above."[92] Professor Duesenberry further observes that:

> the evolution of the structure of the American economy in the period between 1900 and the end of World War I tended to reduce the rate of growth of demand and to reduce the stability of the system. The special virulence of the great depression of the 1930's can be explained in two ways. On the one hand, we can

[90] From *Business Cycles and Economic Growth* by James S. Duesenberry. Copyright 1958 by McGraw-Hill Book Company. Used with permission of McGraw-Hill Book Company.

[91] From *Business Cycles and Economic Growth* by James S. Duesenberry. Copyright 1958 by McGraw-Hill Book Company. Used with permission of McGraw-Hill Book Company.

[92] From *Business Cycles and Economic Growth* by James S. Duesenberry. Copyright 1958 by McGraw-Hill Book Company. Used with permission of McGraw-Hill Book Company.

believe that the depression would have occurred, even without the boom and collapse of speculation in securities and real estate, because the system was incapable of sustained growth. On the other hand, we can believe that sustained growth was possible but that the system was so unstable that the market crash pushed income below the critical point mentioned above. In any case, it will be argued that the depression which began in 1929 was much worse than its predecessors because of changes in the structure of the economy which affected both the growth potential and the stability of the system.[93]

## Investment in Human Capital

A second landmark of the post-Keynesian theory of investment is the group of studies devoted to "investment in human capital."[94] As pointed out by Professor Theodore W. Schultz, "Much of what we call consumption constitutes investment in human capital. Direct expenditures on education, health, and internal migration to take advantage of better job opportunities are clear examples. Earnings foregone by mature students attending school and by workers acquiring on-the-job training are equally clear examples. Yet nowhere do these enter into our national accounts. The use of leisure time to improve skills and knowledge is widespread and it too is unrecorded. In these and similar ways the *quality* of human effort can be greatly improved and its productivity enhanced. I shall contend that such investment in human capital accounts for most of the impressive rise in the real earnings per worker."[95]

Professor Schultz further observes that many paradoxes and puzzles about the United States' economic growth can be resolved once investment in human capital is taken into account. For instance, the decline in the estimated capital-output ratio could be explained by the fact that "human capital has been increasing relative not only to conventional capital but also to income."[96] In other words, Professor Schultz believes that investment in human capital holds the key to the explana-

---

[93] From *Business Cycles and Economic Growth* by James S. Duesenberry. Copyright 1958 by McGraw-Hill Book Company. Used with permission of McGraw-Hill Book Company.

[94] See the collection of essays, "Investment in Human Beings," *Journal of Political Economy*, Vol. LXX, Supplement (October, 1962).

[95] T. W. Schultz, Presidential Address before the American Economic Association (December, 1962), reprinted in *The Goal of Economic Growth*, Edmund S. Phelps, ed. (New York: W. W. Norton & Co., Inc., 1962), p. 106.

[96] *Ibid.*, p. 110.

tion of our increase in productivity per man-hour and per unit of capital, and that human capital has been growing much faster than either tangible capital or output. He suggests that if we want to have a higher growth rate, we should increase our investment in human capital.

This thesis has been examined further by Professors Gary S. Becker, Edward F. Denison, and others.[97] Although the question of whether there is presently substantial underinvestment in human beings is not yet settled, post-Keynesian discussions on the relation between investment and economic growth must take human capital into consideration.[98]

### Technical Progress versus Investment as a Source of Economic Growth

The third landmark of post-Keynesian theory of investment is connected with the question of technical progress versus investment as a source of economic growth. In the mid 1950's Professors Solow, Massell, Fabricant, Kendrick, and others attempted to measure the respective contributions of investment and technological progress to output growth.[99] In these studies, technical progress was treated as

---

[97] See "Investment in Human Beings," *Journal of Political Economy*. This collection includes the following papers: Gary S. Becker, "Investment in Human Capital: A Theoretical Analysis"; Jacob Mincer, "On-the-Job Training: Costs, Returns, and Some Implications"; Larry A. Sjaastad, "The Costs and Returns of Human Migration"; George J. Stigler, "Information in the Labor Market"; Edward F. Denison, "Education, Economic Growth, and Gaps in Information"; Selma J. Mushkin, "Health as an Investment."

[98] For instance, in *The Annual Report of the Council of Economic Advisers*, for 1962, "investment in human resources" is listed as one of the investment policies designed to increase the rate of economic growth. The other investment policies stated by the Council are: investment in technological progress, investment in plant and equipment, investment in natural resources, and investment in public services. In the Council's *Annual Report* for 1966, Chap. 3 is devoted to the problem of "Strengthening Human Resources." Professor Edward F. Denison, in *The Sources of Economic Growth in the United States*, Supplementary Paper No. 13 (New York: the Committee for Economic Development, 1962), assigns an important role to education.

[99] See R. M. Solow, "Technical Change and the Aggregate Production Function," *Review of Economics and Statistics*, Vol. XXXIX (August, 1957); B. F. Massell, "Capital Formation and Technological Change in United States Manufacturing," *Review of Economics and Statistics*, Vol. XLII (May, 1960); M. Abramovitz, "Resources and Output Trends in the United States since 1870," *American Economic Review*, Vol. XLVI (May, 1956); S. Fabricant, *Basic Facts on Productivity Change* (New York: National Bureau of Economic Research, 1959); and John W. Kendrick, "Productivity Trends: Capital and Labor," *Review of Economics and Statistics*, Vol. XXXVIII (August, 1956).

wholly organizational, or "disembodied." Disembodied technical progress refers to those forms of technical change that shift the production function in such a way that, in the long run, the balance between capital and labor in the production process is left undisturbed. Such technical progress can be incorporated in the following form of production function:

$$Y_t = F(K_t, L_t; T)$$

where $(T)$ represents levels of technology. The term is a catch-all for all sources of output growth other than capital accumulation and growth of the labor force. It has come to be known as "the residual." According to studies of Professors Kendrick, Solow, and others, technical progress is the more important source of economic growth. It accounts for more than half of the growth in labor productivity in the United States since 1890.

More specifically, the above-mentioned production function may be written as:

$$Y_t = A_t F(K_t, L_t)$$

where $(Y_t)$, $(K_t)$, and $(L_t)$ represent respectively aggregate output and inputs of capital and labor services at time $(t)$; and $(A_t)$ is an index of technical progress. If we assume that the level of technology $(A_t)$ increases neutrally and exponentially at the rate of $(\lambda)$, the production function may be written as:

$$Y_t = A e^{\lambda t} K_t^b L_t^{1-b}$$

where $(b)$ is the elasticity of production with respect to capital, and $(1 - b)$ is the elasticity of production with respect to the labor employed. Of course, in the case of constant returns to scale, the values of $(b)$ and $(1 - b)$ add up to unity. In other words, this property means that, if each input is paid the amount of its marginal product, the total product will be exhausted exactly by the distributive shares for all the inputs of capital and labor services. This is, of course, the economic version of Euler's theorem as applied to production. Historically, it is often referred to as the "adding-up theorem" of Philip Wicksteed and other neoclassical writers.[100]

The linearly homogeneous production function is the essential ingredient of the neoclassical approach to the theory of economic

---

[100] For lucid presentations of the theorem, see Mark Blaug, *Economic Theory in Retrospect* (revised edition, Homewood, Ill.: Richard D. Irwin, Inc., 1968), pp. 446–466; and George J. Stigler, *Production and Distribution Theories* (New York: The Macmillan Company, 1946), Chap. 12.

growth.[101] It will be recalled that the Harrod-Domar analysis has usually been taken as the point of departure in the post-Keynesian discussions of economic growth. In the Harrod-Domar analysis, the production function explicitly excludes any labor input, and output is stated explicitly as a function of capital alone. The implication is that labor and capital will be combined in fixed proportions. This creates the well known "razor-edge" situation.[102] The stability of steady-state growth equilibrium is thus endangered. In order to assure steady-state growth, it is necessary to relax one or another of the restrictive assumptions of the Harrod-Domar analysis. One way to assure continuous steady-state growth is to make the saving-income ratio ($s$) flexible. This is the approach adopted by Professor Joan Robinson and Professor N. Kaldor.[103]

---

[101] Representative works of the neoclassical approach are: Robert M. Solow, "A Contribution to the Theory of Economic Growth," *Quarterly Journal of Economics*, February, 1956; J. E. Meade, *A Neo-Classical Theory of Economic Growth* (London: Allen and Unwin, 1961); and Edmund S. Phelps, "A New View of Investment: A Neoclassical Analysis," *Quarterly Journal of Economics*, LXXVI (November, 1962), 548–567.

[102] The Harrod Model may be stated as follows:
Equation (1) says that a constant proportion ($s$) of income is devoted to saving and investment:

$$S_t = sY_t \qquad \text{Eq. (1)}$$

Eq. (2) is the acceleration theory of investment:

$$I_t = \beta \left( \frac{dY}{dt} \right) \qquad \text{Eq. (2)}$$

Eq. (3) is the equilibrium condition:

$$S_t = I_t \qquad \text{Eq. (3)}$$

To find the time-path of ($Y$), we use the following procedure:

$$sY_t = \beta \left( \frac{dY}{dt} \right), \text{ or, } \left( \frac{s}{\beta} \right) Y_t = \frac{dY}{dt}$$

After both sides of the equation have been multiplied by ($1/Y$), the equation may be written as:

$$\frac{1}{Y} \frac{dY}{dt} = \frac{S}{\beta}, \text{ or, } \frac{dY}{Y} = \frac{S}{\beta} dt$$

To find ($Y$) as a function of time, we have to integrate. Integration of both sides of the equation yields:

$$\int \frac{dY}{Y} = \int \left( \frac{S}{\beta} \right) dt, \text{ or, } \text{Log } eY = \left( \frac{S}{\beta} \right) t + C$$

To find the solution that gives ($Y$) as a function of ($t$), we translate the logarithmic expression into an exponential expression:

$$Y_t = e^{\frac{s}{\beta}t + C} = e^{\frac{s}{\beta}t} \cdot e^c$$

Let $e^c = A = Y_o$. The final solution becomes: $Y_t = Y_o \, e^{\frac{s}{\beta}t}$.

[103] Joan Robinson, *The Accumulation of Capital* (London: Macmillan & Co., 1965); and N. Kaldor, "Alternative Theories of Distribution," *Review of Economic Studies*, Vol. XXIII (1955–56).

Another possibility is to replace the assumption of fixed coefficients in production by one of substitutability between labor and capital. If the rate of growth of the labor force is exogenously determined by demographic factors, capital may be treated as "putty" which can then be shaped to absorb any size of labor force. This is the neoclassical approach. For instance, Professor Solow, in 1957, introduced the following production function into his model:[104]

$$Y_t = A_{(t)} F(K_t, L_t)$$

The growth rate of output $(\dot{Y}_t / Y_t)$ is equal to the rate of technical progress $(\dot{A}_t / A_t)$ plus a weighted average of the growth rate of capital $(\dot{K}_t / K_t)$ and the growth rate of labor force $(\dot{L}_t / L_t)$, or more specifically:

$$\frac{\dot{Y}_t}{Y_t} = \frac{\dot{A}_t}{A_t} + a_t \frac{\dot{K}_t}{K_t} + (1 - a_t) \frac{\dot{L}_t}{L_t}$$

Since disembodied technical progress may be treated as a separate source of output growth, it permits the inference that income could grow through an increase in knowledge even though investment were zero. This approach tends to down-grade the role of investment in the process of economic growth. As observed by Professor Edmund S. Phelps, "the results of this approach produced a wave of investment pessimism."[105]

A "new view" of investment, however, has since gained currency. "Thesis and antithesis were synthesized by 1960. Investment has been married to Technology. In the new view, the role of investment is to modernize as well as deepen the capital stock. Now investment is priced as the carrier of technological progress."[106]

Since 1961 the new view has been espoused by the Council of Economic Advisers to the President of the United States. The following

---

[104] Solow, *op. cit.*

[105] Phelps, *op cit.*, p. 550.

[106] Phelps, p. 548.

It should be noted that, in the case of disembodied technical progress, capital can be assumed to be homogeneous. Productive capacity depends upon the amount of capital accumulated but not on its age. It follows that investment is taken to be net investment. The time-path of net investment can be described as:

$$I = \frac{dK}{dt} \text{ and } K = \int_0^t I \, dt$$

In "embodied" technical progress models, capital stock can no longer be treated as homogeneous. Each part of the capital stock has to be dated by its year of origin (vintage). It is also assumed that new capital is more productive than capital of older "vintage." It is gross investment in new machines which is relevant to the analysis.

statement, made by the Council in its 1962 Annual Report, further amplifies the view:

> Investment in new equipment serves as a vehicle for technological improvements and is perhaps the most important way in which laboratory discoveries become incorporated in the production process. Without their embodiment in new equipment, many ideas would lie fallow. Conversely, the impact of a dollar's investment on the quality of the capital stock depends on how rapidly increases in knowledge have taken place. This interaction between investment and technological change permits each worker to have not only more tools, but better tools as well.[107]

Theoretically, technological progress is embodied in the current vintage of machines. Capital stock can no longer be treated as homogeneous; it is considered to be made up of machines of different vintages.[108] Thus we need two time variables: one $(t)$ for time in the usual sense, and the second time variable $(v)$ for dating vintages of machines in use at time $(t)$. Furthermore, gross investment in new machines is relevant to the analysis.

The basic model of embodied technical progress was presented by Professor Robert M. Solow in 1959.[109] We limit our attention to this model. On the assumption of Cobb-Douglas and neo-classical orthodoxy, the aggregate production function is written as

$$Y_t = Be^{-\delta(1-\alpha)}L_t^{\alpha}J_t^{1-\alpha}$$

The real difference between this embodied-technical-progress production function and the previous disembodied-technical-progress production function $Y_t = Ae^{\lambda t}L_t^b K_t^{1-b}$ lies in the treatment of the stock of capital, since $(J_t)$ has a more complicated structure than the earlier $(K_t)$. As pointed out by Professor Solow, $(J_t)$ may be called an "effective stock of capital"; it is a productivity-weighted sum of the surviving capital goods representing all earlier technological levels:

$$J_t = \int_{-\infty}^{t} e^{\sigma v}I_v dv$$

---

[107] *Economic Report of the President*, transmitted to the Congress January 1962 (Washington, D.C.: U.S. Government Printing Office, 1964), p. 129.

[108] In its simplest form, the assumption is that technological progress proceeds at some given proportional rate. It affects only new machines. Once installed, the technical features of machines remain "frozen." Thus at time $(t)$, machines of vintage $(v)$ have been affected by technological progress up to time $(v)$ but not thereafter.

[109] Robert M. Solow, *Investment and Technical Progress* from Arrow, Karlin, & Suppes, eds.: Mathematical Methods in the Social Sciences, 1959 (Stanford: Stanford University Press, 1959), pp. 89–104.

According to Professor Solow, the effective stock of capital is derived from the following procedures:

Output from the machines of each vintage is given by the function:

$$Y_{vt} = Be^{\lambda v}L_{vt}{}^{\alpha}K_{vt}{}^{1-\alpha} \qquad \text{Eq. (5-51)}$$

where $(Kvt)$ represents the number of machines of vintage $(v)$ still in existence at time $(t \geqq v)$; $(Lvt)$ denotes the quantity of labor manning the surviving stock of capital of vintage $(v)$ at time $(t)$; $(\alpha)$ and $(1 - \alpha)$ are elasticities of output with respect to $(K)$ and $(L)$; $(Yvt)$ symbolizes the output produced at time $(t)$ using capital of vintage $(v)$; and, finally, $(Be^{\lambda v})$ denotes the level of technology neutrally increasing at the exponential rate of $(\lambda)$.

Total supply of labor to be allocated over capital of all vintages is given by:

$$L_t = \int_{-\infty}^{t} L_{vt}dv \qquad \text{Eq. (5-52)}$$

For total output at time $(t)$, we have:

$$Y_t = \int_{-\infty}^{t} Y_{vt}dv \qquad \text{Eq. (5-53)}$$

Let the quantity $(K_{vv})$ stand for gross investment, which is the output of capital goods at time $(v)$. Suppose we call it $(I_v)$. If the capital goods are exposed to a constant force of mortality (depreciation) symbolized by $(\delta)$, then the average length of life of capital is $(1/\delta)$ and

$$K_{vt} = K_{vve}{}^{-\delta(t-v)} = I_{ve}{}^{-\delta(t-v)} \qquad \text{Eq. (5-54)}$$

Assuming competition in the labor market, all homogeneous labor must receive the same wage regardless of the age of the capital on which it operates. Hence the allocation of labor to capital of various vintages must equalize the marginal productivity of labor in all uses. Let $(M_t)$ be the marginal product of labor at time $(t)$; then from Eq. (5-51) $Y_{vt} = Be^{\lambda v}L_{vt}{}^{\alpha}K_{vt}{}^{1-\alpha}$ we have:

$$M_t = \frac{\partial Y_{vt}}{\partial L_{vt}} = \alpha Be^{\lambda v}L_{vt}{}^{\alpha-1}K_{vt}{}^{1-\alpha} \qquad \text{Eq. (5-55)}$$

Substitute for $(K_{vt})$ from Eq. (5-54): $K_{vt} = I_{ve}{}^{-\delta(t-v)}$ then solve for $(L_{vt})$, and write $[\sigma = \delta + \lambda/(1 - \alpha)]$; the result is:

$$L_{vt} = (\alpha B)^{\frac{1}{1-\alpha}}e^{-\delta t}M_t^{\frac{1}{\alpha-1}}e^{\sigma v}I_v = h_{te}{}^{\sigma v}I_v \qquad \text{Eq. (5-56)}$$

Substitute this expression in Eq. (5-51) and simplify; we have:

$$Y_{vt} = Be^{-\delta(1-\alpha)t}h_t{}^{\alpha}e^{\sigma v}I_v \qquad \text{Eq. (5-57)}$$

Substitute this expression into the total output equation in Eq. (5-53); we obtain:

$$Y_t = Be^{-\delta(1-\alpha)t}h_t^\alpha \int_{-\infty}^{t} e^{\sigma v} I_v dv \qquad \text{Eq. (5-58)}$$

Together Eqs. (5-57) and (5-58) give:

$$Y_t = Be^{-\delta(1-\alpha)t}L_t^\alpha J_t^{1-\alpha} \qquad \text{Eq. (5-59)}$$

Where

$$J_t = \int_{-\infty}^{t} e^{\sigma v} I_v dv \qquad \text{Eq. (5-60)}$$

## TECHNOLOGICAL AND STRUCTURAL UNEMPLOYMENT

It will be recalled that Keynesian economics addresses itself mainly to the problem of "demand-shortage" unemployment. Since the end of the Korean war, a new type of unemployment problem has been identified. During the period from late 1957 to 1964 in the United States, the unemployment rate averaged nearly six percent. The persistence of the high unemployment rate caused some retrogression in the general acceptance of Keynesian remedies.[110] It also led various economists to search for explanations other than that of demand shortage. In particular, technological unemployment once again became the focus of public discussion.[111]

---

[110] The retrogression in the general acceptance of Keynesian economics has been discussed under various names, such as the "Uneasy Triangle," the "cost-push thesis," the nonreversible character of the aggregate supply function, etc. For further readings see Abba P. Lerner, "Keynesian Economics in the Sixties," in *Keynes' General Theory: Reports of Three Decades*, Robert Lekachman, ed., pp. 222–234; Tibor and Anne Scitovsky, "Inflation Versus Unemployment: An Examination of Their Effects," in *Inflation, Growth and Employment*, a series of research studies prepared for the Commission on Money and Credit (Englewood Cliffs, N.J.: Prentice-Hall, Inc., 1964); also Arthur F. Burns, *The Management of Prosperity* (New York: Columbia University Press, 1965).

[111] See, for instance, John T. Dunlop, ed., *Automation and Technological Change*, The American Assembly, Columbia University (Englewood Cliffs, N.J.: Prentice-Hall, Inc., 1962); Paul Einzig, *The Economic Consequences of Automation* (London: Secker & Warburg, 1957); Walter Buckingham, *Automation: Its Impact on Business and People* (New York: The New American Library, Inc., 1961); Charles C. Killingsworth, "Automation, Jobs, and Manpower," in *Men Without Work: The Economics of Unemployment*, Stanley Lebergott, ed. (Englewood Cliffs, N.J.: Prentice Hall, Inc., 1964).

The initial stage of the discussion was dominated by what George Terborgh calls the "alarmists."[112] Since then the problem has been better understood. As pointed out by the Council of Economic Advisers in its 1964 Annual Report, the new unemployment has a variety of causes. It is a juxtaposition of three types of unemployment, namely, "demand shortage," "structural," and "technological." " 'Technological unemployment' is not a third form of unemployment, separate from the other two. Rather, it expresses itself through these other forms. Technological change causes obsolescence of skills and thereby produces some mismatching between available workers and jobs, which we call 'structural' unemployment. Moreover, by raising output per worker, technological change is one of the principal sources of growth in our *potential* total output or GNP—which, if not matched by corresponding growth in *actual* GNP, opens a gap in demand and thereby causes demand-shortage unemployment."[113]

In other words, it may be said that changes in the volume of unemployment are influenced by three basic forces: (1) the growth of aggregate demand, (2) technological change, and (3) the growth of the labor force. "The persistence of a high general level of unemployment in the years following the Korean War was not the result of accelerated technological progress. Its cause was the interaction between rising productivity, labor force growth, and an inadequate growth of aggregate demand."[114] "Thus, in the late 1950's, productivity and the labor force were increasing more rapidly than usual, while the growth of output was slower than usual. This accounts for the persistence of high unemployment rates."[115]

Once the problem is identified, corrective measures can be suitably prescribed. The maintenance of an adequate level of aggregate demand has once again been recognized as a necessary if not sufficient ingredient of an appropriate policy mix. As George Terborgh puts it: "The most effective way to minimize personal hardship from change,

---

[112] See George Terborgh, *The Automation Hysteria* (Washington, D.C.: Machinery and Allied Products Institute and Council for Technological Advancement, 1965), Chap. 1. The "alarmists" mentioned in this chapter include Donald M. Michael (in reference to his *Cybernation: The Silent Conquest*) and members of the Ad Hoc Committee on the Triple Revolution (in reference to views included in the Committee's manifesto).

[113] *Economic Report of the President*, transmitted to the Congress January 1964 (Washington, D.C.: U.S. Government Printing Office, 1964), p. 167.

[114] *Technology and the American Economy*, Report of the National Commission on Technology, Automation, and Economic Progress, I, 1966, 9.

[115] *Technology and the American Economy*, p. 10.

whether technological or other, is to maintain a stable and expanding economy. Desirable as alleviants may be—unemployment insurance, retraining, relocation assistance, labor market services, or what have you—they can never be fully successful without this support. The moral is obvious. The paramount need is for public and private policies conducive to a high-employment economy."[116] This is the official view of the United States Government.[117] Recently, the National Commission on Technology, Automation, and Economic Progress expressed the same conviction, that "the most important condition for successful adjustment to technological change is an adequate level of total income and employment. We recognize that this is not the end of economic policy, but we are confident it is the beginning."[118]

---

[116] Terborgh, *op. cit.*, p. 93.

[117] The Council of Economic Advisers in its *1964 Annual Report* suggested the following policy mixture:
(a) Tax reduction to bolster effective demand.
(b) Important channels of attack on structural problems:
   —improved labor market information services;
   —improved guidance and placement services;
   —improved programs of apprenticeship;
   —strengthened programs to reduce discriminatory hiring and employment practices by race, sex, or national origin;
   —expanded and more effective programs of vocational education, general adult education, and retraining;
   —basic improvements in the quality of our educational system at all levels;
   —measures to enlarge educational opportunities for children of low income families and minority groups;
   —programs to assist the geographical movement of workers;
   —expanded policies to strengthen the economic base and to speed the economic growth of distressed communities and regions.
See *The Economic Report of the President* (1964), pp. 188–190.

[118] *Technology and the American Economy*, p. 34.

# PART TWO

# Monetary
# Theory

# 6

# Pre-Classical
# Monetary Theory

Pre-Classical monetary theory (1650–1776) consists essentially of two strands of thought. The first is the doctrine that "money stimulates trade," which emphasizes the influence of money on output and employment, and largely ignores the possible relationship between money and prices. The second is the quantity theory of money, which concentrates on the relation between money and prices. The outstanding exponents of the first doctrine were John Law, Jacob Vanderlint, and Bishop Berkeley. The important contributors to the development of the quantity theory of money were John Locke, Richard Cantillon, and David Hume. A reconciliation of the two theories was attempted by Hume, the Synthesist.[1]

As mentioned previously, the majority of writers of this period did not embrace the concept of "neutral money." In the economic writings of David Hume, however, the concept of neutral money emerges for the first time. Indeed, as Keynes observed, "Hume had a foot and a half in the classical world."[2]

## The "Money-Stimulates-Trade" Doctrine

The majority of writers of this period associated the chronic shortage of money and high interest rates with depressed trade and unem-

---

[1] See E. A. J. Johnson, *Predecessors of Adam Smith* (New York: Prentice-Hall, Inc., 1937), Chap. 9.

[2] Reprinted from *The General Theory of Employment, Interest, and Money*, p. 343n., by John Maynard Keynes, by permission of Harcourt, Brace & World, Inc.

ployment. Thus, the central issue of preclassical monetary theory was
the role of money as a determinant of output and employment.[3] The
so-called "money-stimulates-trade" doctrine was directly addressed to
this issue.

### Sir William Petty (1632–1687)

A basic building block of the money-stimulates-trade doctrine is the
notion that, given the volume of trade, there is an appropriate amount
of money required for transactions purposes. This idea was formulated
by Petty, who pointed out: ". . . there is a certain measure, and proportion of money requisite to drive the trade of a Nation, more or less
than which would prejudice the same."[4] Professor Viner calls this idea
the "due proportions of money and trade doctrine."[5] The essence of
this doctrine may be explained with the aid of the cash-balance equation, $M = kPY$. If changes in $(P)$ are abstracted from consideration,
then we can derive the truism that, given $(k)$, an increase in $(M)$ would
lead to increase in output $(Y)$. Thus the basic idea was to highlight the
transactions demand for money.

Petty was the first English writer who approached the theory of
money from the cash-balances angle.[6] He pointed out that the "due
proportions," or the Marshallian $(k)$, were largely determined by the

---

[3] Douglas Vickers in his *Studies in the Theory of Money 1690–1776* (Philadelphia: Chilton Book Company, 1959) also comes to the conclusion: "In the
last analysis, the important characteristic of the preclassical literature was that
it developed a theory of money which was addressed to the explanation of the
problems of employment, prosperity, and economic development" [p. 25].

[4] Charles Henry Hull, ed., *Economic Writings of Sir William Petty* (London:
Cambridge University Press, 1899), I, 112–113. Petty derived this concept from
his national income estimates. In his statistical computation of national income,
he found that coined money was a small item quantitatively. Thus he realized that
a small amount of money could drive a large trade if the velocity of circulation
(which he called "revolutions") were adequate.

[5] See Jacob Viner, *Studies in the Theory of International Trade* (New York:
Harper & Row, Publishers, 1937), p. 49.

[6] See Alfred Marshall, *Money, Credit, and Commerce* (reprinted in New York
by Augustus M. Kelley, Publishers, 1960), p. 47; also A. E. Monroe, *Monetary
Theory Before Adam Smith* (Cambridge: Harvard University Press, 1923), p. 146;
and J. A. Schumpeter, *History of Economic Analysis* (New York: Oxford University Press, Inc., 1955), p. 316.

Marshall pointed out: "Petty thought that the money 'sufficient for' a nation is
'so much as will pay half a year's rent for all the lands of England and a quarter's
rent of the Houseing, for a week's expense of all the people, and about a quarter
of the value of all the exported commodities.' (*Quantulumcunque*, Queries 23 and
25; see also his *Political Arithmetic*, ch. ix, and *Verbum Sapienti*, ch. vi)."

system of payments, laws and customs, and the availability of credit in the country. He wrote:

> . . . for the Expence being 40 Millions, if the revolutions were in such short Circles, viz. weekly, as happens among poorer artizens and labourers, who receive and pay every Saturday, then 40/52 parts of 1 Million of Money would answer those ends. But if the Circles be quarterly, according to our Custom of paying rent, and gathering Taxes, then 10 Millions were requisite.[7]

Petty held that money was an important determinant of aggregate spending. He stated:

> . . . if the largeness of a public exhibition should leave less money than is necessary to drive the Nations Trade, then the mischief thereof would be the doing of less work, which is the same as lessening the people, or their Art and Industry.[8]

In this quotation it appears that Petty believed that an adequate money supply is just as important as an increase in the labor force, or a rise in the productivity of the existing labor force through an increase in the workers' "Art and Industry," which, in modern terminology, amounts to technological advance.[9]

Petty was not concerned with the possible effects of an increase in the quantity of money on prices. He thought that an excess of money over and above the "due proportion" could be hoarded by the state by turning it into plates and vessels. Thus he was able to bypass the problem of the value of money, or its reciprocal, the price level.

On the question of the rate of interest, Petty held a monetary theory of interest. He considered "the natural fall of Interest" to be "the effect of the increase of money."[10]

### John Law (1671–1792)

The most elaborate exposition of the money-stimulates-trade doctrine was made by John Law, who made the following assertion:

> Domestic trade depends on money: A greater quantity employs more people than a lesser quantity. A limited sum can only set a

---

[7] Hull, ed., *Economic Writings of Sir William Petty*, I, 112–113.

[8] Hull, ed., *Economic Writings of Sir William Petty*, I, 36.

[9] Petty and his contemporaries believed that a numerous and increasing population was one of the greatest assets that a nation could have. This is what Schumpeter calls the "populationist attitude." See *History of Economic Analysis*, pp. 251–252.

[10] Hull, ed., *Economic Writings of Sir William Petty*, I, 304.

number of people to work proportioned to it, and it is with little success laws are made, for employing the poor and idle in countries where money is scarce; good laws may bring the money to the full circulation it is capable of, and force it to those employments that are most profitable to the country; But no law can make it go further, nor can more people be set to work, without more money to circulate so as to pay the wages of a greater number.[11]

Law by-passed the price level problem by implicitly assuming the presence of unemployed resources and an elastic supply of goods and services. In terms of the quantity equation, Law's arguments may be illustrated by the following expression:

$$Y = \frac{MV}{P}$$

With constant prices $(P)$, due to elastic supply of goods and services, the increase of $(MV)$ would cause a proportional increase in $(Y)$.

Law advocated paper money as the best way to increase the money supply. His argument may be summarized as follows. (1) If money is to function properly it must be stable in value. (2) The precious metals are defective as circulating medium because they are demanded both for monetary and industrial uses. Hence, changes in the demand and supply of the precious metals would affect their value. (3) Paper money is superior because it can be managed and issued according to the "needs of trade."

The preceding "needs-of-trade" argument of John Law shows that he had anticipated the "real-bills doctrine" of the nineteenth-century Banking School (See Chapter 9). In his emphasis on the demand for precious metals, Law also contributed to our understanding of the forces determining the value of metallic money. Unfortunately, his theoretical contributions were obscured by the failure of his financial adventure in France. The burst of the "Mississippi Bubble" (1720) had such a profound influence on eighteenth-century ideas about money and credit that it became one of the major factors in shaping the concept of neutral money.[12] The critics of John Law were quite right in

---

[11] John Law, *Money and Trade Considered, with a Proposal for Supplying the Nation with Money* (London: 1720), p. 11.

[12] See Charles Rist, *History of Monetary and Credit Theory from John Law to the Present Day*, Jane Degras, trans. (New York: The Macmillan Company, 1940), p. 41. Professor Rist observes:

The efforts made in the course of the century by so many writers, including Smith, Hume and Turgot, to reduce the role of money in the national economy to nothing or to insignificance, were directed against Law rather than against mercantilist ideas about money, which had already worn thin.

condemning the abuses of credit. In over-emphasizing the financial aspects of economic development, Law failed to grasp the real problems of an underdeveloped economy such as that of eighteenth-century France. However, as Professors Gurley and Shaw put it, "development involves finance as well as goods."[13] In their analysis, the classical economists' preoccupation on the "real" or "goods" aspects of development also appeared to be lopsided.

### Bishop George Berkeley (1685–1753)

Bishop Berkeley, writing after Law, was another exponent of managed currency. A careful reading of his *The Querist* shows that Berkeley was not an inflationist, or a believer in monetary panaceas.[14] In his consideration of the problems of economic development in Ireland, Berkeley emphasized both the real aspects and the financial aspects of economic growth. On the real side, he named three determinants of output growth, namely, the supply of labor, savings, and the enterprising spirit of the people. The following query illustrates this point:

> Whether the real Foundation for Wealth must not be laid in the Numbers, the Frugality, and the Industry of the People? And whether all attempts to enrich a Nation by other Means, as raising the Coin, Stock-jobbing, and such Arts, are not in vain?[15]

Berkeley further pointed out:

> Whether even Gold and Silver, if they should lessen the Industry of its Inhabitants, would not be ruinous to a country? And whether Spain be not an instance of this?[16]

On the financial side, Berkeley insisted that a distinction should be made between the abuses of money and credit, and the function of

---

[13] See John G. Gurley and E. S. Shaw, "Financial Aspects of Economic Development," *American Economic Review*, Vol. XLV (September, 1955), p. 515.

[14] Berkeley employed the peculiar stylistic device of terse and seemingly disconnected interrogations in *The Querist*. See George Berkeley, *The Querist*, Jacob Hollander, ed. (Baltimore: The Johns Hopkins Press, 1910). This peculiar style has prompted Professor Schumpeter to remark: "The idea of putting a prolonged argument into an endless string of wearying questions may not be to everyone's taste." [*History of Economic Analysis*, p. 289]. This peculiar style might also be a cause for misunderstanding Berkeley's theoretical position.

[15] Berkeley, *op. cit.*, Part I, Question 197, p. 31.

[16] Berkeley, Part I, Qu. 45, p. 14.

money and credit in promoting economic growth. He asked the following question:

> Whether, therefore, the circulating Paper, in the late ruinous Schemes of France and England, was the true Evil, and not rather the circulating thereof without Industry; And whether the Bank of Amsterdam, where Industry had been for so many Years subsisted, and circulated by Transfers on Paper, doth not clearly decide this Point?[17]

Berkeley was of the opinion that where idle resources existed, an increase in money and credit would lead to an increase in economic activity. Mindful of Law's failure, Berkeley insisted that note-issues and bank credit should be placed under public regulation. He asked: "Whether the same Evils would be apprehended from Paper Money under an honest and thrifty regulation?"[18] He suggested that bank credit should be increased in step with increases in the volume of transactions of real goods and services. He further suggested that, whenever necessary, a credit ceiling might be imposed by the monetary authorities in order to preclude excessive credit expansion.[19] He believed there would be more danger of abuse, if monetary affairs were entrusted entirely to private hands.[20]

It should be noted that Berkeley, like Petty, did not make an attempt to reconcile the money-stimulates-trade doctrine with the quantity theory of money. Their failure to analyze prices could probably be attributed to their faith in monetary policy. Petty advocated state hoarding and dishoarding of excess metallic money to solve the problems of inflation and deflation; Berkeley stressed strict regulation of bank credit. Both of these suggestions may be considered, in modern terminology, as "discretionary" monetary policy.

### Jacob Vanderlint (?–1740)

Jacob Vanderlint's only economic book was entitled *Money Answers All Things* (1734). The title was misleading and obscured his true theoretical insight; for, like Berkeley, he was not a believer in monetary panaceas. Vanderlint perceived that there were alternative ways to increase the money supply: (1) by permitting prices to fall, thereby

---

[17] Berkeley, Part I, Qu. 283, p. 41. The "ruinous Schemes of France and England" were the "Mississippi Bubble" and the "South Sea Bubble." By "Industry" Berkeley meant the spirit of enterprise.

[18] Berkeley, Part II, Qu. 22, p. 51.

[19] Berkeley, Part I, Qu. 235, p. 36.

[20] Berkeley, Part III, Qu. 22, 26, pp. 81–82.

stimulating exports and effecting an inflow of precious metals, or (2) by directly increasing money and credit through the monetary system. Like his contemporaries, he was concerned with the problem of un-employment. As he saw it, the basic cause of unemployment was high domestic manufacturing costs which hampered British exports.[21] The high manufacturing costs, in turn, were traced to insufficient agricul-tural production and high food prices that augmented the total wage bill. Thus, Vanderlint suggested the following indirect ways of in-creasing the quantity of money and removing unemployment:

1. Increase the supply of agricultural products in order to lower food prices, thereby permitting the reduction of money-wage rates (but not of real wage rates which, in his system, is the irreducible subsistence wage).
2. Lower costs of production and improve the international com-petitive position of British manufacturers, thereby increasing exports, stimulating an inflow of money, and expanding em-ployment.

It is interesting to note that Vanderlint anticipated Keynes in his counsel against wage reduction as a remedial measure to remove un-employment. Like Keynes, he argued that wage-earners were con-sumers; therefore, wage reduction would cause a decline in aggre-gate demand, which tended to offset its cost-reduction effect. How-ever, this is not to say that Vanderlint was a forerunner of Keynesian economics. In the economics of John Maynard Keynes, as Professor Dillard so aptly put it, "money holds the key to explaining unemploy-ment but not to its remedy."[22] In the economics of Jacob Vanderlint, as well as the other exponents of the money-stimulates-trade doctrine, money holds not only the key to *explaining* unemployment, but also the effective *remedy* for unemployment. The explanation of this phenome-non lies in the fact that none of these writers paid any attention to the role of expectations in the economic decision-making process. Hence, the theory of liquidity preference is conspicuously absent in their writings. Without the speculative (asset)-demand-for-money func-tion, the elasticity of aggregate demand with respect to an increase in the quantity of money will be equal to unity. It is, therefore, ironical that their analysis of money and economic activity is substantially the same as that of the quantity theorists.

---

[21] See Vickers, *op. cit.*, Chap. 9.

[22] See Dudley Dillard, "The Theory of a Monetary Economy," in *Post-Keynes-ian Economics*, K. K. Kurihara, ed. (New Brunswick, N.J.: Rutgers University Press, 1954), p. 20.

## THE QUANTITY THEORY OF MONEY

### John Locke (1632–1704)

John Locke has often been credited with the first clear English formulation of the quantity theory of money. From the time of Jean Bodin
(1530–1596), many of the mercantilists held one or another simple
version of the quantity theory.[23] However, as pointed out by Professor Viner, "in most cases they failed to incorporate it as an integral
part of their foreign-trade doctrine and failed also to show any concern about its consistency with the rest of their doctrine."[24] Locke
made some advance in incorporating the quantity theory into the
foreign-trade doctrine, but a satisfactory synthesis occurred only later
in David Hume's work. Locke also failed to reconcile the money-
stimulates-trade doctrine with the quantity theory of money. Thus,
Keynes remarked: "Locke was the parent of the twin quantity theories."[25] The twin quantity theory was expounded by Locke in his two
essays: *Consequences of the Lowering of Interest and Raising the
Value of Money* (1691) and *Further Considerations Concerning Raising
the Value of Money* (1696).

In the first essay, Locke seems to have grasped the interrelationship
between the money and product markets. He appears to have perceived that the link between money and output (economic activity)
was the rate of interest. Locke considered the rate of interest a purely
monetary phenomenon. Interest was the price for hiring money; and,
like any other price, it was determined by the market forces of demand
and supply. In his analysis, the demand for loanable funds consisted of
borrowings for trade activity; the total money supply in circulation
constituted the supply of loanable funds.[26] Given the level of trade ac-

---

[23] Jean Bodin was probably the first to explain the relation between the quantity of money and prices. In his *Reply to the Paradoxes of Malestroit*, he said: "I
find that the dearness we observe comes from four or five causes. The principal
and almost the only one (to which no one has heretofore referred) is the abundance
of gold and silver, which is much greater in this kingdom today than it was four
hundred years ago." Reprinted in *Readings in Economics*, Kapp and Kapp, eds.
(New York: Barnes & Noble, Inc., 1949), p. 37.

[24] Viner, *Studies in the Theory of International Trade*, pp. 76–78.

[25] Reprinted from *The General Theory of Employment, Interest, and Money*,
p. 343, by John Maynard Keynes by permission of Harcourt, Brace & World, Inc.

[26] Locke's loanable funds analysis was inferior to that of his contemporary, Sir
Dudley North (1641–1694). In North's analysis, the demand for loanable funds
consisted of consumer loans, government borrowing, and borrowing by foreigners;
the supply of loanable funds consisted of savings, dishoarding, injections of new
money, and inflows of foreign money capital. See Sir Dudley North, *Discourses
Upon Trade*, Jacob H. Hollander, ed. (Baltimore: The Johns Hopkins Press, 1907),
pp. 17–21.

tivity, the rate of interest was a function of the quantity of money. A shortage of money meant a high rate of interest, which, in turn, would lead to a reduction of trade activity. This is Locke's money-stimulates-trade doctrine in a nutshell. It was for this reason that he argued against the Child-Culpeper proposal for reducing the rate of interest by legal means.[27] He maintained that their proposal would be self-defeating because lenders would be reluctant to make loans at such an artificially low rate, thus further aggravating the money shortage. This argument leads to the conclusion that the consequence of lowering the rate of interest by legal means would be a reduction of economic activity. Here we have in embryo the integration of monetary theory with the theory of employment. The major analytical shortcoming in this theory was, as pointed out by Keynes in the preceding quotation, the absence of a liquidity preference analysis.

Regarding the quantity theory of the value of money, Locke asserted that the value of money $(1/P)$ depended only on its quantity and not on the demand for money $(k)$. His argument may be illustrated in terms of the familiar Cambridge equation:[28]

$$M = kPY$$

By focusing exclusively on the medium-of-exchange function of money (abstracting from liquidity preference) and by a rigid interpretation of Petty's "due proportion of money and trade doctrine," Locke was able to rule out fluctuations in $(k)$.[29] The constancy of $(k)$ implies the constancy of $(Y)$. Hence, the value of money $(1/P)$ depends exclusively on its quantity.

Locke did not make any explicit attempt to reconcile the two theories. In the first theory, Locke appears to have vaguely perceived the interdependence between the money and commodity markets via the interest rate mechanism. In the second theory, by focusing exclusively on the medium-of-exchange function of money, he completely ignored this interdependence. The implication of the proposition that the value of money is determined by its quantity alone is that prices will vary strictly in proportion to the quantity of money.[30]

---

[27] A good description of the Child-Culpeper position is given by William Letwin, *The Origins of Scientific Economics* (New York: Doubleday & Company, Inc., 1964), Chap. I.

[28] Pre-Marshallian writers who employed the cash-balances approach are: Petty, Locke, Cantillon, Senior, Thornton, Giffen, and Bagehot. See Eprime Eshag, *From Marshall to Keynes* (London: Basil Blackwell & Mott Ltd., 1963), pp. 13–18.

[29] Professor Vickers gives a very good explanation of this point in his *Studies in the Theory of Money 1690–1776*, pp. 52–53.

[30] Professor Blaug relates the Lockean version of the quantity theory to Say's Identity. He observes: "The pure Lockean version of the quantity theory of

The Lockean analysis was conducted in a static framework. He had defined certain fundamental monetary relationships, but failed to provide an adequate explanation of the functional relations of the strategic variables in his system. Nor did he grasp the subtler aspects of economic processes. This analytical gap was filled by Richard Cantillon, who has been referred to as "First of the Moderns."[31]

### Richard Cantillon (1680?–1734)

Cantillon criticized Locke for his failure to trace systematically the effects of an increase in the quantity of money on prices:

> . . . he has clearly seen that the abundance of money makes everything dear, but he has not considered how it does so. The great difficulty of this question consists in knowing in what way and in what proportion the increase of money raises prices.[32]

Cantillon's contributions to the development of the quantity theory of money may be summarized as follows. (1) Cantillon pointed out that the relation between money and prices was not a direct one. Whether or not an increase in the quantity of money would lead to a proportionate increase in prices depended on whether an increase in money would lead to increased spending. The extent of the induced increase in spending, in turn, depended upon the way in which the new money was injected into the system. Since the propensity to spend among different social groups varied, the induced increase in spending would also be different. For instance, if the new money came into the hands of entrepreneurs (the savers), the increase in prices would not be proportional to the increase in money. The explanation was that a part of the new money would be used to augment the supply of loanable funds, which would cause the equilibrium rate of interest to fall. Simultaneously, the composition of total output would also be altered in favor of investment. In Cantillon's words:

> I conclude that by doubling the quantity of money in a State the prices of products and merchandise are not always doubled.

---

money . . . implies Say's Identity, and vice versa. Indeed, the quantity theory was the chief element making for the dichotomization of the pricing process."

Reprinted with permission from Mark Blaug, *Economic Theory in Retrospect* (Homewood, Ill.: Richard D. Irwin, Inc.), p. 135.

[31] See Joseph J. Spengler, "Richard Cantillon: First of the Moderns," reprinted from *Journal of Political Economy*, Vol. LXII (1956), in *Essays in Economic Thought*, Spengler and Allen, eds.

[32] Richard Cantillon, *Essay on the Nature of Trade*, Henry Higgs, trans. and ed. (London: Frank Cass & Co., 1959), p. 161.

The proportion of the dearness which the increased quantity of money brings about in the State will depend on the turn which this money will impart to consumption and circulation. Through whatever hands the money which is introduced may pass it will naturally increase the consumption; but this consumption will be more or less great according to circumstances. It will be directed more or less to certain kinds of products or merchandise according to the idea of those who acquire the money. Market prices will rise more for certain things than for others however abundant the money may be.[33]

I conceive that when a large surplus of money is brought into a State the new money gives a new turn to consumption and even a new speed to circulation. But it is not possible to say exactly to what extent.[34]

(2) Cantillon's analysis recognized the interdependence of the component parts of the economic system. Thus, he held that a change in the monetary side would affect the magnitude of the real variables. The rate of interest in equilibrium would be determined by the interaction of monetary factors with real factors.[35]

Cantillon denied that the rate of interest was a purely monetary phenomenon. He was of the opinion that the rate of interest was essentially determined by saving and productivity; an increase in the quantity of money had no effect on the rate of interest, unless it could lead either to an increase in the supply of savings or an increase in the productivity of capital. Cantillon wrote:

Interest of Money in a State is settled by the proportionate number . . . of Lenders and Borrowers.[36]

Plenty or Scarcity of Money in a State always raises or lowers the price of everything in bargaining without any necessary connecnection with the rate of interest.[37]

It should also be noted that Cantillon in his *Essay* had developed a dynamic analysis of the equilibrating process. His work is notably more advanced than the definitional and static description of monetary affairs presented by John Locke.

(3) Finally, Cantillon's *Essay* reconciled the "twin quantity theory" by employing a general equilibrium analysis, which brought money, in-

---

[33] Cantillon, pp. 177–179.

[34] Cantillon, p. 181.

[35] For a lucid discussion on this point see Becker and Baumol, *The Classical Monetary Theory: The Outcome of the Discussion,* reprinted in *Essays in Economic Thought,* Spengler and Allen, eds. (Chicago: Rand McNally & Co., 1960), pp. 735–771.

[36] Cantillon, p. 199.

[37] Cantillon, p. 215.

terest, employment, wage rates, prices, and population into one inter-related system.[38] The major differences between Cantillon's "general theory" and that of Keynes are: first, Cantillon did not employ a closed-economy model by abstracting from foreign trade; second, Cantillon did not treat population as an exogenous variable; and third, Cantillon, like his predecessors, employed a "loanable-funds" approach to the theory of interest and did not develop an analysis of the asset demand for money.

### David Hume (1711–1776)

It was at the hands of David Hume that the quantity theory of money took the form of its commonly accepted version. Hume antici-pated Irving Fisher in his treatment of the quantity theory. His "inter-val," or "intermediate situation," is analogous to the Fisherian "transi-

---

[38] For instance, Cantillon said:

If the increase of actual money comes from Mines of gold and silver in the State the Owners of these Mines, the Adventurers, the Smelters, Refiners, and all the other workers will increase their expenses in proportion to their gains. They will consume in their households more Meat, Wine, or Beer than before, will accustom themselves to wear better cloaths, finer linen, to have better fur-nished Houses. . . . They will consequently give employment to several Mechanicks . . . all this increase of expense in Meat, Wine, Wool, etc., . . . will not fail to raise their prices. These high prices will determine the Farm-ers to employ more land to produce them in another year. . . . Those then who will suffer from this dearness and increased consumption will be first of all the Landowners, during the term of their Leases, then their Domestic Servants . . . which will compel a large number of them to emigrate to seek a living elsewhere . . . the rest will demand an increase of wages to enable them to live as before. It is thus, approximately, that a considerable increase of Money from the Mines increases consumption, and by diminishing the number of inhabitants entails a greater expense among those who remain.
  If more money continues to be drawn from the Mines all prices will owing to this abundance rise to such a point that not only will the landowners raise their rents considerably when the leases expire and resume their old style of living, increasing proportionately the wages of their servants. . . . This will naturally induce several people to import many manufactured articles made in foreign countries, where they will be found very cheap; this will gradually ruin the Mechanics and Manufacturers of the State. . . .
  When the excessive abundance of money from the Mines has diminished the inhabitants of a State, accustomed those who remain to a too large ex-penditure, raised the produce of the land and the labour of workmen to ex-cessive prices, ruined the manufactures of the State by the use of foreign productions on the part of the Landlords and mine workers, the money pro-duced by the Mines will necessarily go abroad to pay for the imports: this will gradually impoverish the State and render it in some sort dependent on the Foreigner. . . . The great circulation of Money, which was general at the beginning, ceases: poverty and misery follow and the labour of the Mines appears to be only to the advantage of those employed upon them and the Foreigners who profit thereby.
  This is approximately what has happened to Spain since the discovery of the Indies. . . .
Richard Cantillon, *op. cit.*, pp. 163–167.

tion period."[39] Hume stated that during the intermediate situation an increase in the quantity of money would lead to an increase in economic activity:

> . . . though the high price of commodities be a necessary consequence of the encrease of gold and silver, yet it follows not immediately upon the encrease; but some time is required before the money circulates through the whole state, and makes its effect be felt on all ranks of people. At first, no alteration is perceived; by degrees the price rises, first of one commodity, then another; till the whole at last reaches a just proportion with the new quantity of specie which is in the Kingdom. In my opinion, it is only in this interval or intermediate situation, between the acquisition of money and rise of prices, that the encreasing quantity of gold and silver is favourable to industry.[40]

Hume then stated the quantity theory of money as a long-run view. He pointed out that if the prevailing class structure and the basic saving and investment habits of the community remained unchanged, an injection of new money would eventually result in a new equilibrium, where prices would have increased in proportion to the increase in money, and the equilibrium rate of interest would have remained unchanged. He wrote:

> After the new mass of gold and silver has been digested, and has circulated through the whole state, affairs will soon return to their former situation; while the landlords and new moneyholders, living idly, squander above their income; and the former daily contract debt, and the latter encroach on their stock till its final extinction. The whole money may still be in the state, and make itself felt by the encrease in prices: But not being now collected into any large masses or stocks, the disproportion between the borrowers and lenders is the same as formerly and consequently the high interest returns.[41]

It is interesting to note that Hume arrived at the quantity-theory conclusion (namely, in equilibrium, prices increase in proportion to the new money with the equilibrium rate of interest unchanged) not via the real-balances effect, but through an argument based on class structure. According to Hume, the rate of interest was determined by real factors, namely, thrift and productivity. Given the level of pro-

---

[39] See Chap. 7 of this book.

[40] Eugene Rotwein, ed., *David Hume: Writings on Economics* (London: Thomas Nelson & Sons, 1955), pp. 37–38.

[41] *David Hume: Writings on Economics*, p. 58.

ductivity, an increase in thrift would lower the equilibrium rate of interest. Thus, in Hume's analysis, we see the beginning of real analysis. As aptly summarized by Professor Hansen, "Here are the root ideas that permeated monetary thinking in much of the nineteenth century. Thrift and productivity determine the rate of interest; the money supply determines the level of prices. The demand for money is interest-inelastic. Internationally, gold and silver are distributed in proportion to the level of industry and commerce in each country and thereby the price levels of different countries are kept in line."[42]

Following Cantillon, Hume noticed that the proposition that doubling the quantity of money would double prices, applied to a special case only. This was the case in which the increased quantity of money was equiproportionately distributed in relation to the initial money holdings. Otherwise, as pointed out by Cantillon, the relationship would lose its precision.

## SIR JAMES STEUART (1712–1780) AND THE CONTRA-QUANTITY THEORY OF MONEY

Steuart criticized the quantity theory of money by pointing out that prices were not only a function of the quantity of money:

> Here I am led into an examination of the opinion of Messrs. De Montesquieu and Hume, who think that the price of everything depends upon the quantity of specie in the country, which they consider as the representation of everything vendible; as if these two quantities, the commodities, and the specie, were divided into aloquot parts, exactly proportioned to one another.[43]

According to Steuart, whether or not an increase in the quantity of money would lead to a proportionate increase in prices depended upon the following two considerations: (1) Whether an increase in the quantity of money would lead to an increase in aggregate demand; and (2) whether the supply of goods and services was elastic with respect to changes in aggregate demand. He wrote:

> Increase the money, nothing can be concluded as to prices, because it is not certain, that people will increase their expences in

---

[42] From *Monetary Theory and Fiscal Policy*, by Alvin H. Hansen, p. 218. Copyright 1949 by McGraw-Hill Book Company. Used with permission of McGraw-Hill Book Company.

[43] Sir James Steuart, *Principles of Political Oeconomy* (London: 1767), I, 515.

proportion to their wealth; and although they should, the moment their additional demand has the effect of producing a sufficient supply, prices will return to the old standard.[44]

Steuart noted that, if the increased quantity of money was hoarded, there would not be any increase in aggregate demand:

> But if upon this revolution it is found that the state of demand remains without any variation, then the additional coin will probably be locked up, or being converted into plate; because they who have it, not being inspired with the desire of increasing their consumption, and far less with the generous sentiment of giving their money away, their riches will remain without producing more effect than if they had remained in the mine.[45]

In the preceding quotation, Steuart was explicit in stating the role of hoarding in the determination of aggregate demand. He did not, however, make a systematic analysis of the determinants of hoarding.

Steuart, like Petty and Berkeley, was more concerned with the problem of full employment and the relation between money and economic activity than with the question of the value of money. Their faith in the discretionary policies of statesmen also made them less fearful of inflation. They seemed to believe that inflation was not to be feared when there was large-scale unemployment. Steuart's advice to the statesman was:

> He ought at all times to maintain a just proportion between the produce of industry, and the quantity of circulating equivalent, in the hands of the subjects, for the purchases of it; that, by a steady and judicious administration, he may have it in his power at all times, either to check prodicality and hurtfull luxury, or to extend industry and domestic consumption, according as the circumstances of his people shall acquire the one or the other corrective, to be applied to the natural bent and spirit of the times.[46]

His theory of interest also reflected his main concern for full employment. He wrote:

> I entirely agree with Sir Josiah Child, that low interest is the soul of trade, the most active principle for promoting industry, and the improvement of land; and a requisite, without which it is hardly possible that a foreign commerce can long be supported.[47]

---

[44] Steuart, I, 413.
[45] Steuart, I, 400.
[46] Steuart, I, 375.
[47] Steuart, II, 129.

But he disagreed with Child concerning the way to control the rate of interest. Steuart advocated that, instead of controlling the rate by legal means, the statesman could effectively control it by controlling the money supply. Broadly speaking, Steuart's monetary theory had a family resemblance to that of Keynes. Both of them recognized that the influence of money on prices is indirect; both of them also recognized that the market mechanism might set a rate of interest too high for a flourishing trade, and that money could be managed to compensate for such disturbing forces in the economy.[48]

---

[48] That is probably the reason why Samar Ranjan Sen wrote the essay entitled, "Sir James Steuart's General Theory of Employment, Interest, and Money," *Economica*, XIV (1947), 19–36.

# 7

# Classical
# Monetary Theory

The quantity theory of money, as formulated by Cantillon and Hume, was accepted by the classical economists. It represented the mainstream of thought in classical monetary theory. For instance, in discussions on the external value of money (foreign exchange rates), the quantity theory approach was adopted by the "Bullionists";[1] in the realm of the monetary theory of international trade (balance-of-payments adjustment mechanism), the quantity theory was the chief ingredient of the price-specie flow mechanism;[2] and in the theory of money and banking, the same approach was adopted by the "currency school."[3]

The dissenters in the classical period were not few in number. They included the "anti-bullionists"[4] and the exponents of the so-called

---

[1] The bullionists were Walter Boyd, John Wheatley, Ricardo, Francis Horner, Henry Thornton, etc. The theory of foreign exchange rate expounded by them has been called the purchasing power parity theory. For further readings on the subject, see Jacob Viner, *Studies in the Theory of International Trade* (New York: Harper & Row, Publishers, 1937), pp. 218–224; J. A. Schumpeter, *History of Economic Analysis* (New York: Oxford University Press, Inc., 1955), pp. 706–717; and Paul Einzig, *The History of Foreign Exchange* (New York: St. Martin's Press, Inc., 1962), Chap. 17.

[2] See P. T. Ellsworth, *International Economics* (New York: The Macmillan Company, 1938), pp. 16–18; also Gottfried Haberler, *The Theory of International Trade* (New York: The Macmillan Company, 1936), pp. 26–29.

[3] See Lionel Robbins, *Robert Torrens and the Evolution of Classical Economics* (London: Macmillan & Co., 1958), Chap. 5.

[4] The anti-bullionists included Sir Francis Baring, C. W. Bosanquet, and Thomas Smith.

income approach to the theory of money and prices (the "banking school").

The classical theory of the external value of money and the development of the price-specie flow mechanism are not within the purview of this book. In this chapter we limit ourselves to a brief survey of the two approaches to the theory of money and prices expounded by the classical economists and their critics.


## THE QUANTITY THEORY OF MONEY

The quantity theory of money, as indicated earlier, is a long-run view. It is, therefore, consistent with the real analysis of the classical school, which also focuses on a long-run equilibrium, wherein all disturbing elements have worked themselves out. Money is considered neutral in the long-run equilibrium, so it is quite legitimate for the classical economists to have treated money as a veil superimposed on the underlying real relationships.[5] This was, probably, the explanation for the repeated blanket assertions affirming Say's Law (in the sense of Say's Identity).[6] Had the classical economists been more careful and precise in spelling out the equilibrating adjustment process by which deviations from full employment equilibrium tend to be self-correcting, they would have taken much of the wind out of the sails of Keynesian economics.

The outcome of the re-examination of classical and neo-classical monetary theory made by post-Keynesian writers has shown that the classical writers were not guilty of upholding the concept of Say's Identity. What they really meant was that, with flexible prices (including the money-wage rate and the interest rate), the economic system automatically tends toward full-capacity equilibrium. This notion has been called by post-Keynesian writers, Say's Equality (discussed earlier in this book).

---

[5] Professor Don Patinkin made the following interesting observation:
Actually it can be said that everyone simultaneously accepts and rejects Say's law: rejects it, in the sense that no one believes the short-run expenditure function must [always coincide with the 45° line]; accepts it, in the sense that everyone recognizes that in the long run people want goods, and not money.
"Involuntary Unemployment and the Keynesian Supply Function," *The Economic Journal* (September, 1949), p. 378.

[6] See David Ricardo, *The Principles of Political Economy and Taxation*, Everyman's Library No. 590 (London: J. M. Dent & Sons, Ltd., 1955), pp. 192–194; John Stuart Mill, *Essays on Some Unsettled Questions of Political Economy*, reprinted by the London School of Economics and Political Science, 1948, pp. 69–74.

## Henry Thornton (1760–1815)

The classical writers were well aware of the crucial interdependence between money and output markets via the indirect interest-rate mechanism. An outstanding example of this awareness is Henry Thornton's *Enquiry into the Nature and Effects of the Paper Credit of Great Britain* (1802).[7]

Thornton's book was an inquiry into two related questions: (1) whether, apart from convertibility, there existed a natural tendency in the credit mechanism to prevent an over-expansion of bank credit, and resultant price inflation; and (2) whether sound banking practice—such as discounting real bills only—would constitute such a natural restriction.[8] Thornton pointed out:

> In order to ascertain how far the desire of obtaining loans at the Bank may be expected at any time to be carried, we must enquire into the subject of the quantum of profit likely to be derived from borrowing there under the existing circumstances. This is to be judged of by considering two points: the amount, first, of interest to be paid on the sum borrowed; and, secondly, of the mercantile or other gain to be obtained by the employment of the borrowed capital. The gain which can be acquired by the means of commerce is commonly the highest which can be had; and it also regulates, in a great measure, the rate in all other cases. We may, therefore, consider this question as turning principally on a comparison of the rate of interest taken at the bank with the current rate of mercantile profit."[9]

Thornton believed that if the loan rate were kept below the investors' rate of return on capital in the commodity market, there would not be any natural tendency to check an overexpansion of credit. His argument may be illustrated by using a familiar loanable-funds diagram. In Fig. 7-1, amounts of investment (borrowing) and savings (lending) are plotted on the horizontal axis; and the rate of interest is plotted

---

[7] Henry Thornton was a member of Parliament and director of the Bank of England.

[8] The Bank of England suspended specie payment in 1797. The gold standard had been abandoned and the price of gold in terms of the inconvertible paper money had risen along with other prices. The external value (exchange rate) of pound sterling also declined. The Bank of England became the whipping boy for this war inflation. The "bullionists," led by Ricardo, attacked the Bank for excessive note-issue. As a director of the Bank, Thornton was in a difficult position. He put the blame of the overissue of notes on the existing legal maximum rate of 5 per cent, which was below the profit rate of investment in the output market.

[9] Henry Thornton, *An Enquiry into the Nature and Effects of the Paper Credit of Great Britain* (London: J. Hatchard, 1802), p. 287.

on the vertical axis. The investment-demand function is depicted as inversely related to the rate of interest; and the supply of savings as positively related to the rate of interest. The intersection of these two schedules determines the natural rate. Monetary equilibrium exists, if the loan rate $(r_0)$, is equal to the natural rate $(r_n)$. If the loan rate is $(r_1)$, which is below the natural rate $(r_n)$, the demand for loans would be insatiable; and inflationary pressure would be created in the output market. The cumulative process of inflation would come to an end only when the bank rate had been raised to again equal the natural rate. In equilibrium, prices would be higher than before, but the equilibrium rate of interest would be unchanged. The quantity-theory conclusions have been verified.

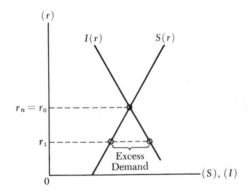

Figure 7-1

Professor Hayek has found that Thornton was the first English writer who stated the "forced-saving" doctrine in print.[10] Although Jeremy Bentham had shortly before expounded the same doctrine, his

---

[10] F. A. von Hayek, "A Note on the Development of the Doctrine of 'Forced Saving,'" *Quarterly Journal of Economics*, Vol. XLVII (November, 1932). The relevant passage from Thornton's *Enquiry* follows:

> It must also be admitted that, provided we assume an excessive issue of paper to lift up, as it may for a time, the cost of goods though not the price of labour, some augmentation of stock will be the consequence; for the labourer, according to this supposition, may be forced by his necessity to consume fewer articles, though he may exercise the same industry. But this saving, as well as any additional one which may arise from a similar defalcation of the revenue of the unproductive members of the society, will be attended with a proportionate hardship and injustice [pp. 263–264].

exposition, according to Professor Viner, "remained in manuscript form until published in 1843 as his *Manual of Political Economy.*"[11] It has been generally recognized that both Thornton's two-rate theory and his forced-saving doctrine anticipated the Wicksellian analysis.

Professor Schumpeter observed that Thornton in his book also mentioned the possibility that, under conditions of unemployment, an increase in bank credit would lead to an increase in output and employment, and not in prices.[12]

The significance of Thornton's analysis is that we cannot give an unqualified summary of classical monetary theory in terms of the veil of money. In the first place, the concept of "unneutral money" was invoked in the elaboration on the forced-saving doctrine and in the exposition on the relation between money and employment under conditions of unemployment. Secondly, as pointed out by Professor Patinkin, "this distinction between the short-run variability of interest in the face of a monetary increase and its long-run invariability in no way represents the 'unbridged conflict' in classical theorizing that Keynes made it out to be. It represents instead the well-reasoned conclusion of the analysis . . . which takes account of the effect of a rising price level in the commodity market on the rate of interest in the loan market."[13]

### David Ricardo (1772–1823)

Ricardo accepted Thornton's two-rate analysis in his pamphlet entitled, *The Price of Gold* (1809). He used this piece of analysis to support his argument for convertibility. This analysis was reiterated by Ricardo in his *The High Price of Bullion* (1810). On the short-run variability and long-run invariability of the rate of interest, Ricardo wrote:

> It is contended that the rate of interest, and not the price of gold or silver bullion, is the criterion by which we may always judge of the abundance of paper money; as that if it were too abundant, interest would fall, and if not sufficiently so, interest would rise. It can, I think, be made manifest, that the rate of interest is not

---

[11] Viner, *op. cit.*, p. 188.

[12] Schumpeter, *op. cit.*, p. 723.

[13] From *Money, Interest, and Prices*, 2nd Edition, p. 369, by Don Patinkin. Copyright © 1965 by Don Patinkin. Reprinted by permission of Harper & Row, Publishers.

regulated by the abundance or scarcity of money, but by the abundance or scarcity of that part of capital not consisting of money.[14]

The rate of interest, though ultimately and permanently governed by the rate of profit, is, however, subject to temporary variations from other causes. With every fluctuation in the quantity and value of money, the prices of commodities naturally vary. They vary also . . . from the alteration in the proportion of supply and demand, although there should not be either greater facility or difficulty of production. When the market prices of goods fall from an abundant supply, from a diminished demand, or from a rise in the value of money, a manufacturer naturally accumulates an unusual quantity of finished goods, being unwilling to sell them at very depressed prices. To meet his ordinary payments, for which he used to depend on the sale of his goods, he now endeavours to borrow on credit, and is often obliged to give an increased rate of interest. This, however, is but of temporary duration; for either the manufacturer's expectations were well grounded, and the market price of his commodities rises, or he discovers that there is a permanently diminished demand, and he no longer resists the course of affairs: prices fall, and money and interest regain their real value. If, by the discovery of a new mine, by the abuses of banking, or by any other cause, the quantity of money be greatly increased, its ultimate effect is to raise the prices of commodities in proportion to the increased quantity of money; but there is probably always an interval during which some effect is produced on the rate of interest.[15]

This passage is quoted in full because it shows that the classical proposition of the realness of the equilibrium rate of interest was the result of careful analysis. Clearly, Ricardo took into consideration the expectations of sellers and a variety of other causes of short-run variability in the rate of interest.

Unfortunately, Ricardo and his followers held the quantity theory of money in a stricter sense.[16] They did not consider the possible relation between money and output. As observed by Professor Hutchison, "Ricardo, in fact, could see nothing at all in Bentham's (forced-saving) doctrine, just as he could see nothing at all in Malthus's ideas on effective demand, and J. B. Say's ideas on utility and value."[17] It is prob-

---

[14] Ricardo, *The High Price of Bullion*, reprinted in *Readings in the History of Economic Thought*, S. H. Patterson, ed. (New York: McGraw-Hill Book Company, 1932), p. 198.

[15] Ricardo, *The Principle of Political Economy and Taxation* (Homewood, Ill.: Richard D. Irwin, Inc., 1963), pp. 171–172.

[16] See Schumpeter, *History of Economic Analysis*, p. 703.

[17] T. W. Hutchison, "Bentham as an Economist," reprinted from *Journal of Political Economy*, Vol. LXVI (June, 1956), in *Essays in Economic Thought*, Spengler and Allen, eds. (Chicago: Rand McNally & Co., 1960), p. 339.

ably true, as some writers point out, that it is to Thornton, and not to Ricardo, that we should look for the exposition of classical monetary theory.[18]

In sum, Ricardo's theory of the value of money in the short run was the rigid quantity theory of money, which was applicable to both paper and metallic money.[19] In the long run, both the quantity and value of metallic money were governed by the same laws as in his theory of value.

Ricardo's view dominated the Bullion Report of 1810, and also provided an immediate inspiration for the "currency principle" subsequently formulated by members of the "currency school."[20] The essence of the "currency principle" is the prescription that a mixed currency (i.e., a currency of coins and paper money) would operate properly only if it operated precisely as would a metallic currency. This it would do only if the note issues were strictly regulated by requiring the issuing banks to keep 100 per cent reserves.

It will be recalled that England had in 1821 adopted the gold standard and that her currency was fully convertible. The "bullionists" agitated for convertibility as a safeguard against excessive note-issues and inflation. The members of the currency school went a step further with their contention that not only should the convertibility of note issues be enforced but the volume of notes should be strictly regulated.

It would be an over-simplification to say that the currency school completely overlooked the influence of demand deposits on the value

---

[18] See, for instance, Charles Rist, *History of Monetary and Credit Theory*, Jane Degros, ed. (New York: The Macmillan Company, 1940); see also B. A. Corry, and others.

[19] Charles Rist observes:
The concept of quantity completely dominates Ricardo's monetary theory: the level of prices depends on the quantity of money, whether that money is metallic or paper. The influence exercised by paper money on prices is the same whether the paper is convertible or not, its influence being strictly proportional to the quantity issued. Exchange rates are determined solely by the quantity of paper money issued in a country. . . . The idea of money as a means of storing value has completely disappeared. . . .
*History of Monetary and Credit Theory* (New York: The Macmillan Company, 1940), pp. 170–171.

[20] The *Bullion Report* was drafted by Francis Horner, Huskisson, and Henry Thornton. It pointed out that there was an excess of paper money in circulation and that convertibility would be the remedy. Although the *Report* was rejected by Parliament, it started a public debate on the proper role of the Bank of England that lasted for some thirty years.
The most prominent members of the currency school were Lord Overstone (Samuel Jones Loyd), G. W. Norman, Robert Torrens, and William Ward. Detailed discussion of the currency school-banking school controversy may be found in Viner, *Studies in the Theory of International Trade*, pp. 220–289; and in Lionel Robbins, *Robert Torrens and the Evolution of Classical Economics* (London: Macmillan & Co., Ltd., 1958), Chap. 5.

of money. In fact, Robert Torrence and other members of the school
made extensive inquiries into the subject in 1844, before the passage
of the Bank Charter Act. At first, Torrens and others held the optimistic view that control over note issue, in line with the currency principle, would indirectly control derivative-deposit creation by the banking
system, because, they believed, the customary reserve ratio would help
to check any over-expansion of bank credit. After the crisis of 1847,
Torrens and others began increasingly to realize the potential instability of a fractional reserve system. However, at this stage in the
development of monetary management, the functions of the lender-of-
last-resort had yet to be clearly perceived by the members of either
the currency or the banking schools.

### John Stuart Mill (1806–1878)

The mainstream of thought in classical monetary theory was restated
by John Stuart Mill. The quantity-theory conclusions that, in equilibrium, money is neutral and the rate of interest is independent of the
quantity of money, were explicitly stated by Mill in his *Principles of
Political Economy* (1848). On the value of money, Mill wrote:

> The value of money, other things being the same, varies inversely
> as its quantity; every increase of quantity lowering the value, and
> every diminution raising it, in a ratio exactly equivalent.[21]

The sequence of causation was described by Mill as follows:

> Supposing the money in the hands of individuals to be increased,
> the wants and inclinations of the community collectively in respect
> to consumption remaining exactly the same, the increase of de-
> mand would reach all things equally, and there would be a uni-
> versal rise in prices. Let us rather suppose, therefore, that to every
> pound, or shilling, or penny in the possession of any one, another
> pound, shilling, or penny were suddenly added. There would be an
> increased money demand, and consequently an increased money
> value, or price, for things of all sorts. This increased value would
> do no good to any one; would make no difference, except that of
> having to reckon (dollars and cents) in higher numbers. It would
> be an increase of values only as estimated in money, a thing only
> wanted to buy other things with; and would not enable any one
> to buy more of them than before. Prices would have risen in a
> certain ratio, and the value of money would have fallen in the
> same ratio.[22]

---

[21] J. S. Mill, *Principles of Political Economy*, abr. and ed. by J. Laurence Laughlin (New York: D. Appleton & Co., 1885), p. 297.

[22] *Ibid.*, p. 296.

It is clear that Mill was quite aware of the necessary assumption on which the quantity theory rests. This is the assumption of an equiproportionate distribution of new money relative to initial money holdings. (Cantillon and Hume had mentioned this point before him.) Mill in the preceding passage realized that the quantity-theory conclusions depend upon the necessary assumption of an absence of distribution effects. (This is why he said, "This increased value would do no good to any one. . . .") If this assumption were dropped, the relationship between money and prices would lose its precision.

The equation of exchange as a vehicle for expounding the quantity theory was explicitly stated by Mill:

> If we assume the quantity of goods on sale, and the number of times those goods are resold, to be fixed quantities, the value of money will depend upon its quantity, together with the average number of times that each piece changes hands in the process. . . . Consequently, the amount of goods and of transactions being the same, the value of money is inversely as its quantity multiplied by what is called the rapidity of circulation. And the quantity of money in circulation is equal to the money value of all the goods sold, divided by the number which expresses the rapidity of circulation.[23]

Again, Mill cautioned:

> The proposition which we have laid down respecting the dependence of general prices upon the quantity of money in circulation must be understood as applying only to a state of things in which money—that is, gold or silver—is the exclusive instrument of exchange, and actually passes from hand to hand at every purchase, credit in any of its shapes being unknown. When credit comes into play as a means of purchasing, distinct from money in hand, we shall hereafter find that the connection between prices and the amount of circulating medium is much less direct and intimate, and that such connection as does exist no longer admits of so simple a mode of expression. That an increase of the quantity of money raises prices, and a diminution lowers them, is the most elementary proposition in the theory of currency, and without it we should have no key to any of the others. In any state of things, however, except the simple and primitive one which we have supposed, the proposition is only true, other things being the same.[24]

Mill's words clearly demonstrate that the simple quantity-theory proposition was not a dogmatic First Principle of Faith (borrowing an expression from Professor Patinkin) of the classical writers.

---

[23] *Ibid.*, p. 298.
[24] *Ibid.*, pp. 299–300.

It is interesting to note that, whereas Thornton followed Petty, Locke, and Hume in adopting the cash-balance approach to the theory of money, Mill employed the transactions-velocity approach.

Mill followed his predecessors in adopting a "loanable-funds" approach to the theory of interest. He stated that "the rate of interest will be such as to equalize the demand for loans with the supply of them."[25] On the long-run invariability of the rate of interest, Mill wrote:

> . . . how great an error it is to imagine that the rate of interest bears any necessary relation to the quantity or value of the money in circulation. An increase of the currency has in itself no effect, and is incapable of having any effect, on the rate of interest.[26]

Once more we should note that the classical economists did not deny that in some measure the rate of interest would be jointly determined by monetary forces. Mill, in his earlier essay, *"On Profits, and Interest"* (1830), pointed out that the increase in bank credit under full-employment conditions would create "forced saving" by pushing down the rate of interest:

> The introduction of banks, which perform the function of lenders and loan-brokers, with or without that of issuers of paper-money, produces some further anomalies in the rate of interest, which have not, so far as we are aware, been hitherto brought within the pale of exact science.[27]

Mill further commented:

> If the paper is inconvertible, and instead of displacing specie depreciates the currency, the banker by issuing it levies a tax on every person who has money in his hands or due to him. . . . The depreciation of the currency, when affected in this way, operates to a certain extent as a forced accumulation.
>
> In any supposable case, however, the issue of the paper money by bankers increases the proportion of the whole capital of the country which is destined to be lent. The rate of interest must therefore fall, until some of the lenders give over lending, or until the increase of borrowers absorbs the whole.[28]

---

[25] *Ibid.*, pp. 440–441.

[26] *Ibid.*, p. 447.

[27] Mill, *Essays on Some Unsettled Questions of Political Economy*, reprinted by the London School of Economics and Political Science, University of London, 1948, p. 114.

[28] Mill, *Essays*, p. 118.

In the above passages, Mill explicitly stated that if distribution effects were present, an increase in the quantity of money would not be neutral and the equilibrium rate of interest could be permanently affected. Thus, it is not quite true to say that the distinguishing characteristic of classical monetary theory is the proposition that the rate of interest was independent of the quantity of money.

Mill was not unaware of the function of money as a store of value:

> Interchange by means of money is therefore, as has been often observed, ultimately nothing but barter. But there is this difference—that in the case of barter, the selling and the buying are simultaneously confounded in one operation. . . . Now the effect of the employment of money, and even the utility of it, is, that it enables this one act of interchange to be divided into two separate acts or operations; one of which may be performed now, and the other a year hence, or whenever it shall be most convenient. Although he who sells, really sells only to buy, he need not buy at the same moment when he sells; and he does not therefore necessarily add to the immediate demand for one commodity when [he] adds to the supply of another.[29]

In the preceding passage, Mill clearly denied Say's Identity. Thus, classical monetary theory, when carefully interpreted, can withstand such charges as the "homogeneity postulate," or the "dichotomization of the pricing process."

Like the majority of classical writers, however, Mill showed disapproval of capital accumulation via forced saving on moral grounds:

> This, indeed, is no palliation of its iniquity. Though A might have spent his property unproductively, B ought not be permitted to rob him of it because B will expend it on productive labour.[30]

## Thomas Tooke and the Contra-Quantity Theory of Money

A departure from the spirit of the classical school was found in the theoretical position of Thomas Tooke (1774–1858), the leading exponent of the banking principle.[31] The departure stemmed from his start-

---

[29] Mill, *Essays*, p. 70.

[30] Mill, *Essays*, p. 118.

[31] The members of the banking school were Thomas Tooke, James Wilson (founder of the *Economist*), and J. W. Gilbert. Professor Viner has stated:

> The discussion between the two schools turned wholly, however, on short-run issues. On the question of what determined the quantity and value of metallic currency in the long run, both schools followed the "classical" or "Ricardian" doctrine.

*Studies in the Theory of International Trade*, p. 221.

ling contra-quantity theory proposition. The quantity theory, in terms of the equation of exchange, stresses a left-side to right-side causality. Tooke, on the other hand, argued the opposite:

> . . . the prices of commodities do not depend upon the quantity of money indicated by the amount of bank notes, nor upon the amount of the whole of the circulating medium; but that, on the contrary, the amount of the circulating medium is the consequence of prices.[32]

> That it is the quantity of money, constituting the revenues of the different orders of the State, under the head of rents, profits, salaries, and wages, destined for current expenditure, that alone forms the limiting principle of the aggregate of money prices, the only prices that can properly come under the designation of general prices. As the cost of production is the limiting principle of supply, so the aggregate of money incomes devoted to expenditure for consumption is the determining and limiting principle of demand.[33]

Professor Hansen is of the opinion that the above passages constitute "one of the earliest and perhaps the first clear statement of the income theory of prices."[34] Since Tooke and the members of the banking school considered that it was the increase in aggregate demand that caused the money supply to grow, the banking system would be playing only a passive role. Therefore, Tooke pointed out: "The Bank of England has not the Power to add to the Circulation."[35]

Here lies the essential difference between the two schools.[36] As mentioned earlier, it was the contention of the currency school that convertibility should be reinforced by a strict regulation of the volume of

---

[32] Thomas Tooke, *An Inquiry into the Currency Principle* (London: Longman, Brown, Green, and Longmans, 1844), pp. 123–124.

[33] Tooke, p. 123.

[34] From *Monetary Theory and Fiscal Policy* by Alvin H. Hansen. Copyright 1949 by McGraw-Hill Book Company. Used with permission of McGraw-Hill Book Company.

[35] Heading of Chap. xi of Tooke's *Inquiry*.

[36] It should be noted that the following ideas were shared by the currency school and the banking school: (1) They were firm supporters of the gold standard. (2) They were against all supporters of inconvertible currency, such as the "Birmingham School" under the leadership of Thomas and Matthias Attwoods, who wanted to insulate the economy from the external impact of the gold standard. (3) They rejected discretionary management of the currency. The currency school wanted the volume of note-issue to be ruled by law or "rule" and not by discretion or "authority." Thus, as Professor Robbins observes in *Torrens and the Evolution of Class. Econ.*, "automatism was one of the central features of the Bank Act [p. 117]." The banking school rejected even this rule of law.

note issue. The banking school, on the other hand, argued that convertibility was sufficient to assure monetary stability and that no further regulation was necessary. This contention was based on the argument that, under a regime of convertibility, the banknotes were a part of the credit structure and, in principle, could always be converted into their metallic equivalent. Thus, Fullarton wrote:

> New gold coin and new conventional notes are introduced in the market by being made the medium of *payments*. Bank-notes, on the contrary, are never issued *but on loan*, and an equal amount of notes must be returned into the bank whenever the loan becomes due. Bank-notes never, therefore, can clog the market by their redundance, nor afford a motive to anyone to pay them away at reduced value in order to get rid of them. The banker has only to take care that they are lent on sufficient security, and the *reflux* and the issue will, in the long run, always balance each other.[37]

The preceding argument has sometimes been called the "law of reflux," which is evidently a sophisticated version of the real-bills doctrine expounded earlier by the anti-bullionists, such as Bosanquet.[38] The essential fallacy of the doctrine had already been exposed by Thornton, Ricardo, and Joplin. During the currency- versus banking-school debate, Torrens followed Ricardo's arguments, and made further rebuttals.[39] The most important point raised by the quantity theorists was that the exponents of the real-bills doctrine failed to understand the full implications of Thornton's two-rate analysis. Overissue was possible because an expansion of loans (even based on real bills) could be induced by a lower loan rate.

For our purposes, it is important to consider Tooke's income theory and the real-bills doctrine as representing the attack on the quantity theory during the time of the classical economists. In the twentieth century, the main line of attack has been associated with Keynesian economics.

---

[37] John Fullarton, *On the Regulation of Currencies* (2nd ed.; London: John Murray, 1845), p. 64 (italics added).

[38] Professor Robbins observes that the argument was precipitated by Bosanquet and evoked Ricardo's famous *Reply to Bosanquet*. See Robbins, *Robert Torrens and the Evolution of Classical Economics*, pp. 128–129.

[39] For detailed discussion of these points, see Viner, *Studies in the Theory of International Trade*, pp. 237–243; also Robbins, *Robert Torrens and the Evolution of Class. Econ.*, pp. 126–143.

# 8

# Neoclassical
# Monetary Theory

The mainstream of thought in neoclassical monetary theory was the quantity theory of money. Expositions of the theory centered around three approaches: (1) the transactions-velocity approach associated primarily with Irving Fisher, (2) the cash-balances approach, whose outstanding exponents were Walras, Marshall, Wicksell, Pigou, and Keynes (author of *A Tract on Monetary Reform*), and (3) the income approach developed by Wicksell, Aftalion, and Keynes (author of *A Treatise on Money*). Basically, the three approaches were but variants of the quantity theory. The latter two approaches, however, suggested possible developments in a new direction. For instance, the Marshallian cash-balances approach anticipated Keynes's liquidity-preference theory;[1] and the Wicksellian theory of aggregate demand and supply provided a theoretical framework into which the Keynesian theory of employment could be fitted with little difficulty.

As described in the two preceding chapters, Cantillon, Hume, Thornton, Ricardo, and J. S. Mill had established the quantity-theory tradition as follows. First, the causal relationship between the quantity of

---

[1] Professor Lorie Tarshis made the following observation on the "Keynesian Revolution":

Indeed, a good case can be made for the assertion that the doctrine of *The General Theory* was mothered by the *Treatise* and fathered by neoclassical economics. If so, we should have to admit that the child suffered from an extreme Oedipus complex.

See "An Exposition of Keynesian Economics," reprinted from *American Economic Review*, Supplement (May, 1948), in *Readings in Economic Analysis*, R. V. Clemence, ed. (Cambridge, Mass.: Addison-Wesley Publishing Co., Inc., 1950), I, 198.

money and the absolute price level was not a mechanical one; the increased quantity of money first had to influence total spending on goods and services either through a direct mechanism (i.e., increased spending in the output markets directly) or through the indirect mechanism (via the rate of interest). Second, money was neutral in equilibrium, but non-neutral during the transition period. The non-neutral money thesis was generally expounded under the forced-saving doctrine. None of these writers, however, attempted to formulate a precise analysis of the stability of equilibrium or to define the stability conditions.

With the exception of Wicksell (and perhaps Fisher), the neoclassical writers did not recognize the need to fill the analytical gap. As observed by Professor Patinkin, "there is a basic chapter missing in practically all neoclassical monetary theory—the chapter which presents a precise dynamic analysis of the determination of the equilibrium absolute level of money prices through the workings of the real-balance effect."[2] In other words, the majority of the neoclassical writers failed to see the full implications of the real-balance effect; consequently, they inadvertently stumbled into such pitfalls as the "dichotomization of the pricing process," and the "homogeneity postulates." They did not perceive that the real-balance effect would be an essential equilibrating mechanism that works to assure the stability of equilibrium in both the output and money markets.[3] This amounts to a direct denial of the "pitfalls."

## Fisher's Transactions-Velocity Approach

The basis of Irving Fisher's transactions-velocity approach was the equation of exchange[4] (at the top of the next page).

---

[2] From *Money, Interest, and Prices*, 2nd Edition, p. 168, by Don Patinkin. Copyright © 1965 by Don Patinkin. Reprinted by permission of Harper & Row, Publishers.

[3] Professor William J. Baumol points out:
The real balance effect is an essential piece of tha machinery which works to produce equilibrium in the money market. Suppose, for example, that for some reason prices fall below their equilibrium level. This will increase the real wealth of cash holders, lead them to spend more money, and that in turn will drive prices back toward equilibrium. Thus, the real balance effect is a part of the equilibrating mechanism of the money market. It is a force behind the working of the quantity theory or whatever analysis we wish to use to explain the determination of the equilibrium price level.
*Economic Theory and Operations Analysis* (1st ed.; Englewood Cliffs, N.J.: Prentice-Hall, Inc., 1965), p. 239.

[4] Irving Fisher, *The Purchasing Power of Money* (1911), reprinted in New York by Augustus M. Kelley, Publishers, 1963), p. 48.

$$MV + M'V' = pQ = PT$$

where $(M)$ is the stock of currency (coins and paper money outside of the banking system); $(V)$ is its velocity of circulation; $(M')$ represents total demand deposits subject to transfer by checks; $(V')$ expresses the velocity of circulation of checks; $(P)$ is an index of prices, and $(T)$ is an index of the physical volume of transactions. The equation of exchange is a truism. Fisher, however, pointed out that "truisms" should never be neglected: "To throw away contemptuously the equation of exchange because it is so obviously true is to neglect the chance to formulate for economic science some of the most important and exact laws of which it is capable."[5]

In order to use the equation of exchange to expound the quantity theory, Fisher made the following four significant assumptions:

> . . . normally the effect of doubling money in circulation (M) is to double deposits (M') because under any given conditions of industry and civilization deposits tend to hold a fixed or normal ratio to money in circulation.[6]

> . . . the velocity of circulation either of money or deposits is independent of the quantity of money or of deposits. No reason has been, or, so far as is apparent, can be assigned, to show why the velocity of circulation of money, or deposits, should be different, when the quantity of money, or deposits, is great, from what it is when the quantity is small.[7]

> . . . the volume of trade, like the velocity of circulation of money, is independent of the quantity of money. An inflation of the currency cannot increase the product of farms and factories, nor the speed of the freight trains or ships. The stream of business depends on natural resources and technical conditions, not on the quantity of money. The whole machinery of production, transportation, and sale is a matter of physical capacities and technique, none of which depend on the quantity of money.[8]

> . . . *the price level is normally the one absolutely passive element in the equation of exchange.* It is controlled solely by the other elements and the causes antecedent to them, but exerts no control over them.[9]

Therefore, he concluded, the equation

---

[5] *Ibid.*, p. 157.
[6] *Ibid.*, p. 151.
[7] *Ibid.*, p. 154.
[8] *Ibid.*, p. 155.
[9] *Ibid.*, p. 172.

is true in the sense that one of *the normal effects of an increase in the quantity of money is an exactly proportional increase in the general price level.*[10]

Fisher qualified this conclusion by pointing out "the fact that the strictly proportional effect on prices of an increase in $M$ is only the normal or ultimate effect after transition periods are over."[11] During the transition period, "an increase in $M$ produces effects not only on the $p$'s, but on all the magnitudes in the equation of exchange."[12] It will be recalled that this analysis had been anticipated by David Hume during the pre-classical period.

Fisher apparently perceived that the factor which assured the stability of equilibrium was the real-balance effect.[13] He pointed out that an increase in the quantity of money, other things being equal, would upset the optimum relation between individuals' cash balances and expenditures. The explanation for this disturbance was that, at the existing price level, individuals' cash balances in real terms would be larger than desired, so that they would attempt to reduce the excess real balances by increasing their money expenditures. If output remained unchanged, the increased monetary demand would lead to an increase in prices. A new equilibrium would finally be reached when the price level had increased in proportion to the increased quantity of money.

---

[10] *Ibid.*, p. 157.

[11] *Ibid.*, p. 159.

[12] *Ibid.*, p. 159. Fisher devoted Chapter 4 to this subject.

[13] Fisher's real-balance effect is as follows:

Suppose, for a moment, that a doubling in the currency in circulation should not at once raise prices, but should halve the velocities instead; such a result would evidently upset for each individual the adjustment which he had made of cash on hand. Prices being unchanged, he now has double the amount of money and deposits which his convenience had taught him to keep on hand. He will then try to get rid of the surplus money and deposits by buying goods. But as somebody else must be found to take the money off his hands, its mere transfer will not diminish the amount in the community. It will simply increase somebody's else's surplus. Everybody has money on his hands beyond what experience and convenience have shown to be necessary. Everybody will want to exchange this relatively useless extra money for goods, and the desire so to do must surely drive up the price of goods. No one can deny that the effect of every one's desiring to spend more money will be to raise prices. Obviously this tendency will continue until there is found another adjustment of quantities to expenditures, and the V's are the same as originally. That is, if there is no change in the quantities sold (the Q's), the only possible effect of doubling M and M' will be a doubling of the $p$'s; for we have just seen that the V's cannot be permanently reduced without causing people to have surplus money and deposits, and there cannot be surplus money and deposits without a desire to spend it, and there cannot be a desire to spend it without a rise in prices. In short, the only way to get rid of a plethora of money is to raise prices to correspond.
*The Purchasing Power of Money*, pp. 153–154.

Fisher, however, did not make effective use of the real-balance effect. In the first place, he did not consider the indirect mechanism—i.e., that the excess money might be used to purchase bonds, thereby pushing bond prices up and the interest rate down. The lowering of the rate of interest would stimulate investment demand. Thus, the increased quantity of money could cause an increase in monetary demand indirectly via the interest rate mechanism.[14] Secondly, Fisher failed to make use of this mechanism to illustrate the inter-dependence between the output and money markets, for the real-balance effect amounts to a direct denial of both the "homogeneity postulate" and the "dichotomization assumption." Instead, Fisher perpetuated the dichotomization of the pricing process by insisting that the determination of the absolute price level occurs entirely in the monetary sector [i.e., the absolute price level is determined by the quantity equation, $P = (MV + M'V')/T$ and that the determination of relative prices takes place in the real sector of the economy (i.e., relative prices are determined by the supply and demand equations for goods and services).[15] The reconstructed neoclassical model, as described in Chapter 3, essentially follows this type of reasoning.

Finally, Fisher's equation of exchange does not explicitly contain the rate of interest. This is because the equation states an equilibrium condition. In equilibrium, the quantity theorists argue, money is neutral and the rate of interest is independent of the quantity of money. By concentrating on the analysis of full-employment equilibrium,

---

[14] See Don Patinkin, "Keynesian Economics and the Quantity Theory." in *Post-Keynesian Economics*, Kurihara, ed. (New Brunswick, N.J.: Rutgers University Press, 1954).

[15] Fisher pointed out:

Another may now receive attention, viz. the fallacious idea that the price level cannot be determined by other factors in the equation of exchange because it is already determined by other causes, usually alluded to as "supply and demand." This vague phrase has covered multitudes of sins of slothful analysts in economics. Those who place such implicit reliance on the competency of supply and demand to fix prices, irrespective of the quantity of money, deposits, velocity, and trade, will have their confidence rudely shaken if they will follow the reasoning as to price causation of separate articles. They will find that there are always just one *too few equations* to determine the unknown quantities involved. The equation of exchange is needed in each case to supplement the equations of supply and demand. . . . But the compatibility of the equation of exchange with the equations which have to deal with prices individually may be brought home to the reader sufficiently for our present purposes by emphasizing the distinction between (1) individual prices relatively to each other and (2) the price *level*. The equation of exchange determines the latter (the price level) only, and the latter only is the subject of this book. . . . It should be clearly recognized that price *levels* must be studied independently of individual *prices*.
The Purchasing Power of Money, pp. 174–175.

Fisher's theory of interest becomes a nonmonetary one.[16] According to him, the equilibrium rate of interest is determined purely by real factors, namely, the productivity of capital, time preference, and risk. In other words, Fisher's equilibrium rate of interest equates desired saving and investment. In Keynesian terminology, this is the typical classical savings-investment theory of interest, which the "Keynesian Revolution" rejected.

Criticisms of Fisher's transactions-velocity approach center around his assumptions concerning $(V)$ and $(T)$. Fisher classified the determinants of $(V)$ as follows:[17]

1. *Habits of the individual.*
   a) As to thrift and hoarding.
   b) As to book credit.
   c) As to the use of checks.
2. *Systems of payments in the community.*
   a) As to frequency of receipts and disbursements.
   b) As to regularity of receipts and disbursements.
   c) As to correspondence between times and amounts of receipts and disbursements.
3. *General Causes.*
   a) Density of population.
   b) Rapidity of transportation.

All these determinants suggest stability of $(V)$.

Fisher considered the following to be the most important determinants of $(T)$:[18]

1. *Conditions affecting producers.*
   a) Geographical differences in natural resources.
   b) The division of labor.
   c) Knowledge of techniques of production.
   d) The accumulation of capital.
2. *Conditions affecting consumers.*
   a) The extent and variety of human wants.
3. *Conditions connecting producers and consumers.*
   a) Facilities for transportation.
   b) Relative freedom of trade.
   c) Character of monetary and banking systems.
   d) Business confidence.

By making $(T)$ solely dependent on real forces, Fisher minimized the relationship between the quantity of money and output. These are the

---

[16] Irving Fisher, *The Theory of Interest* (New York: The Macmillan Company, 1930).

[17] Fisher, *The Purchasing Power of Money*, p. 79.

[18] Fisher, *The Purchasing Power of Money*, pp. 74–75.

elements contributing to his dichotomization of the pricing process in the real and monetary sectors of the economy.

## MARSHALL'S CASH-BALANCES APPROACH

As founder of the Cambridge cash-balances approach, Alfred Marshall (1842–1924) maintained that monetary theory should be integrated with value theory.[19] He considered the determination of the value of money in terms of supply and demand, by applying conventional value theory to monetary theory. Marshall pointed out that the mechanical concept of velocity of circulation obscures the motives and decisions of people behind it. On the other hand, the concept of demand for money focuses attention on the process of individual choice among competing alternatives. As his successor, Professor Pigou, put it, the concept of demand for money "brings us at once into relation with volition—an ultimate cause of demand—instead of with something that seems at first sight accidental and arbitrary."[20]

With regard to the demand for money, Marshall wrote:

> To give definiteness to this notion, let us suppose that the inhabitants of a country . . . find it just worth their while to keep by them on the average ready purchasing power to the extent of a tenth part of their annual *income*, together with a fiftieth part of their *property*; then the aggregate value of the currency of the country will tend to be equal to the sum of these amounts.[21]

---

[19] J. M. Keynes wrote:
He [Marshall] always taught that the value of money is a function of its supply on the one hand, and the demand for it, on the other, as measured by "the average stock of command over commodities which each person cares to keep in a ready form."
*Essays in Biography* (London: Macmillan & Co., 1933), pp. 198–199.
Sir Denis H. Robertson, another Marshall successor, points out:
Money is only one of the many economic things. Its value therefore is primarily determined by exactly the same two factors as determine the value of any other thing, namely, the conditions of demand for it, and the quantity of it available.
*Money*, Cambridge Economic Handbook (Chicago: University of Chicago Press, 1959), p. 23.

[20] A. C. Pigou, "The Value of Money," reprinted from *Quarterly Journal of Economics*, Vol. XXXII (1917), in *Readings in Monetary Theory*, p. 174.

[21] Alfred Marshall, *Money, Credit, and Commerce*, reprinted by Augustus M. Kelley, Publishers, 1960, p. 44.
Alvin H. Hansen points out that this analysis could be summarized in terms of the following equation: $M = kY + k'A$, where $(Y)$ is $(PY)$ money income; $(k')$ is the fraction of assets $(A)$ which people wish to hold in the form of money. See his *Monetary Theory and Fiscal Policy* (New York: McGraw-Hill Book Company, 1949), p. 2.

In this statement, Marshall laid the foundation not only for the Keynesian liquidity-preference theory, but also for the post-Keynesian developments in integrating the theory of demand for money into a "general-asset" theory. (See Chapter 10.) Unfortunately, he dropped the asset or wealth consideration on the very next page; apparently, not recognizing the full implications of his pioneering formulation.

Marshall treated the supply of money as an exogenous variable. Given the demand and supply of money, the value of money (the reciprocal of the price level) would be determined. The Marshallian analysis could then be summarized in terms of the equation, $M = kPY$. Where $(M)$ is the exogenously determined supply of money; $(k)$ is that fraction of money income $(PY)$ which the community wishes to hold in the form of cash and demand deposits; $(P)$ is the general price level; and $(Y)$ is total output. It should be noted that Marshall did not put his theory in this algebraic form. The Pigouvian version was the first algebraic expression of Marshall's theory. Pigou in *The Value of Money* (1917) stated the quantity theory in the following algebraic form:[22]

$$M = \frac{kR}{P}[c + h(1 - c)]$$

where $(k)$ is the proportion of total resources $(R)$, expressed in real terms, which the public chooses to keep in the form of legal tender; $(M)$ is the quantity of legal tender; $(P)$ is the general price level; $(c)$ is the proportion of total resources which are kept in actual legal tender; $(1 - c)$ is the proportion which are kept in bank notes and bank balances; and $(h)$ is the proportion of actual legal tender that bankers choose to keep against the notes and balances held by their customers.

In the Pigouvian version, $(k)$ and $(R)$ are constants and the demand curve for legal tender is visualized as a rectangular hyperbola (uniform unitary elasticity).[23] Fluctuations in $(k)$ caused by sudden shifts in the public's liquidity preference are not treated.

A similar formulation was provided by Keynes in *A Tract on Monetary Reform* (1923).[24] In this book, Keynes considered the quantity theory a fundamental truth. "Its correspondence with fact," he said, "is not open to question."[25] Like Marshall, Keynes concentrated on

---

[22] Pigou, *op. cit.*, pp. 162–183.

[23] Pigou, *op cit.*, p. 165. Pigou pointed out in the same article: "the demand schedule just described is represented by the equation $P = kR/M$. When $k$ and $R$ are taken as constant, this is, of course, the equation of a rectangular hyperbola."

[24] J. M. Keynes, *A Tract on Monetary Reform* (London: Macmillan & Co., 1923).

[25] Keynes, p. 74.

the medium-of-exchange function of money. He believed that the quantity theory "flows from the fact that money as such has no utility except what it derives from its exchange-value." Like Pigou, Keynes extended the Marshallian analysis to include the banking system. The cash-balances equation in his hands becomes:[26]

$$n = p(k + rk')$$

where $(n)$ is the cash in circulation; $(p)$ is the price level; $(k)$ is the number of consumption units which the public decides to hold in cash; $(r)$ represents the proportion of bank deposits kept by banks in the form of cash, or the reserve ratio; and $(k')$ is the number of consumption units which the public decides to hold in demand deposits. Keynes pointed out: "So long as $k$, $k'$, and $r$ remain unchanged, we have the same results as before, namely, that $n$ and $p$ rise and fall together."[27] Keynes thought that $k$, $k'$, $r$, and $n$ were institutionally given parameters: "The proportion between $k$ and $k'$ depends on the banking arrangements of the public; the absolute value of these on their habits generally; and the value of $r$ on the reserve practices of the banks."[28]

Over the course of the business cycle, Keynes pointed out, $(k)$ and $(k')$ would fluctuate. Thus, he suggested:

> The usual method of exercising a stabilising influence over $k$ and $k'$, especially over $k'$, is that of bank-rate. A tendency of $k'$ to increase may be somewhat counteracted by lowering the bank-rate, because easy lending diminishes the advantage of keeping a margin for contingencies in cash. Cheap money also operates to *counterbalance* an increase of $k'$, because, by encouraging borrowing from the banks, it prevents $r$ from increasing or causes $r$ to diminish. But it is doubtful whether bank-rate by itself is always a powerful enough instrument, and, if we are to achieve stability, we must be prepared to vary $n$ and $r$ on occasion."[29]

The speculative demand for money is entirely absent from the *Tract*. Although "the Marshallian version of the quantity theory represents a fundamentally new approach to the problem of money and prices,"[30]

---

[26] Keynes, p. 77.

[27] Keynes, p. 77.

[28] Keynes, pp. 77–78.

[29] Keynes, p. 85.

[30] From *Monetary Theory and Fiscal Policy* by Alvin H. Hansen. Copyright 1949 by McGraw-Hill Book Company. Used with permission of McGraw-Hill Book Company. Hansen further comments:
It is not true, as is often alleged, that the "cash-balance" equation is merely the quantity theory in new algebraic dress. . . . The difference can be stated

the neglect of the asset (wealth) factor conveys the misleading impression that the demand for money depends solely on money income, thus ignoring the rate of interest ($r$). The omission of the rate of interest led to several unfortunate developments in neoclassical monetary theory. In the first place, it gave rise to the assumption that the demand for money is interest-inelastic. This amounts to saying that money serves only as a medium of exchange and has no utility of its own. Secondly, it led the majority of neoclassical writers to overlook the interdependence between the output and the money markets. As pointed out by Professor Patinkin, "all too often this humanizing of the demand for money led to an undue concentration on the money market, a corresponding neglect of the commodity markets, and a resulting 'dehumanizing' of the analysis of the effects of monetary changes."[31] This "dehumanizing analysis" is evidenced by their concentration on comparative statics and a corresponding neglect of an analysis of equilibrium stability. Although the professed aim of the Cambridge school was to integrate monetary theory with value theory, as observed by Professor Patinkin, there is an asymmetry in their analyses, for they failed to apply the stability test, which they used in value theory, to monetary theory. The primary explanation for this deficiency is that most of the writers did not recognize the full implications of the real-balance effect, which "is inherent in the Cambridge equation." The Cambridge equation, $M = kPY$, states the equilibrium condition in the money market. This equation can be rearranged to become an excess-demand equation, $kPY - M = E$, where ($kPY$) is the demand for money, ($M$) the supply of money, and ($E$) is excess-demand for money. In equilibrium, of course, $E = 0$. A change in ($P$) alone, other things being equal, will generate a real-balance effect, because the expression $kPY - M$ would be positive. Since an excess demand for money means a reduced demand for goods and services, the real-balance effect in this case will cause a non-proportionate change in ($kPY$). "Thus, if properly interpreted, the Cambridge function does not imply uniform unitary elasticity."[32] But, in their attempt to validate the quantity-

---

as follows: In the terms of the Marshallian approach, sudden and rapid *shifts* in the desire of the public to hold money may profoundly affect prices even though the monetary authority successfully maintains a high stability in the money supply. . . . It is $k$, not $M$, that holds the stage [pp. 49–50].

[31] From *Money, Interest and Prices*, 2nd Edition, pp. 166–167, by Don Patinkin. Copyright © 1965 by Don Patinkin. Reprinted by permission of Harper & Row, Publishers.

[32] From *Money, Interest and Prices*, 2nd Edition, pp. 177–188, by Don Patinkin. Copyright © 1965 by Don Patinkin. Reprinted by permission of Harper & Row, Publishers.

theory conclusions, the majority of neoclassical writers made the invalid assumption that the demand curve for money was a rectangular
hyperbola. The preceding statement by Pigou regarding the demand
curve for money is an outstanding example. This pitfall, as noted by
Professor Patinkin, was due to their failure to make a clear distinction
between the "market-equilibrium curve"—relevant in comparative-
static analysis—and the demand curve for money, as can be gleaned
from the following illustration.

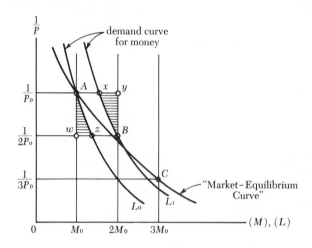

**Figure 8-1**

Figure 8-1 shows the nominal amount of money demanded and supplied. The value of money $(1/P)$ is plotted on the vertical axis. The
nominal amount of money supplied $(M)$ and the amount of nominal
money demanded $(L)$ are plotted on the horizontal axis. The demand
for nominal money is inversely related to the value of money $(1/P)$. It
is a downward sloping function, because at a higher $(P)$, which means
lower $(1/P)$, the typical individual will want to hold larger money
balances. It should be noted that the demand curve for money $(L)$
does not have the property of uniform unitary elasticity. For if there
is an increase in $(P)$, unaccompanied by a proportional increase in $(M)$,
the amount of real money balances $(M/P)$ demanded will decline. (The
rectangle $M_0 \cdot 1/P_0$ is larger than the rectangle $M_0 \cdot 1/2\ P_0$.) At the
same time, an excess demand for nominal money would be created, as
indicated by the distance $(wz)$. Hence, the slope of the demand curve
at point $(z)$ is less than unity.

Suppose the initial money supply is $(M_0)$, and the demand curve for money is $(L_0)$. The equilibrium price level $(P_0)$ is determined at the point of intersection $(A)$. Now, assume that the initial money holdings are all doubled, so that the total amount of nominal money supplied rises from $(M_0)$ to $(2M_0)$. Thus, the supply curve for money shifted rightward. Turning now to the demand curve $(L_0)$, the increased quantity of nominal money at the original price level $(P_0)$ will create a real-balance effect both in the output markets and in the money market. The real-balance effect in the money market is reflected by the increased liquidity preference of individuals. They now feel that they should be able to indulge in a higher level of liquidity. This is the reason for the rightward shift of the demand curve for money from $(L_0)$ to $(L_1)$; the increased liquidity preference is indicated by the distance $(Ax)$. The excess money is measured by the distance $(xy)$, which is equivalent to the excess demand for output in the commodity markets. The increased spending in the output markets (assuming output is fixed, being determined by real factors) will lead to price increases. As prices increase, the demand for nominal money for transactions and precautionary purposes also increases (sliding down the curve $L_1$). A new equilibrium will be reached when the excess supply of money (excess demand for goods) has been eliminated. This new equilibrium is indicated by the intersection point $(B)$. In equilibrium, the price level has increased to $(2P_0)$, which is proportional to the increased quantity of money $(2M_0)$; the quantity theory is validated. Similarly, if the supply of money is increased to $(3M_0)$, the new demand curve for money must intersect the new supply curve at point $(C)$, corresponding to $(3P_0)$.

If we connect the market-equilibrium points, $(A)$, $(B)$, and $(C)$, we get the Patinkin "market-equilibrium curve." This curve is a rectangular hyperbola. But this is not the demand curve for money. What the neoclassical writers had in mind was the "market equilibrium curve," which only indicates comparative static positions. They did not bother to formulate a dynamic analysis of the stability of equilibrium.

Knut Wicksell (1851–1926) was free of this error.[33] Furthermore, he also recognized that the real-balance effect was the automatic mechanism which assures the stability of equilibrium. He wrote:

> Now let us suppose that for some reason or other commodity prices rise while the stock of money remains unchanged, or that the stock of money is diminished while prices remain temporarily unchanged. The cash balances will gradually appear to be too small *in relation to the new level of prices* (though in the first case they

---

[33] See Knut Wicksell, *Lectures on Political Economy*, E. Classen, trans., and L. Robbins, ed. (New York: The Macmillan Company, 1935), II, 142–143.

have not on the average altered in absolute amount. It is true that in this case I can rely on a higher level of receipts in the future. But meanwhile I run the risk of being unable to meet my obligations punctually, and at best I may easily be forced by shortage of ready money to forego some purchase that would otherwise have been profitable.) I therefore seek to enlarge my balance. This can only be done—neglecting for the present the possibility of borrowing, etc.—through a *reduction* in my *demand* for goods and services, or through an *increase* in the *supply* of my own commodity (forthcoming either earlier or at a lower price than would otherwise have been the case), or through both together. The same is true of all other owners and consumers of commodities. But in fact nobody will succeed in realising the object at which each is aiming—to increase his cash balance; for the sum of individual cash balances is limited by the amount of the available stock of money, or rather is identical with it. On the other hand, the universal reduction in demand and increase in supply of commodities will necessarily bring about a continuous fall in all prices. This can only cease when prices have fallen to the level at which the cash balances are regarded as *adequate*. (In the first case prices will now have fallen to their original level.)[34]

This is the "missing chapter" in neoclassical monetary theory. Wicksell filled in this analytical gap.

## WICKSELL'S RESTATEMENT OF THE QUANTITY THEORY OF MONEY

The main purpose of Wicksell's monetary analysis was to defend the quantity theory of money against its critics, such as Thomas Tooke. What Wicksell had in mind was "to follow up the logical consequences of the fundamental conception which had given rise to the Quantity Theory, so as to arrive at a theory which should be both self-consistent and in full agreement with the facts."[35] In pursuing this course, Wicksell not only supplied the missing chapter in neoclassical monetary theory, but also formulated an income approach to the problem of money and prices, which "contained the embryo of 'a theory of output as a whole.'"[36]

---

[34] Knut Wicksell, *Interest and Prices*, R. F. Kahn, trans. (London: Macmillan & Co., 1936), pp. 39–40.

[35] Wicksell, *Interest and Prices*, pp. xxiii–xxiv.

[36] See the comment of Bertil Ohlin in "Some Notes on the Stockholm Theory of Savings and Investment," reprinted from *Economic Journal*, Vol. XLVII (Part I, March 1937, and Part II, June 1937), reprinted in *Readings in Business Cycle Theory*, selected by a Committee of the American Economic Association (Philadelphia: The Blakiston Co., 1951), p. 88.

Wicksell considered the theoretical side of the Tookean analysis "purely critical in general outlook and negative in concept."[37] There was much truth in Tooke's "incomes-determine-prices" thesis, according to Wicksell. But he pointed out that Tooke "never mentions the factors on which the value of money must ultimately depend; it simply leaves the question an open one."[38] However, Wicksell thought that Tooke had raised one highly suggestive point—namely, the relationship between income and aggregate demand—which could be used as a starting point for his restatement of the quantity theory. Wicksell's sequence of thought, from the partial equilibrium analysis of Marshallian value theory to an aggregate-demand and supply analysis of the price level, is neatly summarized in the following passage:

> Every rise or fall in the price of a particular commodity presupposes a disturbance of the equilibrium between the supply of and demand for that commodity, whether the disturbance has actually taken place or is merely protective. What is true *in this respect* of each commodity separately must doubtless be true of all commodities collectively. A general rise in prices is therefore only conceivable on the supposition that the general demand has for some reason become, or is expected to become, greater than the supply. . . . Any theory of money worthy of the name must be able to show how and why the monetary or pecuniary demand for goods exceeds or falls short of the supply of goods in given conditions.[39]

The concluding sentence of this quotation is of decisive importance. It means that monetary theory in the short run must reject Say's Identity.[40]

Wicksell's aggregate-demand and supply analysis laid special emphasis on the relationship between savings and investment. This approach was developed in the following way. Changes in the price level (the reciprocal of the value of money) are determined by the interaction of aggregate demand and aggregate supply. Equilibrium of aggregate demand and aggregate supply is attained when the supply of savings is equal to the demand for savings (investment demand). Savings enter into the loan market as the supply of loanable funds, which is determined by the loan rate of interest. Investment demand (the de-

---

[37] Wicksell, *Interest and Prices*, p. 44.

[38] Wicksell, *Interest and Prices*, p. 44.

[39] Wicksell, *Lectures on Political Economy*, II, pp. 159–160.

[40] See Oscar Lange, *Say's Law: A Restatement and Criticism;* also C. G. Uhr, "Knut Wicksell—A Centennial Evaluation," *American Economic Review*, Vol. XLI (December, 1951); also Bertil Ohlin, "Some Notes on the Stockholm Theory of Savings and Investment," in *Readings in Business Cycle Theory*, Gottfried Haberler, ed. (Philadelphia: The Blakiston Company, 1951).

mand for savings) is determined by the loan rate in relation to the real rate, which is the expected yield on new capital (analogous to the marginal efficiency of capital). Equilibrium in the loan market is attained when the loan rate of interest is equal to the real rate. This means that the demand for savings is just matched by the supply. Consequently, the output markets are also in equilibrium, and the price level has no tendency to change. The condition for equilibrium in both the output and loan markets was expressed by Wicksell:

> The rate of interest at which *the demand for loan capital and the supply of savings* exactly agree, and which more or less corresponds to the expected yield on the newly created capital will then be the normal or natural real rate. It is essentially variable. If the prospects of the employment of capital become more promising, demand will increase and will at first exceed supply; interest rates will then rise and stimulate further saving at the same time as the demand from entrepreneurs contracts until a new equilibrium is reached at a slightly higher rate of interest. And at the same time equilibrium must *ipso facto* obtain . . . in the market for goods and services, so that wages and prices will remain unchanged. The *sum* of money incomes will then usually exceed the money value of the consumption goods annually produced, but the excess income—i.e., what is annually saved and invested in production—will not produce any demand for present goods but only for labor and land for future production.[41]

If we pause to consider the Wicksellian proposition, we shall note that Wicksell had juxtaposed the Tookean proposition of income-determined prices and the Thornton-Ricardo two-rate analysis. In discussing the doctrinal antecedents of the Wicksellian monetary analysis, Professor Carl G. Uhr maintains that "it is most unlikely that Wicksell ever read Thornton's work in his early monetary studies, because he never referred to it, while on the other hand, he discussed the writings of Tooke and Ricardo on the currency debate at length."[42]

We shall also note that Wicksell had explicitly brought into the limelight the role played by the interest rate in monetary theory. Thus, Professor Hansen comments, "By concentrating upon the rate of interest, he swept away the narrow foundations of the quantity theory."[43]

Furthermore, the Wicksellian analysis could easily be extended to

---

41 Wicksell, *Lectures on Political Economy*, II, 193.

42 Carl G. Uhr, *Economic Doctrines of Knut Wicksell* (Berkeley, Calif.: University of California Press, 1960), p. 200.

43 From *Monetary Theory and Fiscal Policy* by Alvin H. Hansen. Copyright 1949 by McGraw-Hill Book Company. Used with permission of McGraw-Hill Book Company.

become the loanable-funds theory of interest.[44] For instance, the equilibrium condition of $(I = S)$ can be extended as follows:

Demand for loanable funds = Supply of loanable funds

$$I + H = S + DH + \Delta M$$

where $(H)$ is hoarding; $(DH)$ represents dishoarding; and $(\Delta M)$ expresses the incremental increase in new money.

Professor Conard observed that in terms of monetary or real theories of interest,

> Wicksell explicitly synthesizes monetary and nonmonetary theories, for his "natural" rate of interest is that of a nonmonetary theory, and his money rate is that of a monetary theory. Wicksell, like Ricardo, regarded the money rate as a kind of aberration from the rate determined by nonmonetary theory (except in those instances when the two were identical), the true character and importance of the latter being well revealed by its title, "natural," or "normal." Yet Wicksell, unlike Ricardo, did not brush aside the monetary theory as unimportant because ephemeral. Instead, he made the divergence between the two the central feature of his dynamic analysis.[45]

The dynamic analysis of Wicksell is his famous "cumulative process," the essence of which may be illustrated with the aid of the familiar saving-and-investment diagram. In Figure 8-2, the initial monetary equilibrium is indicated by the intersection of the $(I_0)$ schedule and the $(S_0)$ schedule. The initial natural rate is $(rn_0)$, which coincides with the loan rate $(r_0)$. A disturbance is introduced in the form of innovation and technological progress, which shifts the investment demand schedule upward from $(I_0)$ to $(I_1)$. This, in turn, causes the natural rate to rise from $(rn_0)$ to $(rn_1)$. If the banking system fails to raise the loan rate, an excess demand will be created in the output market. Since the analysis is conducted under a full-employment assumption, the increased monetary demand will only lead to an increase in prices. As long as the loan rate remains below the natural rate, the price increase will be cumulative. However, there is a limit to this cumulative process under normal conditions. The increase in prices will create two restrictive effects which will prevent the banking system from maintaining the loan rate indefinitely below the natural rate. The restrictive effects are: (1) an external drain on monetary reserves resulting from

---

[44] See Joseph W. Conard, *Introduction to the Theory of Interest* (Berkeley, Calif.: University of California Press, 1959), Chap. 9.

[45] Conard, p. 155.

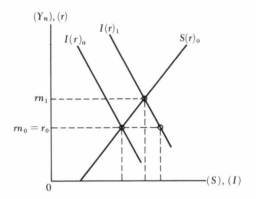

$(Y_n), (r)$

$I(r)_1$

$I(r)_0$

$S(r)_0$

$rn_1$

$rn_0 = r_0$

$(S), (I)$

0

Figure 8-2

the price-induced balance-of-payments disequilibrium, and (2) an internal drain due to increased volume of transactions demand. These two factors will eventually force the banking system to raise the loan rate. A new equilibrium will be reached when the loan rate is again equal to the natural rate. Consequently, the excess demand in the output market is eliminated. Thus, as Professor Patinkin observed, "the cumulative process in Wicksell's analysis plays the role of the fundamental equilibrating mechanism forcing the banks to eliminate any discrepancy between the rate they set and the real rate, and thus restoring equilibrium to the loan market."[46]

The Wicksellian analysis also highlights the fact that it is the fluctuations in the marginal productivity of capital and the lagged adjustment of the loan rate which cause aggregate demand to change; consequently, the general price level and the rate of interest will change in the same direction:

> But the explanation suggested by the Quantity Theory—that rising prices are due to an excess of money, falling prices to a scarcity—does not accord with actually observed movements of the rate of interest. If it were correct, we should expect that at a time of rising prices there would be a temporary reduction in the rate of interest, at a time of falling prices a temporary increase; and that when prices had become accommodated to the change in the stocks of precious metal, the rate of interest would once again return to its normal position. Observation teaches us, however, that

[46] From *Money, Interest and Prices*, 2nd Edition, p. 592, by Don Patinkin. Copyright © 1965 by Don Patinkin. Reprinted by permission of Harper & Row, Publishers.

when prices are rising there is a continual *rise* in rates of interest, and that when prices are falling there is a continual *fall* in rates of interest.[47]

Wicksell observed that, although primary attention should be directed to changes in aggregate demand in analyzing the causes of short-run price movements, changes in the supply of money and credit could sometimes be the leading cause of price-level changes:

> It still remains true, however, that they *may* take their origin in independent causes (the production of precious metals, issue of paper money, development of the credit system, etc.), and that they then have an independent significance in regard to movements of prices, in so far as they accelerate or retard the movement of the money rate of interest to the new position of the natural rate.[48]

The preceding analysis has another implication; it provides a solution to "Gibson's Paradox."[49] According to A. H. Gibson's empirical study, published in the *Banker's Magazine*, January, 1923, and November, 1926, there was a close correlation between the interest rate and prices over a period of more than a hundred years. Wicksell had shown that this phenomenon could be explained by a lagging bank rate. This line of reasoning leads to the following practical application: All proposals for stabilizing the value of money (or the price level), according to Wicksell, can "attain their objective only in so far as they exert an indirect influence on the *money rate of interest*, and bring it into line with the natural rate, or below it, more rapidly than would otherwise be the case."[50]

The Wicksellian version of neoclassical monetary theory, however, did not depart greatly from the mainstream of thought. In regard to

---

[47] Wicksell, *Interest and Prices*, p. 167.

[48] *Ibid.*

[49] Reprinted from *A Treatise on Money*, II, 198, by John Maynard Keynes, by permission of Harcourt, Brace & World, Inc.

Professor Blaug explains this paradox as follows:

The expansion of bank credit, Thornton had argued, can express itself or become effective only through a reduction in the money rate of interest. As soon as the addition of credit ceases, prices adjust themselves to the new size of the money stock and the rate of interest returns to its former equilibrium level determined by the rate of return on real capital. Following this argument, one would expect the bank rate and the general price level to move in opposite directions. But the foremost critic of Ricardian monetary theory, Thomas Tooke, author of the influential *History of Prices* (1838–57), showed that, on the contrary, the market rate of interest and price level were positively correlated. This finding, corroborated in later days, was dubbed Gibson's Paradox by Keynes in *The Treatise on Money*.

Reprinted with permission from Mark Blaug, *Economic Theory in Retrospect* (Homewood, Ill.: Richard D. Irwin, Inc.), p. 560.

Wicksell's discussion of the paradox is contained in *Interest and Prices*, Chap. 11.

[50] Wicksell, *Interest and Prices*, p. 188.

long-run equilibrium, the relevant theory of money is still the quantity theory. In the short run, the relevant monetary theory is the preceding analysis of cumulative change. In the words of Professor Gardner Ackley, "Wicksell's analysis differed from the simple quantity theory only in the *process* by which its results were achieved, not in its results. *In equilibrium*, prices were proportional to the money supply, and both were constant in time. *In equilibrium*, there were no idle balances flowing into the capital market nor additions needing to be made to cash balances in order to finance a larger money volume of transactions."[51] This point may be illustrated with the equilibrium equation in the loan or capital market:[52]

$$S + DH + \Delta M = I$$

where $(\Delta M)$ is the rate of addition to the money supply; and $(DH)$ is "dishoarding," which refers to the rate at which cash balances are used to buy securities. If $(DH)$ is negative, it signifies "hoarding" or an increase in cash-balances.[53] $(DH)$ may be defined as $(DH = M - kPY)$, which states that $(DH)$ occurs when the actual cash balances $(M)$ are greater than the transactions demand for money $(kPY)$.

In equilibrium, $(S)$ will be equal to $(I)$. To have $(S=I)$, $(\Delta M + DH) = 0$ is required. When this happens, the identity, $DH = M - kPY$, becomes $M = kPY$ — the cash-balances equation.

Although Wicksell's short-run analysis is an outstanding contribution to the theory of income determination, he did not have

> an explicit theory of income and employment in the sense of the contemporary "Stockholm" and "Keynesian" schools, for, *inter alia*, he had no clear understanding of the consumption function and its impact on the determination of income. Yet, and herein lies perhaps his greatest merit, he developed the all-essential analytic framework within which these and other schools have generated theories by using substantially the same variables he used but

---

[51] Gardner Ackley, *Macroeconomic Theory* (New York: The Macmillan Company, 1961), p. 161.

The same idea is presented by Professor Edward S. Shaw:

In Wicksell's version, for example, money is neutral vis-à-vis output and employment only in monetary equilibrium—in the long run. In transition intervals the supply of money is relevant to output and its composition. Both in the long run and in the short run, money is a determinant of absolute prices or price levels as distinct from price relationships.

*Money, Income and Monetary Policy* (Chicago: Richard D. Irwin, Inc., 1950), pp. 359–360.

[52] See Ackley, *Macroeconomic Theory.*

[53] Wicksell did not consider the Keynesian speculative demand for money. He held that the motives for holding cash consisted only of transactions and precautionary motives. See his *Lectures*, II, 71.

assigning different values or roles to them and dismantling some of his restrictive assumptions concerning perfect competition, perfect foresight, and so forth.[54]

## KEYNES' A TREATISE ON MONEY

Keynes' *A Treatise on Money* (1930) marks the beginning of his departure from neoclassical monetary theory.[55] In the preface of the book, Keynes wrote:

> The ideas with which I have finished up are widely different from those with which I began. The result is, I am afraid, that there is a good deal in this book which represents the process of getting rid of the ideas which I used to have and of finding my way to those which I now have.[56]

The ideas which Keynes had acquired clearly reflected the influence of continental writers. Regarding business-cycle theory, Keynes said:

---

[54] C. G. Urh, *Knut Wicksell—A Centennial Evaluation.*
Hansen expresses a similar opinion in *Monetary Theory and Fiscal Policy:*
. . . his work falls short of an adequate theory of income determination. It related mainly to one determinant of income—the investment function.
Hansen further points out:
the multiplier analysis, based on the consumption function, was missing. There is, moreover, implicit in much of Wicksell's work an excessively optimistic view with respect to the interest-elasticity of investment. And he saw very dimly the relation of the demand for cash holdings to the rate of interest . . . he enormously exaggerated the power of the banking system to control, by means of interest-rate manipulations, the flow of aggregate demand and the level of prices [p. 93].

[55] Hansen has stated:
Keynes' *Treatise on Money* (1930) could perhaps be described as a belated, and in some measure confused, effort to catch up with Continental thinking on the saving-investment problem, the natural rate and the money rate of interest, factors affecting the natural rate, and basic factors underlying fluctuations in the rate of investment.
*Business Cycles and National Income* (New York: W. W. Norton & Co., Inc., 1951), p. 334.
Dudley Dillard points out:
During his early career, Keynes was primarily a specialist in monetary theory and monetary policy. His great work prior to his *General Theory* was a two volume *Treatise on Money.* When he moved from the narrower field of monetary theory to the broader field of general economic theory, Keynes took money along with him and gave it a place of tremendous importance in the determination of employment and production in the economic system as a whole.
*The Economics of John Maynard Keynes* (New York: Prentice-Hall, Inc., 1948), p. 5.

[56] Reprinted from *A Treatise on Money* by John Maynard Keynes, I, vi, by permission of Harcourt, Brace & World, Inc.

Accordingly I find myself in strong sympathy with the school of writers—Tugan-Baranovski, Hull, Spiethoff and Schumpeter—of which Tugan-Baranovski was the first and most original, and especially with the form which the theory takes in the works of Tugan-Baranovski himself, and of two American Amateur-economists (cranks, some might say), Rorty and Johannsen.[57]

Regarding monetary theory, Keynes admitted that he was influenced by Wicksell:

In substance and intention Wicksell's theory is closely akin (much more closely than Cassel's version of Wicksell) to the theory of this Treatise, though he was not successful, in my opinion, in linking up his Theory of Bank-rate to the Quantity Equation.[58]

Thus, the *Treatise* can be described as a juxtaposition of three theories: The saving-investment theory of the business cycle developed by the continental writers; the theory of the bank rate formulated by Wicksell; and the cash-balance version of the quantity theory. Like the Wicksellian analysis, the *Treatise* contains the embryo of "a theory of output as a whole," but Keynes had not yet found his way to it specifically. His primary interest was still the value of money (or its reciprocal, the general price level).[59]

Like Wicksell, Keynes attempted to improve the quantity theory. He was not satisfied with the traditional view on the relation between the rate of interest and the general price level:

No systematic treatment of the subject exists in the English language, so far as I am aware. You will search in vain the works of Marshall, Pigou, Taussig or Irving Fisher. Even Professor Cassel's

---

[57] Reprinted from *A Treatise on Money* by John Maynard Keynes, II, 100, by permission of Harcourt, Brace & World, Inc.

[58] Reprinted from *A Treatise on Money* by John Maynard Keynes, I, 186, by permission of Harcourt, Brace & World, Inc.

[59] Lawrence R. Klein observes:
The whole aim of the *Treatise* was to tell us how to keep prices stable; or, what is the same, to keep savings and investment equal; or, what is the same, to keep the market rate of interest equal to the natural rate. Thus Keynes' concrete proposals were schemes of monetary control; the banks by manipulation of the rate of interest would influence the level of investment until equilibrium could be achieved with the more stable rate of savings.
*The Keynesian Revolution* (New York: The Macmillan Company, 1954), pp. 16–17.

Lorie Tarshis has observed that: "in the *Treatise*, Keynes was interested directly in the general price level; and in the *General Theory*, in the national income." "An Exposition of Keynesian Economics," in *Readings in Economic Analysis*, Clemence, ed., p. 198.

treatment, which is somewhat fuller, does not examine the train of causation in any detail.[60]

The traditional quantity-theory view was that the rate of interest and the general price level were inversely related. The reason for this belief was that an increase in the bank-rate was generally regarded as a signal for the contraction of money and credit. Since $P = f(M)$, the traditionalists would infer that the price level would fall. Hence, a high bank-rate was associated with a low price level; and, by similar reasoning, a low bank rate with a high price level. As mentioned earlier, this had been questioned first by Thomas Tooke and then by A. H. Gibson. Keynes' solution to "Gibson's Paradox" was similar to that of Wicksell:

> The explanation of this on my theory is, of course, the movements of bank-rate have so often represented a belated and inadequate effort to follow a movement of the natural rate.[61]

To bring out all these refinements of the traditional quantity theory, Keynes gave a great deal of emphasis to his fundamental equations.[62] He summarized the factors that affect the general price level in the "Fundamental Equation of Price":

$$Y = IIO = E + Q$$

where ($Y$) is actual money income; ($II$) denotes the general price level; ($E$) is normal income level, at which investment is equal to savings and total windfall profits are equal to zero. Keynes counted only "normal" profits (a part of Marshallian total costs) as part of ($E$). ($Q$) denotes windfall profits, which "are the difference between the value of current output and ($E$), its cost of production."[63] Keynes further pointed out: "Thus we have Profits = Value of Output − Cost of Pro-

---

[60] Reprinted from *A Treatise on Money* by John Maynard Keynes, I, 186, by permission of Harcourt, Brace & World, Inc.

[61] Reprinted from *A Treatise on Money* by John Maynard Keynes, I, 196 n, by permission of Harcourt, Brace & World, Inc.

[62] Klein observes in *The Keynesian Revolution:*
Keynes apparently thought that he was bringing out the heart of his theory in the exposition of his pretentious "fundamental equations," but the "fundamental equations" were not the essential contribution of the book, and it is quite unfortunate that the reviews and discussions of the book always centered on these equations, instead of on more useful material [p. 17].

[63] Reprinted from *A Treatise on Money*, I, 151, by John Maynard Keynes, by permission of Harcourt, Brace & World, Inc.

duction = Value of Investment − Savings."[64] Equilibrium requires that
(Q) should be zero. In other words, the equilibrium money income is:
$Y = IIO = E$. For "if the total profits (Q) are not zero, the entrepreneurs
will tend, so far as they can, to alter the total volume of employment
which they offer to the Factors of Production at a given rate of renumeration—upwards or downwards."[65] Hence, as observed by Professor Lutz, the difference between S and I is supposed to be the
cause of the profits or losses of the system, and consequently of the
inception of a cumulative process.[66] A rearrangement of the fundamental equation gives us the following expression:

$$II = \frac{E}{0} + \frac{Q}{0} = \frac{E}{0} + \frac{I - S}{0} = \frac{E + (I - S)}{0}$$

Keynes was well aware that the equation is also an identity:

> The Fundamental Equations of Chapter 10 are in themselves no
> more than identities, and therefore not intrinsically superior to
> other identities which have been propounded, connecting mone-
> tary factors.
>
> The main advantage, however, to be claimed for the new Funda-
> mental Equations is for the purposes of qualitative investigation.
> For they are, I think, a much more powerful instrument of analysis
> than their predecessors, when we are considering what kind of
> monetary and business events will produce what kind of conse-
> quences.[67]

Although the rate of interest is not explicitly stated in it, the equation has an advantage over the cash-balance equation in that it directs
attention to the saving-investment nexus. The relation between the rate
of interest and the price level can now be stated in terms of the investment function:

> Bank-rate does not appear explicitly as a factor in the Fundamental
> Equation of Price. It cannot, therefore, affect the price-levels di-
> rectly but only indirectly through its influence on one or more of
> the factors which do appear in the Fundamental Equation.[68]

[64] Reprinted from *A Treatise on Money*, I, 151, by John Maynard Keynes, by
permission of Harcourt, Brace & World, Inc.

[65] Reprinted from *A Treatise on Money*, I, 151–152, by John Maynard Keynes, by
permission of Harcourt, Brace & World, Inc.

[66] Friedrich A. Lutz, "The Outcome of the Saving-Investment Discussion," reprinted from *Quarterly Journal of Economics*, Vol. LII (August, 1938), in *Readings
in Business Cycle Theory*, G. Haberler, ed., p. 133.

[67] Reprinted from *A Treatise on Money*, I, 221–222, by John Maynard Keynes, by
permission of Harcourt, Brace & World, Inc.

[68] Reprinted from *A Treatise on Money*, I, 185, by John Maynard Keynes, by
permission of Harcourt, Brace & World, Inc.

The "Fundamental Equation of Price" was the parade ground on which Keynes put the Wicksellian theory of the bank rate and the saving-investment theory of business cycles through their paces. With one foot still in the neoclassical world, Keynes had as yet no conception of an underemployment equilibrium. Neither did he have a clear idea on the role played by aggregate demand in the determination of income and employment.[69] Like his neoclassical contemporaries, Keynes considered the variable (0) in the fundamental equation as fixed and given:

> My so-called "fundamental equations" were an instantaneous picture taken on the assumption of a given output. They attempted to show how, assuming the given output, forces could develop which involved a profit disequilibrium, and thus required a change in the level of output.[70]

Secondly, Keynes considered ($E$) as a stable equilibrium value. Thus ($Q$) is the only strategic factor that would cause the general price level to fluctuate. In other words, the theory of price fluctuations could be stated in terms of saving and investment.[71]

It has been generally recognized that the most important contribution made by Keynes in his *Treatise* is his analysis of the asset demand for money or liquidity preference.[72] Earlier writers had, of course, recognized the store-of-value function of money, as evidenced by their discussions of hoarding. Keynes, however, was the first to integrate

---

[69] Klein in *The Keynesian Revolution* makes the following comments:
The variable E which represents income paid out to the factors of production was never adequately accounted for by Keynes, this being the principal fault of the *Treatise*. This variable represents effective demand, and the lack of any theory of effective demand was precisely the fault which prevented Keynes from producing a satisfactory result at this time [pp. 20–21].

[70] Reprinted from *The General Theory of Employment, Interest, and Money*, p. vii, by John Maynard Keynes, by permission of Harcourt, Brace & World, Inc.

[71] Hansen in *Business Cycles and National Income*, p. 336, observes:
Keynes' "S" is not actual savings, but the savings which would be made if the actual income were at normal (level). . . . If investment is just sufficient to offset what people would save, S, at a normal income, then the actual income . . . will be at normal, E. Income is driven up or down if investment exceeds or falls below this level. It is the fluctuation of I around S that produces the business cycle.

[72] For instance, John Lintner asserts: "The importance of this innovation in monetary theory can scarcely be over-emphasized—only the integration of the theory of money with a theory of output as a whole can take precedence." *The New Economics*, Harris, ed., p. 516.
J. R. Hicks, in his article, "A Suggestion for Simplifying the Theory of Money," reprinted from *Economica*, New Series, No. 2 (1935), in *Readings in Monetary Theory*, pp. 13–32, also attaches signal importance to this innovation. Klein in *The Keynesian Revolution* makes similar observations.

liquidity preference into a theory of money and prices. Hence the demand for money can now be related to the rate of interest as well. This innovation involves a qualitative distinction between cash balances for spending—income deposits—and savings deposits, which are "not required for the purpose of current payments and could, without inconvenience, be dispensed with if, for any reason, some other form of investment were to seem to the depositor to be preferable."[73] The decisions of the wealthholder are described by Keynes as follows:

> When a man is deciding what proportion of his money-income to save, he is choosing between present consumption and the ownership of wealth. In so far as he decides in favour of consumption, he must necessarily purchase goods—for he cannot consume money. But in so far as he decides in favour of saving, there still remains a further decision for him to make. For he can own wealth by holding it either in the form of money (or the liquid equivalent of money) or in other forms of loan or real capital. This second decision might be conveniently described as the choice between "hoarding" and "investing," or alternatively, as the choice between "bank-deposits" and "securities."[74]

This innovation is worthy of being named a "marginal revolution," as Professor Hicks put it.[75] Hicks pointed out in his 1935 article that the works of Pareto, Wicksteed, and others in value theory, have made us realize the significance of the marginal-utility concept. We now understand that ". . . marginal utility analysis is nothing else than a general theory of choice, which is applicable whenever the choice is between alternatives that are capable of quantitative expression." This analysis should be applied to monetary theory. Wicksell and Mises had tried their hands at it but failed to develop a marginal utility theory

---

[73] Reprinted from *A Treatise on Money,* I, 36, by John Maynard Keynes, by permission of Harcourt, Brace & World, Inc.

[74] Reprinted from *A Treatise on Money,* I, 140–141, by John Maynard Keynes, by permission of Harcourt, Brace & World, Inc.

[75] Hicks observes:
Mr. Keynes' "Treatise," so far as I have been able to discover, contains at least three theories of money. One of them is the Savings and Investment theory, which, as I hinted, seems to me only a quantity theory much glorified. One of them is a Wicksellian natural rate theory. But the third is altogether much more interesting. It emerges when Mr. Keynes begins to talk about the price-level of investment goods; when he shows that this price-level depends upon the relative preference of the investor—to hold bank-deposits or to hold securities. Here at last we have something which to a value theorist looks sensible and interesting!
*A Suggestion for Simplifying the Theory of Money,* reprinted in *Readings in Monetary Theory,* pp. 15–16.

of money. In Keynes' exposition of the price level of investment goods, we "at last . . . have a choice at the margin!"[76]

Keynes' theory of the determination of the general price level may be summarized as follows:

1. The general price level $(II)$ is stated as $II = E + [I - S]/0$. The general price level $(II)$ consists of two components: the price level of consumption goods, $(P)$, and the price level of investment goods, $(P')$. The implication is that, in order to stabilize the $(II)$, the central bank must stabilize $(P)$ and $(P')$ simultaneously.

2. The price level of consumption goods, $(P)$, is expressed in the equation, $P = E/0 + [I' - S]/R$.[77] Like $(II)$, it can be controlled through the bank rate.

3. The price level of investment goods, $(P')$, is, however, determined by a different set of forces. $(P')$ is determined by the demand for savings deposits and the supply of savings deposits. The demand for savings deposits is functionally related to the price level of investment goods. This schedule is Keynes' "bearishness function." The supply of savings deposits is under the direct control of the banking system. $(P')$ is determined by the intersection of these two schedules. "A fall in the price-level of securities is therefore an indication that the 'bearishness' of the public . . . has been insufficiently offset by the creation of savings-deposits by the banking system—or that the 'bullishness' of the public has been more than offset by the contraction of savings-deposits by the banking system. It follows that the

---

[76] *Ibid.*, p. 16.

[77] This equation is derived in the following way (see Keynes' *Treatise*, I, 135):

Let   $(E) = $ the total money-income or Earnings of the community in a unit of time;

    $(I') = $ the part of $(E)$ which has been earned by the production of investment goods (cost of production of new investment);

  $E - I' = $ cost of production of the current output of consumption-goods;

  $E - S = $ the current expenditure on consumption-goods;

Let   $(0) = $ total output; $(R) = $ physical volume of consumption-goods;

    $(C) = $ physical volume of investment-goods;

    $(0) = R + C;\ I' = E(C/0)$

  $P \cdot R = $ current expenditure on consumption-goods

  $P \cdot R = E - S = $ current expenditure on consumption-goods

  $P \cdot R = E - S = E([R + C]/0) - S = E(R/0) + E(C/0) - S$

  $P \cdot R = E(R/0) + I' - S$

  $\therefore P = E/0 + (I' - S)/R$

actual price-level of investment is the resultant of the senti-
ment of the public and the behaviour of the banking system."[78]
4. Thus the general price level, $(II)$, and the amount of total profits
"depend on all four factors—(1) the rate of saving, (2) the cost
of new investment, (3) the 'bearishness' of the public, (4) the
volume of savings-deposits; or, if you like, on the two factors—
(1) the excess of saving over cost of investment, and (2) such
excess of bearishness on the part of the public unsatisfied by
the creation of deposits by the banking system. Thus, given
the rate of new investment and the cost of production, the price-
level of consumption-goods is solely determined by the disposition of the public toward 'saving.' And given the volume of
savings-deposits created by the banking system, the price-level
of investment-goods (whether new or old) is solely determined
by the disposition of the public towards 'hoarding' money."[79]
5. To relate the general price level to the quantity of money, total
cash balances are divided into income deposits $(M_1)$, business
deposits $(M_2)$, and savings deposits $(M_3)$. $E = M_1V_1$. Keynes
assumed $(V_1)$ to be constant. He wrote, "Generally speaking,
one would expect the average value of $k_1$ in a given economic
society to be a fairly stable quantity from year to year. But this
average stability may be accompanied by considerable season-
able fluctuations, if income, though accruing steadily day by
day, is not received and disbursed daily but at intervals."[80]
Now the fundamental equation for the general price level could
be rewritten: $IIO = M_1V_1 + Q$. Keynes maintained that interest
rate fluctuations would cause fluctuations only in $(Q)$, not $(V_1)$.
Thus Professor Klein observed: "*We may conclude that the
classical theory took a fraction of $E + Q = Y$ as a stable given
value, while Keynes took a fraction of merely $(E)$ as a stable
given value.*"[81] Professor Klein further suggested that if Keynes
wrote $M_1V_1 = E$, we can legitimately write $M_2V_2 = Q$. Hence
the fundamental equation can be written as $M_1V_1 + M_2V_2 =
E + Q = Y = IIO$. It should be noted that Keynes excluded the

[78] Reprinted from *A Treatise on Money*, I, 142, by John Maynard Keynes, by
permission of Harcourt, Brace & World, Inc.

[79] Reprinted from *A Treatise on Money*, I, 143–144, by John Maynard Keynes, by
permission of Harcourt, Brace & World, Inc.

[80] Reprinted from *A Treatise on Money*, I, 144, by John Maynard Keynes, by
permission of Harcourt, Brace & World, Inc.

[81] Klein, *The Keynesian Revolution*, pp. 22–23.

savings-deposits $(M_3)$ from this fundamental equation. $(M_1 + M_2)$ subsequently became his $(L_1)$ and $(M_3)$ his $(L_2)$.

6. In equilibrium, $(Q)$ is equal to zero. The fundamental equation becomes: $II0 = M_1V_1$. This equation "evidently bears a family relationship to Professor Irving Fisher's familiar equation $P \cdot T = M \cdot V$, except that 0 represents current output, whereas $T$ is the volume, not of output, but of transactions, and that $M_1 V_1$ represent the income-deposits and their velocity, whereas $M$, $V$ are the cash-deposits and their velocity."[82]

Thus we see that Keynes, in his *Treatise*, did not depart drastically from the neoclassical framework. In equilibrium, his theory is equivalent to the quantity theory; in disequilibrium, his theory is the theory of cumulative change. Like Wicksell, he had strong faith in the power of monetary policy to stabilize the price level. Their criterion of price stabilization was the equality of savings and investment. But neither of them realized at that time, as pointed out by Professor Klein, that "savings and investment can be in equilibrium at various levels of employment."[83] This mistake could have been avoided, if they had seen their way clear to developing a theory of income determination.

---

[82] Reprinted from *A Treatise on Money*, I, 150, by John Maynard Keynes, by permission of Harcourt, Brace & World, Inc.

[83] Klein, *The Keynesian Revolution*, p. 26.

# 9

# The General Theory as
# Monetary Theory

## THE FUNDAMENTAL ISSUES RAISED BY KEYNES

From the veiwpoint of monetary theory, two fundamental issues are presented in *The General Theory:* (1) Keynes' attack on the traditional separation of monetary theory and value theory, and (2) his emphasis on the demand for money as an asset alternative to other yield-bearing assets.

On the first issue Keynes wrote:

> So long as economists are concerned with what is called the Theory of Value, they have been accustomed to teach that prices are governed by the conditions of supply and demand; and, in particular, changes in marginal cost and the elasticity of short-period supply have played a prominent part. But when they pass in volume II, or more often in a separate treatise, to the Theory of Money and Prices, we hear no more of these homely but intelligible concepts and move into a world where prices are governed by the quantity of money, by its income-velocity, by the velocity of circulation relatively to the volume of transactions, by hoarding, by forced saving, by inflation and deflation *et hoc genus omne;* and little or no attempt is made to relate these vaguer phrases to our former notions of the elasticities of supply and demand.[1]

---

[1] Reprinted from *The General Theory of Employment, Interest, and Money,* p. 292, by John Maynard Keynes, by permission of Harcourt, Brace & World, Inc.

192

"What is wanted is a marginal revolution" in monetary theory; and *The General Theory* came close to such a revolution.[2]

*The General Theory* represents a transition from a monetary theory of prices to a monetary theory of output.[3] In making this transition, Keynes not only attempted to integrate monetary and value theory, but also brought the theory of interest into the realm of monetary theory. This synthesis may be explained by the diagram in Figure 9-1.

The diagram illustrates that the Keynesian theory of money and prices recognizes a higher degree of interdependence among the relevant variables in the system than the quantity theory does. In asserting that the quantity of money affects the price level directly, the quantity theory "tries to determine income [$PY$] without interest, just as the labor theory of value tried to determine price without output."[4] The Keynesian theory, on the other hand, asserts that the relationship between the quantity of money and the price level is an indirect one. The chain of causation, as shown in the diagram, is as follows. The first impact of an increase in the quantity of money will be on the rate of interest. How far the rate of interest will fall depends upon the strength of the community's liquidity preference. If the increase in the quantity of money does push down the interest rate, aggregate demand will be increased via an interest-induced increase in investment demand. Assuming there are unemployed resources in existence, the increased aggregate demand will lead to an increase in output and employment.[5] As output increases, cost conditions will change also. Eventually

---

[2] J. R. Hicks, "A Suggestion for Simplifying the Theory of Money," reprinted from *Econometrica* (1935) in *Readings in Monetary Theory* (Homewood, Ill.: Richard D. Irwin, Inc., 1951), p. 14.

Professor Hicks also comments: "Indeed, Mr. Keynes' innovation is closely parallel . . . to the innovation of the marginalist." See "Mr. Keynes and the *Classics*," reprinted from *Econometrica* (April, 1937), in *Readings in the Theory of Income Distribution*, p. 469.

[3] Keynes in *The General Theory* wrote:

When I began to write my *Treatise on Money* I was still moving along the traditional lines of regarding the influence of money as something so to speak separate from the general theory of supply and demand. When I finished it, I had made some progress towards pushing monetary theory back to becoming a theory of output as a whole. . . . This book, on the other hand, has evolved into what is primarily a study of the forces which determine changes in the scale of output and employment as a whole . . . [pp. vi–vii].

Reprinted from *The General Theory of Employment, Interest, and Money* by John Maynard Keynes, by permission of Harcourt, Brace & World, Inc.

[4] Hicks, "Mr. Keynes and the *Classics*," in *Readings in the Theory of Income Distribution*, pp. 467–470. The symbol in the bracket, ($PY$), is ours.

[5] Stated differently, the link between money and output is the rate of interest. As long as the increase in ($M$) can push down ($r$), both aggregate demand and output will increase.

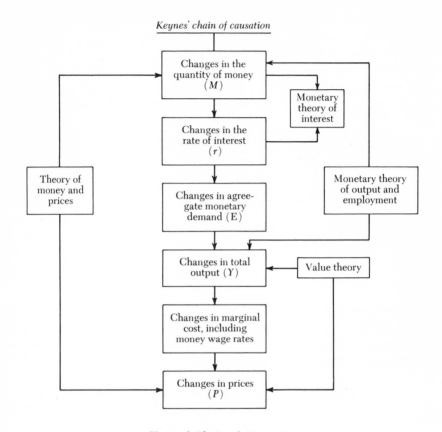

Keynes' chain of causation

**Keynes' Chain of Causation**

**Figure 9-1**

marginal costs (essentially wage costs) will rise and consequently prices will also increase.

The Keynesian theory is more "general" than the neoclassical quantity theory in the sense that, first, it does not overlook the relationship between the quantity of money and the rate of interest and, second, it does not overlook the relationship between the quantity of money and output. This general theory includes the neoclassical theory as a special case. As a first approximation, Keynes wrote: "So long as there is unemployment, *employment* will change in the same proportion as the quantity of money; and when there is full employment, *prices* will change in the same proportion as the quantity of money."[6] However,

---

[6] Reprinted from *The General Theory of Employment, Interest, and Money*, p. 296, by John Maynard Keynes, by permission of Harcourt, Brace & World, Inc.

Keynes considered that the following possible complications would qualify the preceding statement:

(1) Effective demand will not change in exact proportion to the quantity of money.

(2) Since resources are not homogeneous, there will be diminishing, and not constant, returns as employment gradually increases.

(3) Since resources are not interchangeable, some commodities will reach a condition of inelastic supply whilst there are still unemployed resources available for the production of other commodities.

(4) The wage-unit will tend to rise, before full employment has been reached.

(5) The renumerations of factors entering into marginal cost will not all change in the same proportion.[7]

Keynes' general conclusion is: "The general price-level depends partly on the rate of renumeration of the factors of production which enter into marginal cost and partly on the scale of output as a whole, i.e., (taking equipment and technique as given) on the volume of employment."[8]

As stated by Professor Dillard, "it is through the theory of output that value theory and monetary theory are brought into juxtaposition with each other."[9]

Keynes emphasized non-neutral money. He pointed out: "as soon as we pass to the problem of what determines output and employment as a whole, we require the complete theory of a Monetary Economy."[10] It will be recalled that ever since the failure of John Law's scheme, orthodox writers had brushed money aside as of secondary importance in explaining the economic process of reality. It was not until the publication of *The General Theory* that "monetary analysis has once more conquered [triumphed] in our times."[11] This leads us to the second fundamental issue raised by Keynes.

---

[7] Reprinted from *The General Theory of Employment, Interest, and Money*, p. 296, by John Maynard Keynes, by permission of Harcourt, Brace & World, Inc.

[8] Reprinted from *The General Theory of Employment, Interest, and Money*, p. 294, by John Maynard Keynes, by permission of Harcourt, Brace & World, Inc.

[9] Dudley Dillard, *The Economics of John Maynard Keynes* (New York: Prentice-Hall, Inc., 1948), pp. 224–225.

[10] Reprinted from *The General Theory of Employment, Interest, and Money*, p. 293, by John Maynard Keynes, by permission of Harcourt, Brace & World, Inc.

[11] See J. A. Schumpeter, *History of Economic Analysis* (New York: Oxford University Press, Inc., 1965), p. 276.

By monetary analysis, Professor Schumpeter meant that "Monetary Analysis introduces the element of money on the very ground floor of our analytical structure and abandons the idea that all essential features of economic life can be represented by a barter economy model" [p. 278].

Keynes believed that in the "problems of the real world . . . our previous expectations are liable to disappointment and expectations concerning the future affect what we do today. It is when we have made this transition that the peculiar properties of money as a link between the present and the future must enter into our calculations."[12] Therefore, he maintained that discussions of the effects of changing expectations about the future should be stated in monetary terms. This emphasis leads directly to money as an asset alternative to other yield-bearing assets. (It will be recalled that Marshall had envisaged the idea before Keynes, but failed to pursue it.)

Keynes' rejection of the neutrality of money is closely linked with his monetary theory of interest. As observed by Professor Johnson, "The essence of the Keynesian revolution was to shift the subject matter of monetary theory, placing the emphasis on the level of employment as the central subject of monetary theory and posing the determination of the rate of interest as a specifically monetary problem."[13] In rejecting the orthodox saving and investment theory of interest, Keynes wrote:

> The rate of interest is not the "price" which brings into equilibrium the demand for resources to invest with the readiness to abstain from present consumption. It is the "price" which equilibrates the desire to hold wealth in the form of cash with the available quantity of cash; —which implies that if the rate of interest were lower, i.e. if the reward for parting with cash were diminished, the aggregate amount of cash which the public would wish to hold would exceed the available supply, and that if the rate of interest were raised, there would be a surplus of cash which no one would be willing to hold. If this explanation is correct, the quantity of money is the other factor, which, in conjunction with liquidity-preference, determines the actual rate of interest in given circumstances. Liquidity-preference is a potentiality or functional tendency, which fixes the quantity of money which the public will hold when the rate of interest is given; so that if $r$ is the rate of interest, $M$ the quantity of money and $L$ the function of liquidity-preference, we have $M = L(r)$. *This is where, and how, the quantity of money enters in the economic scheme.*[14]

[12] Reprinted from *The General Theory of Employment, Interest, and Money*, pp. 293–294, by John Maynard Keynes, by permission of Harcourt, Brace & World, Inc.

[13] Harry G. Johnson, "Monetary Theory and Keynesian Economics," reprinted from *Pakistan Economic Journal*, Vol. VIII (June, 1958), in *Readings in Money, National Income, and Stabilization Policy*, Smith and Teigen, eds. (Homewood, Ill.: Richard D. Irwin, Inc., 1965), pp. 32–33.

[14] Reprinted from *The General Theory of Employment, Interest, and Money*, pp. 167–168, by John Maynard Keynes, by permission of Harcourt, Brace & World, Inc. (Italics added.)

In the Keynesian system, money is neutral in two situations. The first is the situation of full employment in which the quantity theory of money comes of age; and the second is the special case of the "liquidity trap." [15] Money is non-neutral in the intermediate situation between these two limiting cases.

The most distinguishing feature of Keynes' monetary theory is its emphasis on the demand for money as an asset alternative to other yield-bearing assets.[16] This emphasis led him to make several innovations in monetary theory. In the first place, Keynes made the income velocity of circulation dependent upon the rate of interest or bond yields. Hence, the income velocity of circulation could no longer be assumed to be constant, as was assumed in neoclassical monetary theory.

Secondly, Keynes separated the demand for money into two component parts: transactions demand, which was assumed to be dependent upon income; and a liquidity-preference demand, which was assumed to be dependent upon the rate of interest. Keynes wrote:

> Whilst the amount of cash which an individual decides to hold to satisfy the transactions-motive and the precautionary motive is not entirely independent of what he is holding to satisfy the speculative-motive, it is a safe first approximation to regard the amounts of these two sets of cash-holdings as being largely independent of one another.
>
> Let the amount of cash held to satisfy the transactions- and precautionary-motives be $M_1$, and the amount held to satisfy the spec-

---

[15] Keynes in *The General Theory* wrote:
There is the possibility . . . that, after the rate of interest has fallen to a certain level, liquidity-preference may become virtually absolute in the sense that almost everyone prefers cash to holding a debt which yields so low a rate of interest. In this event the monetary authority would have lost effective control over the rate of interest [p. 207].
This point has prompted Sir Dennis Robertson to make the following stricture: Under the impulse of Keynes's work, the rate of interest was elevated to a position of commanding theoretical importance. Roughly speaking, nothing was ever allowed to happen—money was not allowed to affect prices, wage-rates were not allowed to affect employment. I had almost added, the moon was not allowed to affect the tides—except through the rate of interest. . . . But it became also the villain of the piece, and a very powerful villain. It was the dragon guarding the cave of "liquidity-preference". . . .
"What Has Happened to the Rate of Interest?" *Three Banks Review* (March, 1949), p. 16, cited by J. R. Schlesinger in "After Twenty Years: The General Theory," *Quarterly Journal of Economics*, Vol. LXX (November, 1959).

[16] Professor James Tobin observes:
In a world of financial assets and well-developed capital markets, Keynes was right in perceiving the tactical advantage to the theorist of treating separately decisions determining total wealth and its rate of growth and decisions regarding the composition of wealth.
See "Money, Capital, and Other Stores of Value," *American Economic Review*, Vol. LI (May, 1961), p. 28.

ulative-motive be $M_2$. Corresponding to these two compartments of cash, we then have two liquidity functions $L_1$ and $L_2$. $L_1$ mainly depends on the level of income, whilst $L_2$ mainly depends on the relation between the current rate of interest and the state of expectation. Thus

$$M = M_1 + M_2 = L_1(Y) + L_2(r)$$

where $L_1$ is the liquidity function corresponding to an income $Y$, which determines $M_1$, and $L_2$ is the liquidity function of the rate of interest $r$, which determines $M_2$. It follows that there are three matters to investigate: (*i*) the relation of changes in $M$ to $Y$ and $r$, (*ii*) what determines the shape of $L_1$, (*iii*) what determines the shape of $L_2$.[17]

Thirdly, Keynes explained the existence of a liquidity preference for money by a necessary condition:

> This necessary condition is the existence of *uncertainty* as to the future of the rate of interest, i.e. as to the complex of rates of interest for varying maturities which will rule at future dates. For if the rates of interest ruling at all future times could be foreseen with certainty, all future rates of interest could be inferred from the *present* rates of interest for debts of different maturities, which would be adjusted to the knowledge of the future rates.[18]

Keynes did not set up a theory of expectations. Instead, he only discussed the conventions and habits of thought governing the formation of these expectations.[19] He was of the opinion that the accepted convention is to expect a "normal" long-term rate to prevail, and to which investors expect any deviant rate of interest to return.

Fourthly, Keynes formulated his theory of interest explicitly in "stock" terms. It will be recalled that the traditional loanable-funds theory of interest was formulated in "flow" terms.

Lastly, Keynes employed the Marshallian short-run analysis as a substitute for dynamic analysis. Hence, in the Keynesian analysis, both the accumulation of real capital and the accumulation of debt are excluded from explicit consideration.

The impact of *The General Theory* has been so great "that most of recent theory and research on money can be classified either as application and extension of Keynesian ideas or as counterrevolutionary at-

---

[17] Reprinted from *The General Theory of Employment, Interest, and Money,* pp. 199–200, by John Maynard Keynes, by permission of Harcourt, Brace & World, Inc.

[18] Reprinted from *The General Theory of Employment, Interest, and Money,* p. 168, by John Maynard Keynes, by permission of Harcourt, Brace & World, Inc.

[19] See Keynes, p. 203.

tack on them."[20] Before reviewing some post-Keynesian developments, we shall survey some of the criticisms of *The General Theory* as a monetary theory, for, as we shall see, a great deal of recent work stems from these criticisms.

## Evaluation of Keynesian Monetary Theory

Practically all of Keynes' theoretical innovations mentioned in the previous section have been criticized by subsequent writers. Let us consider some of the criticisms. With regard to Keynes' division of the demand for money into two separate parts, Professor Hansen in 1949 extended the Keynesian analysis by treating the transactions demand for money as a reflection of economic behavior (choice at the margin) and particularly as being interest-elastic at high rates.[21] He wrote: "The quantity theorists believed that the demand for money was interest-inelastic. Even Keynes made the $L_t$ function [our notation] interest-inelastic. But this is not necessarily the case."[22]

Professor Baumol in 1952 further elaborated on the interest-elasticity of the transactions demand for money.[23] He criticized Keynes by saying: "If firms are efficient profit maximizers, Keynes was probably wrong in playing down the influence of the interest rate on the transactions demand for cash."[24]

A significantly different approach from the Keynesian approach to the demand for money has been expounded by modern quantity theorists. For instance, Professor Friedman in his *The Quantity Theory— A Restatement* (1956) writes of his own formulation of the quantity theory that it

> does not use the distinction between . . . "transition balances" and "speculative balances" that is so widely used in the literature. The

---

[20] H. G. Johnson, "Monetary Theory and Policy," *American Economic Review*, LII (June, 1962), 336.

[21] See Alvin H. Hansen, *Monetary Theory and Fiscal Policy* (New York: McGraw-Hill Book Company, 1949), pp. 66–68.

[22] From *Monetary Theory and Fiscal Policy* by Alvin H. Hansen. Copyright 1949 by McGraw-Hill Book Company. Used with permission of McGraw-Hill Book Company.

[23] See William J. Baumol, "The Transactions Demand for Cash: An Inventory Theoretical Approach," *Quarterly Journal of Economics*, Vol. LXVI (November, 1952). The basic ideas of this article have been incorporated by Professor Baumol in his discussion on "Optimal Cash Balances" in *Economic Theory and Operations Analysis* (2nd ed.; Englewood Cliffs, N.J.: Prentice-Hall, Inc., 1965), pp. 241–245.

[24] Baumol, *Economic Theory and Operations Analysis*, 1st ed., p. 244.

distinction between money holdings of ultimate wealth-owners and of business enterprises is related to this distinction but only distantly so. Each of these categories of money-holders can be said to demand money partly from "transaction" motives, partly from "speculative" or "asset" motives, but dollars of money are not distinguished according as they are said to be held for one or the other purpose. Rather, each dollar is, as it were, regarded as rendering a variety of services, and the holder of money as altering his money holdings until the value to him of the addition to the total flow of services produced by adding a dollar to his money stock is equal to the reduction in the flow of services produced by subtracting a dollar from each of the other forms in which he holds assets.[25]

Turning to his analysis of the speculative demand for money, Keynes did not consider the composition of wealth in sufficient detail. In other words, Keynes' alternatives for asset choice are limited to cash and bonds. Professor John Lintner in 1947 observed: "The models of the *General Theory* need to be broadened, to allow separately not only for different liquidity preference schedules of individuals and business firms, but also at least for commercial banks and other financial institutions."[26]

Professor Haberler at the same time (1947) made the following criticism of the speculative demand for money: "The theory of liquidity stands in great need of further elaboration. It will be necessary to distinguish a large number of different types of assets than just money and real goods, or money, securities, and real goods. The different types of assets have to be arranged according to their liquidity, with cash on one end of the scale, certain types of finished goods on the other end, and loans, bonds, equities, raw material, etc., in between."[27]

Professor Robinson in 1952 tried to extend and refine the liquidity preference theory. She wrote: "Keynes' theory treated the rate of interest as determined by the demand and supply of money. This was a useful simplification in the pioneering days of the theory, but it was always obvious that there is no such thing as *the* rate of interest and that the demand and supply of every type of asset has just as much right to be considered as the demand and supply of money. To develop a more refined theory the notion of liquidity preference, measured by

[25] Milton Friedman, ed., *Studies in the Quantity Theory of Money* (Chicago: University of Chicago Press, 1956), p. 14.

[26] John Lintner, "The Theory of Money and Prices," *The New Economics*, Seymour E. Harris, ed. (New York: Augustus M. Kelley, Publishers, 1947), p. 521.

[27] Gottfried Haberler, "The General Theory (4)," *The New Economics*, Seymour E. Harris, ed., p. 165.

the reward required to induce owners of wealth to hold assets other than money, must be broken up into a number of aspects."[28]

Professors Gurley and Shaw in 1955 went a step farther in their criticism of Keynes' theory: "A more decisive break with liquidity-preference theory seems advisable. Liquidity is not the only characteristic that distinguishes bonds from alternatve financial assets. Each financial intermediary offers its own differentiated product for the public to hold. This product is competitive with bonds. It may be more or less liquid than bonds, but it embodies a service, perhaps insurance, that bonds do not. The product is also competitive with money narrowly defined, offering less liquidity perhaps but offering as well security, interest, insurance, and other services. In view of the increasing variety of financial assets, it does seem appropriate to abandon liquidity as the pivotal factor in interest theory."[29]

The criticisms mentioned in the preceding paragraphs concern essentially Keynes' conception of money as an asset. We now turn to criticisms of Keynes' assumption of given wage and price levels and his failure to consider the effects of price expectations on the demand for money. A review of Keynes' views on wage reduction and full employmnt may lend perspective to a discussion of these criticisms.

In Chapter 19 of *The General Theory*, Keynes pointed out that "the reduction in money-wages will have no lasting tendency to increase employment except by virtue of its repercussions either on the propensity to consume for the community as a whole, or on the schedule of marginal efficiency of capital, or on the rate of interest."[30] The last-mentioned route—via the rate of interest—concerns us here. Keynes wrote: "The reduction in the wages-bill, accompanied by some reduction in prices and in money-incomes generally, will diminish the need for cash for income and business purposes; and it will therefore reduce *pro tanto* the schedule of liquidity-preference for the community as a whole. *Cet. par.* this will reduce the rate of interest and thus prove favourable to investment."[31] As observed by Professor Haberler, "this amounts to giving up the idea of under-employment equilibrium under a regime of flexible prices and wages except in two limiting cases: Full

---

[28] Joan Robinson, *The Rate of Interest and Other Essays* (London: Macmillan & Co., 1952), p. 5.

[29] John G. Gurley and E. S. Shaw, "Financial Aspects of Economic Development," *American Economic Review*, XLV (September, 1955), 527–528.

[30] Reprinted from *The General Theory of .Employment, Interest, and Money*, p. 262, by John Maynard Keynes, by permission of Harcourt, Brace & World, Inc.

[31] Reprinted from *The General Theory of Employment, Interest, and Money*, p. 263, by John Maynard Keynes, by permission of Harcourt, Brace & World, Inc.

employment may be prevented from being reached via this route, (*a*) if the liquidity trap prevents a fall in the rate of interest . . . or (*b*) if investment is quite insensitive to a fall in the rate of interest."[32] And as Keynes noted, "There is, therefore, no ground for the belief that a flexible wage policy is capable of maintaining a state of continuous full employment;—any more than for the belief that an open-market monetary policy is capable, unaided, of achieving this result. The economic system cannot be made self-adjusting along these lines."[33]

It is clear from the preceding arguments that Keynes confined the effects of wage reduction only to ($L_1$), and made ($L_2$) depend solely on the rate of interest. Keynes' treatment leads to three unfortunate results: (1) overlooking the liquid-wealth effect (the real-balance effect) on consumption and on the demand for money, (2) assuming a "money illusion" in the speculative demand for money, and (3) neglecting the influence of price-level expectations on the demand for money.

With regard to point (1), Professor Patinkin observes: "It is interesting to speculate on the train of reasoning which caused Keynes to ignore the real-balance effect. It seems likely that he did recognize the influence of wealth on consumption (or rather savings), but thought of this influence only in terms of nonmonetary assets."[34]

With regard to (2), Professor Patinkin observes: "Keynesian monetary theory never permits the speculative demand to absorb an increased supply of money except at a lower rate of interest."[35] This amounts to building a money illusion into the speculative demand for money. Money illusion refers to the notion that an increase in the supply of money causes a change in some real aspect of an individual's economic behavior. For instance, assume that a money illusion exists in the market for money. The equilibrium condition in the money market will be in the form:

$$L_1(PY_0) + L_2(r) = M_0$$

where $L_1(PY_0)$ is the transactions and precautionary demand for money; ($Y_0$) is the full employment output; ($P$) denotes the price level;

---

[32] Haberler, *op. cit.*, p. 169.

[33] Reprinted from *The General Theory of Employment, Interest, and Money*, p. 267, by John Maynard Keynes, by permission of Harcourt, Brace & World, Inc.

[34] From *Money, Interest, and Prices*, 2nd Edition, p. 636, by Don Patinkin. Copyright © 1965 by Don Patinkin. Reprinted by permission of Harper & Row, Publishers.

[35] From *Money, Interest, and Prices*, 2nd Edition, p. 373, by Don Patinkin. Copyright © 1965 by Don Patinkin. Reprinted by permission of Harper & Row, Publishers.

$L_2(r)$ is the speculative demand for money; and $(M_0)$ is the given money supply. It should be noted that this equilibrium condition is stated in nominal terms. In real terms this equation can be written as

$$\frac{L_1(PY_0)}{P} + \frac{L_2(r)}{P} = \frac{M_0}{P}$$

where $L_1(PY_0)/P$ is the demand for real transaction balances; and $L_2(r)/P$ is the demand for real speculative balances.

Suppose that the supply of money increases and consequently under full employment conditions the price level rises. The equation in real terms tells us that the transactions demand for real-balances will not change $[L_1(2PY_0)/2P = L_1(PY_0)/P]$.[36] But the real amount of cash people desire to hold for $(L_2)$ purposes must change, because it varies inversely with the price level. Hence, the rate of interest must fall in order to restore equilibrium in the money and the commodity markets. This is Keynes' way of destroying the classical and neoclassical real theory of interest. "The over-all tone of the *General Theory* leaves little doubt that Keynes intended his liquidity-preference theory to be a fundamental challenge to classical and neoclassical monetary theory. But if this challenge is to meet the latter theory on its own grounds— those of full employment and price flexibility—then Keynes' position cannot be vindicated except by attributing to him the assumption of money illusion in the speculative demand for money."[37]

As to point (3), we must turn to the writings of modern quantity theorists for an explicit analysis of the role of price-level expectations in the demand for money. For instance, Professor Friedman in his *The Quantity Theory of Money—A Restatement* (1956) considers the

---

[36] Professor Patinkin gives the following illustration:

Assume that in a certain economy the old currency is abolished and replaced by a new one. For example, assume that all dollars are suddenly recalled, and replaced by pesos, at the rate of two pesos for every dollar turned in. Correspondingly, whatever previously cost one dollar, now costs two pesos, and every contractual obligation in dollars is replaced by a corresponding one in twice as many pesos. Only the rate of interest is permitted to remain unchanged. Clearly in such a case there would be no reason for the real quantities of goods demanded and supplied to change. Neither would there be any reason for anyone to change his mind about the net amount of real indebtedness which he considers desirable. It is also clear that the real amount of money demanded for transactions purposes would not change; hence, it is equally clear that the real amount demanded for speculative purposes will not change.

"Keynesian Economics and the Quantity Theory," in *Post-Keynesian Economics*, K. K. Kurihara, ed. (New Brunswick, N.J.: Rutgers University Press, 1954), p. 144.

This is the case where "money illusion" is absent. The equilibrium condition in real terms is written as $L_1(Y_0) + L_2(r) = M_0/P$.

[37] From *Money, Interest, and Prices*, 2nd Edition, p. 374, by Don Patinkin. Copyright © 1965 by Don Patinkin. Reprinted by permission of Harper & Row, Publishers.

demand for money as dependent upon bond yields, equity yields, the ratio of non-human to human wealth, or the ratio of wealth to income, the level of real income per capita, the tastes and preferences of wealth-owning units, and the rate of change of the level of prices. The theoretical structure of modern quantity theory will be discussed in the following chapter. At this point, suffice it to note that modern quanity theorists regard the demand-for-money function as stable under normal circumstances. But under abnormal conditions, such as during periods of hyperinflation, the velocity of circulation of money rises drastically owing to the influence of price-level expectations.

In this vein, Professor Richard T. Selden in 1959 observed; "The key to velocity analysis lies in the application of orthodox demand theory to money. The reciprocal of velocity, real balances per unit of output $(M/PY)$, may be regarded as a commodity whose services are in demand. . . . If the public expects the rate of inflation to increase (perhaps because of rapid monetary expansion), the demand for $M/PY$ will fall and velocity will rise."[38]

Another category of criticisms involves Keynes' "short-run" analysis. Professor Leontief in 1947 criticized Keynes as follows: "True to the Cambridge tradition, he resorts to the Marshallian substitute for dynamic theory—the 'short-run' analysis. The short-run analysis is related to the true dynamic approach in the same way as the, also Marshallian, partial equilibrium theory stands in respect to the Walrasian general equilibrium analysis. In both instances the problem at hand is simplified by selective omission of some of the relevant relationships, on the one hand, and treatment as independent of some of the really dependent variables on the other."[39] Subsequently, Professors Leontief, Patinkin, and others further emphasized that involuntary unemployment was a feature of disequilibrium, requiring a dynamic theoretical analysis.[40] Keynes' methodology was deemed inappropriate to dealing with the problem of involuntary unemployment.

Professors Gurley and Shaw in 1955 also criticized the short-run Keynesian model but for a different reason. They wrote: "This model is not an efficient instrument for studying economic development in either its real or its financial aspects. On the side of goods, the model is inefficient because it does not allow for the effects of investment and

---

[38] Richard T. Selden, "Cost Push and Demand Pull Inflation, 1955–57," *Journal of Political Economy*, LXVIII (February, 1959), 7–8.

[39] Wassily Leontief, "Postulates: Keynes' General Theory and the Classicists," in *The New Economics*, Seymour E. Harris, ed., p. 239.

[40] See "Evaluation of The General Theory" in Chap. 4 of this book.

of the growth in the labor supply on output capacity. . . . On the side of finance, the Keynesian model is inefficient because it does not allow for the effects of spending and deficits on debt and on financial capacity of spending units to sustain their spending. Deficits, like investment, leave an economic residue. In the case of investment, the residue is output capacity. In the case of deficit, the residue is debt and a change in financial capacity."[41]

Aside from these methodological criticisms, *The General Theory* as a monetary theory of interest has also been criticized for confusing the "stock" and "flow" analyses. It will be recalled that Keynes in the *Treatise* took over the Wicksellian flow analysis and added his own asset demand for money, which was conducted in stock terms. Thus, Professor Horwich observed: "The *Treatise* was a serious and brilliant contribution to the development of stock-flow monetary theory."[42]

However, Keynes in *The General Theory* stated that interest was not a reward for saving but for parting with liquidity. The rate of interest is determined solely by the supply and demand for money; the equality of saving and investment is maintained by the level of income, and not by the rate of interest. The concept of the "natural" rate, which is prominent in the *Treatise*, disappears in *The General Theory*.

Professor R. F. Harrod in 1963 criticized Keynes for neglecting the flow variables.[43] Professor Horwich maintains that "Keynes falls into a stock-flow confusion that, in an historical perspective, is monumental."[44] Earlier, Professor Robertson also criticized Keynes for overlooking the real forces (namely, saving and investment) in the determination of the rate of interest.[45]

Keynes' neglect of flow variables in his theory of the determination of the interest rate probably stems from his rejection of the concept of a natural rate. Professor Harrod has suggested that Keynes discarded this concept because "he wanted to avoid a connotation of the word 'natural' as used by economists from Adam Smith onwards, namely, an equilibrium price that the ordinary workings of the economic system

[41] Gurley and Shaw, *loc. cit.*, p. 523.

[42] George Horwich, *Money, Capital, and Prices* (Homewood: Ill.: Richard D. Irwin, Inc., 1964), p. 420.

[43] See R. F. Harrod, "Retrospect on Keynes (1963)," in *Keynes' General Theory: Reports of Three Decades*, Robert Lekachman, ed. (New York: St. Martin's Press, Inc., 1964), pp. 139–152.

[44] Horwich, p. 428.

[45] See D. H. Robertson, "Mr. Keynes and the Rate of Interest" in *Essays in Monetary Theory* (London: P. S. King, 1940).

tend to establish in the long run. He wanted to emphasize his view that there was no such equilibrium towards which the system normally gravitated, and he feared to arouse misunderstanding, if he used the word 'natural'."[46] Nonetheless, Keynes never really succeeded in banishing the natural rate. It crept in again when he conceded that in equilibrium, saving and investment are equal at the going rate of interest. In Keynes' own words:

> All these points of agreement can be summed up in a proposition which the classical school would accept and I should not dispute; namely, that, if the level of income is assumed to be given, we can infer that the current rate of interest must lie at the point where the demand curve for capital corresponding to different rates of interest cuts the curve of the amounts saved out of the given income corresponding to the different rates of interest.[47]

Finally, we come to Professor Hicks' qualification of Keynes' explanation of the nature of interest, or the reason for the existence of liquidity preference. In his *Value and Capital* (1939), Professor Hicks dissented from Keynes' view that a part of the interest paid on securities is attributable to a risk of default and that a part of the interest paid, at least on long-term securities, is to be attributed to uncertainty of the future course of interest rates. He wrote: "But to say that the rate of interest on perfectly safe securities is determined by nothing else but uncertainty of future interest rates seems to leave interest hanging by its own bootstraps; one feels an obstinate conviction that there must be more in it than that."[48]

To find the fundamental explanation of the existence of pure interest, Professor Hicks proceeded to consider the problem using a model of a system in which the securities are perfectly safe and perfectly short (i.e., so short that the rate of interest cannot change during its currency). Even in this case, people still would not invest all their surplus funds in securities. Why? Because "to convert this money into bills requires a separate transaction, and the trouble of making that transaction may offset the gain in interest."[49] Professor Hicks concluded: "Securities which are not generally acceptable in payment of debts bear some interest because they are imperfectly 'money'."[50] Accord-

---

[46] Harrod, *op. cit.*, p. 146.

[47] Reprinted from *The General Theory of Employment, Interest, and Money*, p. 178, by John Maynard Keynes, by permission of Harcourt, Brace & World, Inc.

[48] J. R. Hicks, *Value and Capital* (2nd ed.; London: Oxford University Press, 1946), p. 164.

[49] Hicks, pp. 164–165.

[50] Hicks, p. 167.

ing to him, the short-term rates measure the trouble of making trans-actions. He explained the long-run rates in terms of speculation regard-ing the future course of the short rate. "The system of interest rates for loans of various durations can thus be reduced to a standard type of short rate (the rate of interest for loans of one week) combined with a series of forward short rates: rates for loans of one week, to be exe-cuted not in the current week, but in some future week."[51]

Professor Robinson defended Keynes' interpretation. She com-mented: "Both Mr. Hicks and Mr. Kaldor display a lively horror of boot straps, but it is not clear how they propose to escape from them."[52] She pointed out that the Hicksian analysis was made under the as-sumption that "rational expectations must be self-consistent. It cer-tainly does not detach the rate of interest from dependence on its boot straps for, in such a world, the only reason for a difference between the short and long rates is the expectation of a change in the long rate."[53]

Professor Modigliani also maintained that Hicks' analysis was faulty. He pointed out that "it is true that money and securities are close substitutes, but this connection is to be found elsewhere than in de-grees of moneyness; it depends on the fact that both money and securi-ties are alternative forms of holding assets in nonphysical form. Securi-ties are thus close substitutes for money, but not for money as a medium of exchange, only for money as an asset."[54]

In conclusion, it may be said that Keynes' emphasis on treating money as an asset is an important contribution to monetary theory. Unfortunately, he overplayed his hand, and the Keynesian polemics took place. As aptly put by Professor Harrod, "By refusing to concede enough to tradition and going too far in certain respects, Keynes has caused what was new and true and important in his own theory to suffer undue neglect."[55]

---

[51] Hicks, pp. 145–146.

[52] Joan Robinson, *The Rate of Interest and Other Essays*, p. 18n.

[53] *Ibid.*

[54] Franco Modigliani, "Liquidity Preference and the Theory of Interest and Money," in *Readings in Monetary Theory* (Homewood, Ill.: Richard D. Irwin, Inc., 1951), p. 235; see also *Econometrica* (1944), p. 85.

[55] Harrod, *op. cit.*, p. 147.

# 10

# Post-Keynesian Developments in Monetary Theory

We examine post-Keynesian developments in monetary theory under four headings: (1) integration of monetary theory and value theory; (2) neutrality and non-neutrality of money; (3) theory of the demand for money; and (4) theory of the supply of money.

Much of the writing involved here stems from the disputed issues raised by *The General Theory*. Perhaps the most outstanding feature of post-Keynesian monetary theory is the trend towards a formulation of the theory of demand for money as a part of capital theory. As aptly stated by Professor Johnson, "contemporary monetary theorists, whether avowedly 'Keynesian' or 'quantity,' approach the demand for money in essentially the same way, as an application of the general theory of choice, though the former tend to formulate their analysis in terms of the demand for money as an asset alternative to other assets, and the latter, in terms of the demand for the services of money as a good."[1]

Another important development in post-Keynesian monetary economics—the concern with quantitative testing and measurement of empirical monetary relationships—is outside the scope of this book.

---

[1] Harry G. Johnson, "Monetary Theory and Policy," *American Economic Review*, LII (June, 1962), 344.

## INTEGRATION OF MONETARY AND VALUE THEORY

It was mentioned in Chapter 9 that one of the fundamental issues raised by Keynes in *The General Theory* is his attack on the classical separation of monetary theory and value theory. The two theories are integrated through his theory of output and employment.[2]

An alternative method of integration was subsequently suggested by Professor Patinkin in his *Money, Interest, and Prices*. By explicitly introducing the factor of real-balances as a determinant of economic behavior under the assumption of "pure choice," he demonstrated (1) that the "classical dichotomy" could be removed; (2) that the quantity-theory conclusions (i.e., in equilibrium, money is neutral and the rate of interest is independent of the quantity of money) could be validated; and (3) that involuntary unemployment is essentially a phenomenon of disequilibrium. These points were discussed in Chapters 4 and 5 of this book. The basic idea of removing the classical dichotomy and, hence, validating the quantity-theory conclusions, may be recapitulated by using the familiar *IS* and *LM* diagram as an illustration.

Figure 10-1 shows the initial equilibrium at point $(A)$ as a full-employment equilibrium, with full-employment output denoted by $(Y_0)$ and the corresponding equilibrium level of the interest rate indicated by $(r_0)$. The aggregate demand function underlying the $(IS)$ curve is in the form: $E = F(Y, r, M/P)$. Real-balances $(M/P)$ is one of the determinants of this aggregate-demand function $(E)$. The demand-for-money function underlying the $(LM)$ schedule has the form: $L = P \cdot L_1(Y) + P \cdot L_2(r)$. The money-illusion factor is not included in this function.

Now suppose that the quantity of money is increased. At the same $(r_0)$, there is an excess supply of money. The excess supply of money will be disposed of in two ways: (1) by increasing the demand for goods, which creates an inflationary gap in the goods market; and (2) by increasing the demand for bonds, which depresses the rate of interest. The temporary fall of the interest rate from $(r_0)$ to $(r_1)$ stimulates investment, which, in turn, adds to the inflationary pressure in the

---

[2] Keynes' attack was followed by a protracted investigation of the internal logical consistency of classical monetary theory. An excellent summary of the results of this investigation is given by Professors Gary S. Becker and William J. Baumol in "The Classical Monetary Theory: The Outcome of the Discussion," reprinted from *Economica*, n.s., Vol. XIX (November, 1952), in *Essays in Economic Thought*, Spengler and Allen, eds. (Chicago: Rand McNally & Co., 1960), pp. 753–771. One of the issues discussed in the literature is that of Say's Identity—mentioned in Chap. 2 of this book.

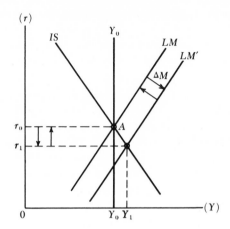

**Figure 10-1**

goods market. The excess money in existence is depicted by the downward shift of the $(LM)$ schedule; and a rising in price level is implicit in the increase in $(Y)$ from $(Y_0)$ to $(Y_1)$. Now, the real-balance effect emerges as an equilibrating mechanism. The desire to replenish cash balances, in order to maintain the same real balances, causes the demand for nominal money to increase. This means that the $(LM)$ curve will shift backward towards its original position. It also means that total spending will decrease and that the interest rate will start rising. Full-employment equilibrium is restored when the $(LM)$ schedule has reverted to its original position.

This simple exercise demonstrates the integration of monetary and value theories: The contradiction between classical value theory (in which demand and supply functions depended solely on relative prices) and the quantity theory (in which the quantity of money determines the absolute price level) is now removed by making the supply and demand functions for goods and services depend not only on relative prices but on real balances as well. This exercise also demonstrates that the quantity-theory conclusions can be visualized by explicitly introducing the real-balance effect in the general equilibrium analysis.

Another attempt to integrate value and monetary theories is implicit in the development of the aggregate-supply and aggregate-demand analysis by Professors Weintraub, Davidson, and Smolensky. The basic ideas of their analysis have been discussed in Chapter 5 above.

## Neutrality and Non-Neutrality of Money

Keynes attacked the neutral-money analysis of the classical school. To emphasize non-neutral money, he invoked the monetary theory of interest (liquidity-preference theory). Yet, in the 1940's, there was a "renaissance of classical economics." The architects of this renaissance were Professors Pigou, Scitovszky, and Haberler.[3] By explicitly introducing the liquid-wealth effect on saving (consumption), they have restored the internal logical consistency of the classical system.

Professor Lloyd A. Metzler in his innovative article *Wealth, Saving, and the Rate of Interest* (1951) further clarified the required assumptions for neutral money.[4] He pointed out that, although the "Pigou-Scitovszky-Haberler effect" had salvaged the "classical" mechanism of price flexibility and automatic full employment, it had unwittingly destroyed another feature of the classical system, namely, the real theory of interest.

According to Professor Metzler, we now have three theories of interest: (1) the classical real theory of interest, (2) the Keynesian monetary theory of interest, and (3) the modified classical system. The first two stand in polar positions and the last one occupies an intermediate position.

In the modified classical system, the capital market is subject to three main influences: (1) current saving and investment, as in the classical and neoclassical theories; (2) the decisions concerning the holding of cash or securities, as in the Keynesian doctrine; and (3) the impact of liquid wealth on current saving, as in the Pigou-Scitovszky-Haberler analysis. The equilibrium rate of interest is determined by the interplay of these three influences.

With the addition of the third influence, it is important to distinguish two types of monetary disturbance. If a change in the quantity of money comes about through the central bank's open-market operations, which affect the public's holdings of assets, the equilibrium rate of interest will be determined by monetary forces. Even in the classical

---

[3] See A. C. Pigou, *Employment and Equilibrium* (London, 1941), especially Chap. 7; also his "The Classical Stationary State," *Economic Journal*, Vol. LIII (December, 1943); Tibor Scitovszky, "Capital Accumulation, Employment and Price Rigidity," *Review of Economic Studies*, Vol. VIII (1940–41); and Gottfried Haberler, *Prosperity and Depression* (3rd ed.; Geneva: 1941); also his "The Pigou Effect Once More," *Journal of Political Economy*, Vol. LX (1952).

[4] Lloyd A. Metzler, "Wealth, Savings, and the Rate of Interest," *Journal of Political Economy*, Vol. LIX (April, 1951).

world of free competition and price flexibility, money is no longer neutral. On the other hand, if the increase in the quantity of money comes about either through an increase in exports or through an increase in gold production, the public's asset holdings will not be changed. In this case, money is neutral in equilibrium and the rate of interest is independent of the quantity of money.

Let us consider the reasoning that leads to the non-neutral money conclusion. The Pigou-Scitovszky-Haberler saving function may be written in the form:

$$S = f(Y, r, W)$$

where $(W)$ denotes wealth. For simplicity's sake, let us assume that the owners of private wealth hold such wealth in only two forms: money and common stock; and that the central bank is authorized to buy and sell the common stock (the only nonmonetary asset in the system). Hence the real value of private wealth may be represented by the equation

$$W = \lambda \frac{dY}{r} + \frac{M}{P}$$

where $(W)$ denotes the value of real wealth; $(\lambda)$ is the proportion of total supply of common stock held by private owners; $(Y)$ is full-employment real income; $(d)$ is the proportion of this real income consisting of business profits; $(dY/r)$ indicates that the real value of common stock is the capitalized value of business profits, where the capitalization is at the prevailing rate of interest $(r)$; and $(M/P)$ represents real balances. This identity equation defines the real value of private wealth as the sum of private security holdings and private money holdings.

Non-neutral money in this model may be illustrated with the *IS-LM* diagram.

Figure 10-2 shows that the initial position of full-employment equilibrium is at the point of intersection of the $(IS)_0$ and $(LM)_0$ curves. Every point on the $(IS)$ curve represents $I(r) = S(Y, r, W)$. The full-employment real income is $(Y_0)$, and the corresponding equilibrium interest rate is $(r_0)$. Now, the central bank increases the money supply by open-market purchases of privately held common stocks. The immediate impact shifts the $(LM)$ schedule from the original position $(LM_0)$ downward to $(LM_1)$. Simultaneously, the rate of interest falls from $(r_0)$ to $(r_1)$. The result is, of course, the emergence of an inflationary gap in the goods market. (Recall that the economy is under full-employment conditions.) At this point the real-balance effect ensues. The $(LM)$ curve starts shifting backward towards its original position.

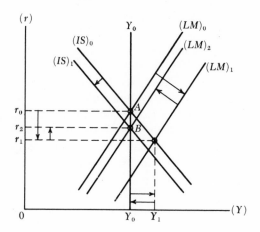

**Figure 10-2**

But the $(IS)$ curve at the same time also begins to shift downward, for $(\lambda)$, the proportion of the total supply of common stock held by private owners, has been reduced by the monetary authority. Consequently, consumption falls. Full-employment equilibrium is finally restored when the lowered $(IS)_1$ intersects the backward shifting $(LM)_1$ at $(B)$. While $(Y_0)$ remains unchanged, the equilibrium rate of interest is now lower than before. This means that the monetary authority can permanently lower the equilibrium rate of interest and can control the rate of economic growth.

Professor Johnson has observed: "Metzler's analysis of open-market operations implicitly rests on a distribution effect (the private sector but not the government being assumed to be influenced by a change in the latter's real debt); but subsequent writers, including Patinkin, have accepted this as a legitimate assumption, and Gurley and Shaw's analysis builds on it."[5]

Professor Patinkin, in *Money, Interest, and Prices,* and Professors Gurley and Shaw, in *Money in a Theory of Finance,* have presented several assumptions which they consider necessary to establish the neutrality of money:

1. *Wage and Price Flexibility:* Professor Patinkin points out: "If this is absent, the dynamic process . . . by which an increasing price level causes a negative real-balance effect in both the

---

[5] Johnson, *loc. cit.,* p. 341.

commodity and bond markets—and thus ultimately eliminates the inflationary pressures created by the initial monetary increase—clearly cannot operate. Hence the economy cannot be brought to a new equilibrium position."[6] Professors Gurley and Shaw agree: "Price flexibility is the unseeen hand that may maintain monetary equilibrium with a given nominal stock of money. Price rigidity shackles the unseen hand."[7]

2. *Absence of "Money Illusion"*: According to Professor Patinkin, "Once we accept the money illusion of his liquidity equation, Keynes' analysis of the effects of an increase in the quantity of money follows as a matter of course."[8] According to Professors Gurley and Shaw, "A . . . friction can be put into the model in the form of money illusion: spending units define their goals and make their plans in nominal rather than in real terms."[9]

3. *Absence of Distribution Effects*: In Professor Patinkin's words, "Assume, for example, that the redistribution of real incomes generated by a price increase is such as to decrease the demand for consumption commodities and increase the demand for bonds and money. That is, the individuals whose real incomes are increased by the price change have a higher propensity to save and lend than those whose real incomes are decreased. Then a doubling of the quantity of money will no longer leave the rate of interest invariant. For the 'forced savings' created by the price rise will cause the rate of interest to decline. The level of national income will remain the same, but its composition will change in favor of investment, as against consumption, commodities."[10] Professors Gurley and Shaw also think that monetary policy ceases to be trivial if there is distribution effect.[11]

4. *Inelastic Expectations*: Professors Gurley and Shaw state: "With some misgivings, spending units hitherto have taken it for granted that any equilibrium price level is the permanent

---

[6] From *Money, Interest, and Prices*, 2nd Edition, p. 275, by Don Patinkin. Copyright © 1965 by Don Patinkin. Reprinted by permission of Harper & Row, Publishers.

[7] John G. Gurley and E. S. Shaw, *Money in a Theory of Finance* (Washington, D.C.: The Brookings Institution, 1960), p. 43.

[8] From *Money, Interest, and Prices*, 2nd Edition, p. 278, by Don Patinkin. Copyright © 1965 by Don Patinkin. Reprinted by permission of Harper & Row, Publishers.

[9] Gurley and Shaw (2nd ed.; New York: Harper & Row, Publishers, 1965), p. 45.

[10] From *Money, Interest, and Prices*, 2nd Edition, pp. 285–286, by Don Patinkin. Copyright © 1965 by Don Patinkin. Reprinted by permission of Harper & Row, Publishers.

[11] See Gurley and Shaw, p. 43.

price level; they have had static price expectations, a special case of unitary elasticity of price expectations."[12] Professor Patinkin concurs that static expectations are a necessary assumption for the neutrality of money.[13]

5. *Absence of Government Debt or Open-Market Operations:* Professor Metzler has already demonstrated this required assumption for neutral money.

6. *Absence of a Combination of Inside and Outside Money:* Professors Patinkin, Gurley and Shaw have demonstrated that money is neutral if money is either entirely of the "outside" variety, or entirely of the "inside" variety. "Outside" money refers to money "based on the debt of a unit (the government) exogenous to the economic system itself."[14] "Inside" money refers to money "based on the debt of endogenous economic units."[15] According to Professors Gurley and Shaw, "Even within a strict neoclassical framework, however, monetary policy may not be neutral on real variables when there exists a combination of inside and outside money; that is, when the Banking Bureau holds both business bonds and 'foreign' securities or gold behind its monetary liabilities. Then an increase in nominal money, owing to the Banking Bureau's purchase of business bonds, increases the Bureau's holdings of real bonds proportionally more than its real monetary liabilities. This means that private sector's real holdings of business bonds are reduced relative to their real holdings of money. Hence, the equilibrium interest rate is lower, and other real variables in the economy will adjust. A combination of inside and outside money, then, permits the monetary authority to get a grip on levels of real income and wealth."[16]

## THEORY OF THE DEMAND FOR MONEY

Broadly speaking, there are two approaches to the study of the demand for money: the Keynesian and the neoclassical. As mentioned earlier, the two approaches have substantial common ground in that

---

[12] Gurley and Shaw, p. 44.

[13] See Patinkin, pp. 310–313.

[14] From *Money, Interest, and Prices*, 2nd Edition, p. 295, by Don Patinkin. Copyright © 1965 by Don Patinkin. Reprinted by permission of Harper & Row, Publishers.

[15] From *Money, Interest, and Prices*, 2nd Edition, p. 295, by Don Patinkin. Copyright © 1965 by Don Patinkin. Reprinted by permission of Harper & Row, Publishers.

[16] Gurley and Shaw, pp. 90–91. Professor Patinkin's discussion is contained in *Money, Interest, and Prices*, pp. 295–310.

they both involve analysis in terms of capital theory and as "an application of the general theory of choice." A related development in this area involves the definition of the money supply, or what Professor Johnson calls "the distinguishing characteristics of money."[17] The definition of money supply is important in this context because "a particular choice of definition may facilitate or blur the analysis of the various motives for holding cash."[18] Furthermore, a particular choice of definition also indicates, or delineates, the area in which monetary policy is effective.

In this section, we first briefly survey some of the developments in liquidity-preference theory; next we summarize the basic arguments underlying the restatement of the quantity theory of money; and finally we turn to the choice of a definition of the money supply.

### Developments in Liquidity-Preference Theory

*Professor Baumol's Analysis.*—The possibility that the transactions demand for money might be interest elastic was first systematically worked out by Professors Baumol and Tobin.[19] This development follows logically from the conception of money as an asset. "If an asset or spectrum of assets not including money can be found which satisfies the asset holder's desires for yield and safety, the simple Keynesian asset-demand hypothesis is no longer relevant to the holding of money balances, but rather determines the prices of the liquid assets or the structure of interest rates." If so, "then any interest elasticity of the demand for money which exists must be due to the interest-responsiveness of transactions demand."[20] In discussing the analysis of the interest elasticity of the transactions demand for money,[21] Professor

---

[17] Johnson, *op. cit.*, p. 351.

[18] See R. J. Ball, *Inflation and the Theory of Money* (Chicago: Aldine Publishing Company, 1964), p. 166.

[19] See William J. Baumol, "The Transactions Demand for Cash: An Inventory Theoretical Approach," *Quarterly Journal of Economics*, Vol. LXVI (November, 1952); and James Tobin, "The Interest-Elasticity of Transactions Demand for Cash," *Review of Economics and Statistics*, Vol. XXXVIII (August, 1956).

[20] Reprinted with permission from Ronald L. Teigen, "The Demand for and Supply of Money," in *Readings in Money, National Income and Stabilization Policy*, W. L. Smith and R. L. Teigen, eds. (Homewood, Ill.: Richard D. Irwin, Inc.), pp. 54–55.

[21] As pointed out by Professor Teigen, the hypotheses of Professors Baumol and Tobin also recognize "that there is an opportunity cost for holding transactions idle: it is the rate of return on time deposits or securities." Reprinted with permission from Ronald L. Teigen, "The Demand for and Supply of Money," in *Readings in Money, National Income and Stabilization Policy*, W. L. Smith and R. L. Teigen, eds. (Homewood, Ill.: Richard D. Irwin, Inc.), p. 55.

Baumol raises the question of "whether there is some way in which an optimum cash balance can be computed and, if so, how this optimum cash balance figure will be affected by changes in incomes and interest rates."[22] In answering this question, he applies the principle of determining the optimum level of inventories to the problem of determining the optimum cash balance held by a firm. The procedure is to first find the cash-balance cost equation. Once this equation is found we have obtained all the information required for the solution of the problem because the equation shows how the firm's objective (cost minimization) is affected by the different values of the variables in the equation. The cost equation is derived in the following way.

Assume that the transactions of the firm in question can be perfectly foreseen and occur in a steady stream. The optimization problem of the firm is to minimize the costs of holding transactions balances. Total costs of holding transactions balances consist of two components: (1) interest cost, and (2) noninterest cost. The former is in the nature of opportunity cost, which is the interest income foregone. The latter includes such cost items as brokerage fees, postage, etc., arising from converting cash into securities and vice versa. Thus the total cost equation may be written

$$TC = r\left(\frac{W}{2}\right) + n\left(\frac{T}{W}\right)$$

where $(TC)$ designates total costs; $(r)$ is the rate of interest; $(W)$ is the size of each cash withdrawal; $(W/2)$ expresses the average cash balance; $(n)$ denotes the noninterest cost of making one withdrawal; $(T)$ is the volume of transactions; $(T/W)$ is the number of withdrawals.

The least-cost combination is found by setting the derivatives $(dTC/dW)$ equal to zero and solving for $(W)$:

$$\frac{dTC}{dW} = \frac{r}{2} - \frac{nT}{W^2} = 0$$

$$\frac{r}{2} = \frac{nT}{W^2}$$

$$\therefore W = \sqrt{\frac{2nT}{r}}$$

It is clear that if the brokerage fee goes up, the number of withdrawals should be decreased. This is equivalent to saying that the optimal cash balance will rise. Similarly, if the level of the interest rate

[22] William J. Baumol, *Economic Theory and Operations Analysis* (1st ed.; Englewood Cliffs, N.J.: Prentice-Hall, Inc., 1961), p. 241.

goes up, it will pay to make withdrawals as small and as late as possible. Thus the optimal balance of idle, noninterest-bearing cash will fall.

*Liquidity Preference As Behavior Towards Risk.*—Turning now to the speculative demand for money, it will be recalled that Keynes introduced the "convention hypothesis" which permitted him to consider the concept of expectations redundant. Keynes' reference to uncertainty in the market was not related to an analysis of subjective doubt in the mind of the individual investor; rather, he apparently referred to the disagreement among investors concerning the future of the interest rate. Professor James Tobin in 1958 suggested an alternative foundation for Keynes' theory.[23] He explains liquidity preference as behavior towards risk.

According to R. Duncan Luce and Howard Raiffa, we have risk when the probability distribution of the outcomes is known to the decision-maker.[24] Thus the expected value of a decision is known to the decision-maker, although the specific result of an action cannot be accurately predicted. Uncertainty, on the other hand, exists when the probability distribution of the "state of nature" is completely unknown.[25] The decision-maker cannot even determine the expected value of a specific decision. Professor Tobin's analysis transforms the problem of uncertainty into one involving risk, for liquidity preference may be interpreted as preference for less risky forms of investment. There is no risk of return in holding money. But the element of risk plays an important part in holding bonds. Since the prospect of the return from bonds consists of many possible outcomes, the risk involved is predominantly the risk of capital loss. For the individual investor, the greater the proportion of his funds invested in bonds, the greater is the risk of capital loss from them. To bear this risk, the individual bond-holder must be compensated by an adequate return from bonds.

Here we have a decision-making problem involving risk. What is the appropriate decision rule? The classical approach is to define,

---

[23] James Tobin, "Liquidity Preference as Behavior towards Risk," reprinted from *Review of Economic Studies*, Vol. XXV, No. 2 (February, 1958), in *Readings in Macroeconomics*, M. G. Mueller, ed. (New York: Holt, Rinehart & Winston, Inc., 1966), pp. 173–191.

[24] Luce and Raiffa, *Games and Decisions* (New York: John Wiley & Sons, Inc., 1957), p. 13.

[25] Those options over which the decision-maker has no control are called "states of nature" in Game-Theory parlance. For instance, in a duopoly situation, the competitors' policies are beyond the control of the duopolist. Such policies are called "states of nature."

first of all, a subjective certainty-equivalent (or sure-prospect equivalent) return function for the individual investor. This function, in essence, is an indifference curve indicating what combinations of risk and return are judged subjectively by the individual to be equivalent. The nature of this function is illustrated in Figure 10-3.

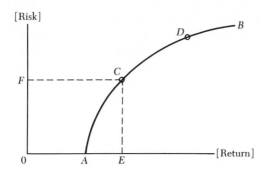

**Figure 10-3**

In Figure 10-3, risk is measured along the vertical axis and returns from investment in bonds along the horizontal axis. The curve (*AB*) is the certainty-equivalent indifference curve. It slopes upward because it shows that if the return of one prospect, such as depicted by point (*D*), is higher than another (say point *C*), its risk must also be greater. The investor is indifferent concerning the two choices. The shape of the certainty-equivalent indifference curve depends upon the investor's tastes and preferences. Suppose (*0E*) is the return of the original prospect. Then (*0F*) is a measure of the risk involved. (*0A*) is the certainty equivalent, for the risk involved is zero. The difference between the level of return and the certainty equivalent is the premium for risk.

Secondly, we need a measure of risk and a measure of the return from investing in bonds. The measure of return is the mean value of possible outcomes of pay-offs; the measure of risk is the standard deviation of the pay-offs.[26]

What are the pay-offs from investing in bonds? Briefly, they are of two kinds: (1) the interest, symbolized by (*i*), from bonds, and (2) the capital gain denoted by (*G*).

---

[26] For instance, a manager is estimating the sales from two projects; if the estimated sales of both projects are $1,000, the mean of each is $1,000.

If we let ($\lambda$) be the proportion of the individual's funds invested in bonds, then the mean value of his total return is:

$$u = \lambda(i + uG)$$

where ($u$) is the mean value of his total return; ($uG$) the mean value of his capital gain.

If the capital gain is zero, then the mean value of the total return depends entirely on two things: ($i$) and ($\lambda$). And $u = \lambda i$.

The risk associated with the return is obviously the risk of the capital gain. The interest is fixed and known; there is no risk involved in that part of the pay-offs. The measure of risk, therefore, is the standard deviation of the capital gain denoted by ($\sigma G$); the standard deviation of the total return can then be written:[27]

$$u = \frac{\sigma}{\sigma G} \cdot i$$

This equation is derived in the following way:

$$\sigma = \lambda \cdot \sigma G$$

$$\lambda = \frac{\sigma}{\sigma G}$$

Substituting this expression into the mean value of the total return equation, we obtain:

$$u = \frac{\sigma}{\sigma G} \cdot i$$

From this last equation, we derive the opportunity curve for the return and risk of various combinations of money and bonds. The nature of the opportunity curve is illustrated in Figure 10-4.

In Figure 10-4, the mean value of total returns from investing in bonds is measured along the vertical axis from the origin in an upward direction, the standard deviation (risk) of total returns and of capital gains along the horizontal axis, and the proportion of funds invested in bonds along the vertical axis from the origin in a downward direction.

Equation [$u = (\sigma/\sigma G) \cdot i$] is illustrated in the upper part of the diagram. Suppose that the standard deviation of capital gains ($\sigma G$) is equal to ($0M$), and that ($MN$) represents the fixed and known interest

---

[27] It will be recalled that the *mean* is a value calculated to be "typical" of the magnitudes in the distribution. The *standard deviation* indicates the extent to which items differ from this "typical" value. More specifically, the standard deviation ($\sigma$) is the square root of the variance.

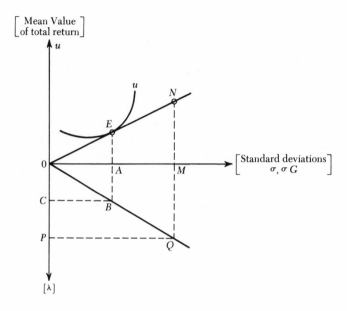

**Figure 10-4**

rate. Then the equation $[u = (\sigma/\sigma G) \cdot i]$ is reduced to $[u = i]$; and the relation can be represented by the line $(ON)$.

The lower part of the diagram represents the relation $[\sigma = \lambda \sigma G]$. If all the funds of the individual are invested in bonds, then the proportion $(\lambda)$ is equal to unity (or 100 per cent). The relation $[\sigma = \lambda \sigma G]$ can, therefore, be expressed as $[\sigma = \sigma G]$. It is depicted by the line $(OQ)$. For $(\lambda) = (OP) = (MQ)$, and the slope of $(OQ)$ is equal to the reciprocal of $(\sigma G)$, which, in turn is equal to $(OM)$.

Now we can superimpose the individual's certainty-equivalent indifference map upon this diagram. The optimum position of the decision-maker can now be represented by the point $(E)$, at which one of the indifference curves is tangent to the opportunity curve $(ON)$. The certainty-equivalent indifference curve is convex downwards, because the axes of risk and return have been reversed in this diagram. The opportunity curve $(ON)$ is represented by a straight line, for the mean value of the return is a weighted average of zero return from holding money and of a given mean value of return from the funds invested in bonds. The optimum position indicates that the individual will invest $(OC)$ proportion of his funds in bonds and will hold the remaining portion $(CP)$ in the form of money.

This is the alternative explanation of liquidity preference. As pointed out by Professor Tobin, "This theory does not depend on inelasticity of expectations of future interest rates, but can proceed from the assumption that the expected capital gain or loss from holding interest-bearing assets is always zero."[28] In other words, the explanation is independent of the Keynesian hypothesis that the individual will hold money if he expects bond prices to fall. Tobin shows this even for the case where the mean value of capital gains is zero. This idea is expressed by the relation $[u = \lambda i]$. Hence, this theory "is a logically more satisfactory foundation for liquidity preference than the Keynesian theory. . . . Moreover, it has the empirical advantage of explaining diversification—the same individual holds both cash and 'consols'—while the Keynesian theory implies that each investor will hold only one asset."[29]

*Professor Ralph Turvey's Analysis.*—With the introduction of a wealth variable as a determinant of liquidity preference, Professor Ralph Turvey in 1960 observed that the $(L)$ function would be different for a change in the quantity of money brought about by open-market operations than for a change brought about by fiscal policy.[30] His basic model may be summarized as follows:

The wealth of the private sector may be written:

$$W = M + NH \qquad\qquad \text{Eq. (10-1)}$$

where $(W)$ denotes wealth in the private sector; $(M)$ the given quantity of money; $(N)$ is the given number of bonds; $(H)$ is the price of bonds $(1/r)$; $(NH)$ is the value of the given number of bonds.

The demand for bonds may be written:

$$Dn = cW + dH \qquad\qquad \text{Eq. (10-2)}$$

where $(Dn)$ denotes the demand for bonds; the equation states that the demand for bonds is a function of $(W)$ and $(H)$; $(c)$ denotes $(\Delta Dn/\Delta W)$, the value of which is assumed to be less than unity; and $(d)$ denotes the marginal responsiveness of the demand for bonds to changes in bond prices $(\Delta Dn/\Delta H)$.

The supply of bonds is assumed to be given:

$$Sn = NH \qquad\qquad \text{Eq. (10-3)}$$

---

[28] Tobin, *op. cit.*, p. 190.

[29] Tobin, p. 190.

[30] Ralph Turvey, *Interest Rates and Asset Prices* (New York: The Macmillan Company, 1960).

Equilibrium requires that the demand for bonds equal the supply of bonds:

$$Dn = NH = cW + dH \qquad \text{Eq. (10-4)}$$

Solving for $(H)$:

$$H = \frac{cM}{(1-c)\,N - d} \qquad \text{Eq. (10-5)}$$

This equation indicates that the price of bonds $(H)$ will rise, if $(N)$ falls, or if $(c)$ rises, or if $(M)$ increases. With a simple monetary system in which money is the only alternative asset, the bond-preference theory is equivalent to liquidity-preference theory.

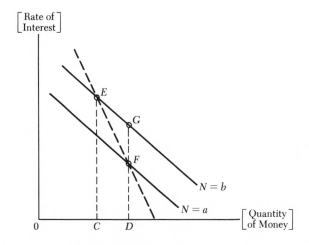

**Figure 10-5**

Professor Turvey points out that an adequate exposition of a liquidity-preference (or bond-preference) theory must explicitly state whether a "constant-number-of-bonds liquidity-preference curve" or an "open-market-operations liquidity-preference curve" is being employed.[31] The difference between the two curves is illustrated by Professor Turvey's own diagram in Figure 10-5. In Figure 10-5, the rate of interest is plotted on the vertical axis; and the quantity of money on the horizontal axis. Suppose that the number of bonds is fixed and equal to $(a)$. The "constant-number-of-bonds liquidity-preference curve" is the

---

[31] Turvey, p. 24.

curve indicated by $(N = a)$. This curve shows the relationship between the rate of interest, the number of bonds, and the quantity of money. It slopes downward because an increase in the quantity of money constitutes an increase in wealth $(W = M + NH)$; and an increase in wealth implies an increase in the demand for bonds $(Dn = cW + dH)$. The higher demand for bonds means lower bond yields (higher bond prices), which constitute an additional increase in wealth. This is shown symbolically by the Equations (10-5) and (10-1). The dotted line is another kind of liquidity-preference curve. This is the "open-market-operations liquidity-preference curve." Here an increase in the quantity of money from $(0C)$ to $(0D)$ is accompanied by a decrease in the number of bonds (open-market purchases of bonds by the Central Bank), and vice versa (open-market sales of bonds by the Central Bank).

In Figure 10-6, the central bank purchases bonds in the open market and thereby increases the quantity of money by $(CD)$. Originally the given number of bonds is $(b)$. The original "constant-number-of-bonds liquidity-preference curve" is indicated by $(N = b)$. Now the $(b - a)$ bonds are bought by the central bank. The given number of bonds is decreased from $(b)$ to $(a)$; and the constant-number-of-bonds liquidity-preference curve" shifts downward to $(N = a)$. The rate of interest falls by $(GF)$. This means that the price of bonds is raised. It should be noted that the fall in the rate of interest in this case is larger than in the case of an increase in the quantity of money brought about by increased gold production. Suppose the increase in the quantity of money $(CD)$ in Figure 10-6 is brought about by a method other than open-market purchases of bonds. There is no decrease in the number of bonds. The "constant-number-of-bonds liquidity-preference curve" will remain in the same position $(N = b)$. In this case, sliding down the curve will indicate a smaller decrease in the rate of interest (smaller increase in bond prices).

*The Gurley-Shaw Thesis.*—Professors Gurley and Shaw have introduced another determinant of the demand for money—the influence of nonmonetary financial intermediaries.[32] They view the functions of such intermediaries as turning "primary securities into indirect securities for the portfolios of ultimate lenders. They give lenders a wide variety of financial assets particularly suited to their needs, and they also make it less necessary for borrowers to issue these types of securities, which are ill-adapted to their own businesses."[33] According to

---

[32] Gurley and Shaw, *Money in a Theory of Finance*.
[33] Gurley and Shaw, p. 197.

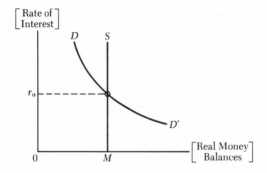

**Figure 10-6**

them, spending units' real demand for nonmonetary indirect assets depends on the following factors: (1) the level of real income, (2) real holdings of financial assets (in both quantity and quality), (3) the rate of interest on primary securities, (4) the explicit deposit rates paid by the monetary system and by nonmonetary intermediaries on their indirect debts, (5) the real rental rate on capital goods, and (6) the ratio of spending units' primary debt to tangible assets. "These are also determinants of spending units' real demand for money and primary securities."[34]

Equilibrium in the money market without the influence of nonmonetary financial intermediaries is depicted by Figure 10-6, which shows that the money market is in equilibrium when the real demand for money ($DD'$) is equal to the real supply (or stock) of money ($SM$). The equilibrium rate of interest is ($r_0$). This is the same as the Keynesian liquidity-preference theory. Now enter the nonmonetary financial intermediaries. Suppose that they offer more attractive deposit rates. This fact will cause the spending units to increase their demand for nonmonetary indirect assets and to reduce their demand for money by the same amount. "Consequently, the demand schedule for money shifts to the left so that there is a reduction in demand for money of $M'M$, at the interest rate $i_0(r_0)$, equal to the purchases of nonmonetary indirect assets. With the nominal stock of money unchanged, and at a given price level, the rate of interest falls from $i_0(r_0)$ to $i_1(r_1)$."[35] This adjustment is shown in Figure 10-7.

The analysis of Professors Gurley and Shaw affects the Keynesian

[34] Gurley and Shaw, p. 203.
[35] Gurley and Shaw, pp. 215–216.

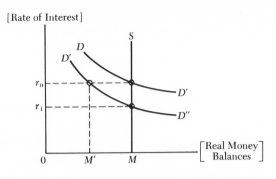

**Figure 10-7**

doctrine in two other related matters: (1) the "liquidity trap" and (2) the relationship between the rate of interest and the velocity of circulation of money.

Wih regard to (1), they point out,

> Again, in the Keynesian model, "the" interest rate may fall to a floor that is established by absolute liquidity preference on the part of spending units. One apparent effect of indirect finance, of the institutionalization of saving and investment, is to reduce this irreducible minimum. Nonbank intermediaries may drive bond prices high both because funds must be invested to cover operating expenses and because, while intermediaries are growing, the continuous net receipts of new funds make asset liquidation unnecessary. Growing intermediaries are "firm hands" that may acquire and hold both bonds and equidities at prices which would be unreasonably high in a more primitive financial system.[36]

Regarding (2), in Keynesian theory the interest rate is positively correlated with velocity given the quantity of money. Although there are many exceptions to the rule. The relationship is still more attenuated when allowance is made for the diversification demand for money and for the substitutability between money and other indirect financial assets. "While income and debt are growing, the public may reject money balances in favor of insurance reserves, pension funds, or perhaps saving and loan shares. Because money becomes a smaller share of total financial assets, velocity becomes a less reliable index of interest rates."[37]

---

[36] Gurley and Shaw, "Financial Aspects of Economic Development," *American Economic Review*, XLV (September, 1955), 531–532.

[37] *Ibid.*, p. 533.

It should be noted that the Keynesian analysis concentrated almost exclusively on the interest elasticity of the demand-for-money function (sliding along the same schedule).[38] On the other hand, the Gurley-Shaw analysis stresses the importance of the shifts of the schedule. The policy implication of this analysis is that " 'financial control' should supplant 'monetary control.' "[39] For "monetary control limits the supply of one financial asset, money. With a sophisticated financial structure providing financial assets, other than money and bonds, in increasing proportion to both, control over money alone is a decreasingly efficient means of regulating flows of loanable funds and spending on goods and services. Financial control, as the successor to monetary control, would regulate creation of financial assets in all forms that are competitive with direct securities in spending units' portfolios."[40]

The Gurley-Shaw analysis may be viewed as an example of the post-Keynesian trend of formulating monetary theory as part of the general theory of asset holding. Earlier, in 1951, Professor Musgrave's pioneering article, "Money, Liquidity and Valuation of Assets," had already set the trend in this direction.[41]

In this article, Professor Musgrave points out: "The central issue of monetary theory is the role of the money supply as a determinant of

---

[38] Professor Gardner Ackley [AER, XLVII (June, 1957), 672] in his comments on Professor S. C. Tsiang's "Liquidity Preference and Loanable Funds Theories, Multiplier and Velocity Analysis: A Synthesis," *American Economic Review*, Vol. XLVI (September, 1956), observed: "Keynes tended, despite formal disclaimers, to assume a stable speculative demand schedule, and to deal only with movements along this schedule. That is, he assumed a given level and structure of interest rate expectations by wealth-holders."

Professor Lawrence S. Ritter made the same point in "The Role of Money in Keynesian Theory," reprinted from *Banking and Monetary Studies*, D. Carson, ed., in *Readings in Macroeconomics*, M. G. Mueller, ed., p. 166.

[39] Gurley and Shaw, "Financial Aspects of Economic Development," p. 537.

[40] *Ibid.*

For criticisms of this thesis see Joseph Aschheim, *Techniques of Monetary Control* (Baltimore: The Johns Hopkins Press, 1961), Chap. 7; and J. M. Culbertson, "Intermediaries and Monetary Theory: A Criticism of the Gurley-Shaw Theory," *American Economic Review*, 48 (March, 1958), 119–131.

[41] R. A. Musgrave, "Money, Liquidity, and Valuation of Assets," in *Money, Trade and Economic Growth: in Honor of John Henry Williams* (New York: The Macmillan Company, 1951), pp. 216–242.

Professor Musgrave cited the following references for earlier contributions to a general asset theory: J. R. Hicks, "A Suggestion for Simplifying the Theory of Money," in *Readings in Monetary Theory* (Homewood, Ill.: Richard D. Irwin, Inc., 1951); J. Marschak, "Money and the Theory of Assets," *Econometrica*, Vol. VI, No. 4 (October, 1938); K. E. Boulding, "A Liquidity Preference Theory of Market Price," *Economica*, New Series XI, No. 42 (May, 1944).

expenditure levels."[42] However, "the importance of money as a determinant of expenditure levels arises in its $M_2$ use."[43] Specifically, "When asset holders, on balance, change their demand for $M_2$ relative to their demand for other assets, a revaluation of assets results and some change in income generating expenditures is likely to follow."[44] "It follows that the very concept of demand for asset money is meaningful only with reference to the demand for alternative assets: with respect to $M_2$ there can be no 'monetary' but only a 'general asset' theory."[45]

*Professor Tobin's "Portfolio-Balance" Approach.*—Professor James Tobin's "portfolio-balance" approach carries this line of development a step further. In his "Money, Capital, and Other Stores of Value" (1961), Professor Tobin outlines the way towards a synthesis of the Keynesian and quantity-theory approaches to monetary theory. He points out:

> A synthesis of the two approaches must, of course, avoid the arbitrary choices of both, abandoning the convenience of assuming that all assets but one are perfect substitutes. The price of this advance in realism and relevance is the necessity to explain not just one market-determined rate of return but a whole structure. The structure of rates may be pictured as strung between two poles, anchored at one end by the zero own-rate conventionally born by currency . . . and at the other end by the marginal productivity of the capital stock. Among assets that are not perfect substitutes, the structure of rates will depend upon relative supplies. In general, an increase in the supply of an asset—e.g., long-term government bonds—will cause its rate to rise relative to other rates, but less in relation to assets for which it is directly or indirectly a close substitute—in the example, short-term securities and money—than in relation to other assets—in the example, capital. In such a synthesis, monetary policy falls in proper perspective. The quantity of money can affect the terms on which the community will hold capital, but it is not the only asset supply that can do so. The net monetary position of the public is important, but so is its composition.[46]

## Restatement of the Quantity Theory of Money

The "orthodox" Keynesians have tended to neglect the role of money in the determination of aggregate demand. Their "anti-monetary doc-

---

[42] Musgrave, *op. cit.*, p. 216.

[43] Musgrave, p. 218.

[44] *Ibid.*

[45] *Ibid.*, p. 219.

[46] James Tobin, "Money, Capital, and Other Stores of Value," *American Economic Review*, LI (May, 1961), 34–35.

trines" implied that "money does not matter."[47] The modern quantity theorists, on the other hand, insist that "money does matter." Thus Professor Friedman points out in *The Quantity Theory of Money—A Restatement:*

> The Chicago tradition was not a rigid system, an unchangeable orthodoxy, but a way of looking at things. It was a theoretical approach that insisted that money does matter—that any interpretation of short-term movements in economic activity is likely to be seriously at fault if it neglects monetary changes and repercussions and if it leaves unexplained why people are willing to hold the particular nominal quantity of money in existence.[48]

Herein lies the essential difference between the quantity theorists and the Keynesians. The modern quantity theorists no longer employ Say's Law to explain the full-employment level of output, nor do they rely on institutional factors to explain the constancy of the velocity of circulation. Professor Friedman calls attention to the fact that

> The quantity theory is in the first instance a theory of the demand for money. It is not a theory of output, or of money income, or of the price level. Any statement about these variables requires combining the quantity theory with some specifications about the conditions of supply of money and perhaps about other variables as well.[49]

Since money is one of the assets in the economy, "the theory of the demand for money is a special topic in the theory of capital."[50] The

---

[47] The term "anti-monetary doctrine" was coined by Professor Culbertson in "United States Monetary History: Its Implications for Monetary Theory" in *The National Banking Review*, I, No. 3 (March, 1964), 359–379. He observed:
The nonmonetary interpretation of the Great Depression is the foundation of the Keynesian Revolution, of much of the macroeconomic theory still taught to the students, and of ideas still reflected in the formulation of economic policy. . . . It seems to me, as is indicated below, that the anti-monetary doctrines are untenable on their face and that the excellent and detailed review of the chronology of the Great Depression provided by Friedman and Schwartz may be what is needed finally to force a reconsideration of this whole period [p. 361].
Professor Lawrence S. Ritter points out that the emphasis on the interest-inelasticity of the aggregate demand function "has typically been construed by most Keynesians to mean that monetary policy is likely to be less effective in combating depression than in stopping inflation." Because of the fear that rising interest will choke off investment, the orthodox Keynesians "have at times objected to the use of monetary policy to stop inflation." "The Role of Money in Keynesian Theory," in *Readings in Macroeconomics*, p. 164.

[48] Milton Friedman, ed., *Studies in the Quantity Theory of Money* (Chicago: University of Chicago Press, 1956), p. 3.

[49] *Ibid.*, p. 4.

[50] *Ibid.*

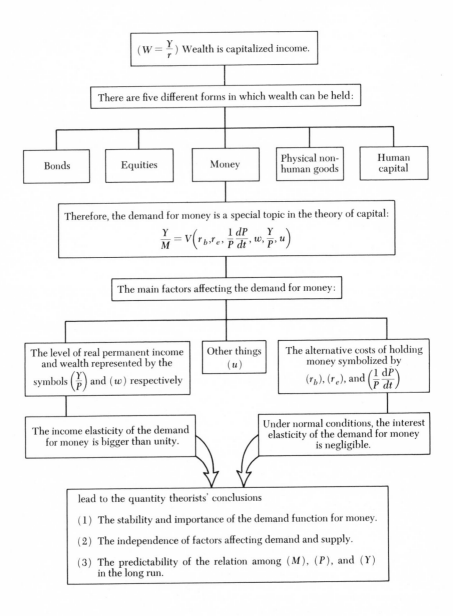

**A Formal Structure of the Factors That Influence the
Amount of Money People Want to Hold**

**Figure  10-8**

central points of Professor Friedman's restatement of the quantity theory of money are summarized in Figure 10-8.

Figure 10-8 demonstrates that Professor Friedman starts his analysis of the demand for money from the broad concept of wealth:

> From the broadest and most general point of view, total wealth includes all resources of "income" or consumable services. One such source is the productive capacity of human beings, and accordingly this is one form in which wealth can be held. From this point of view, "the" rate of interest expresses the relation between the stock which is wealth and the flow which is income, so if $Y$ be the total flow of income, and $r$, "the" interest rate, total wealth is $W = Y/r$.[51]

The concept of "income" relevant to his analysis is not the concept employed in national-income accounting. His "income" is defined as expected yield on wealth, or "permanent income."[52] Since permanent income is measured by an average of incomes in the recent past, it tends to fluctuate much less than "observed income." This is essential to the modern quantity-theory hypothesis that the demand for money is highly stable. We shall come back to this point after stating the other central points of Professor Friedman's theory.

Wealth can be held in five different forms: (1) money, (2) bonds, (3) equities, (4) physical, non-human goods, and (5) human capital. According to Professor Friedman:

> The analysis of the demand for money on the part of the ultimate wealth-owning units in the society can be made formally identical with that of the demand for a consumption service. As in the usual theory of consumer choice, the demand for money (or for any other particular asset) depends on three major sets of factors: (a) the total wealth to be held in various forms—the analogue of the budget restraint; (b) the price of and return on this form of wealth and alternative forms; and (c) the tastes and preferences of the wealth-owning units.[53]

---

[51] *Ibid.*
Professor Johnson observes:
Friedman's application to monetary theory of the basic principle of capital theory—that income is the yield on capital, and capital the present value of income—is probably the most important development in monetary theory since Keynes' *General Theory*. Its theoretical significance lies in the conceptual integration of wealth and income as influences on behavior.
See "Monetary Theory and Policy," *American Economic Review*, Vol. LII (June, 1962), p. 350.

[52] Friedman, p. 19. His "permanent income" hypothesis is discussed in "Theory of Consumer Behavior" in Chap. 5 of this book.

[53] Friedman, p. 4.

Thus, the demand for money (or its alter ego, the income velocity of circulation of money) may be expressed as a function of bond yields $(r_b)$, equity yields $(r_e)$, the rate of change of the price level $(1/p\ dP/dt)$, the ratio of non-human to human wealth or "equivalently, of income from non-human wealth to income from human wealth, which means that it is closely allied to what is usually defined as the ratio of wealth to income"[54] $(w)$, the level of real income per capita $(Y/P)$, tastes and preferences of wealth-owning units, and all other relevant factors $(u)$. Symbolically, the demand-for-money fnnction may be written

$$\frac{Y}{M} = V\left(r_b,\ r_e,\ \frac{1}{p}\frac{dP}{dt},\ w,\ \frac{Y}{p},\ u\right)$$

The three "major sets of factors" affecting the demand for real-balances are represented by the symbols enclosed in the brackets. According to Professor Friedman:

> This is a more sophisticated version of the quantity equation. . . . This $(Y)$ is simply money income. This $(M)$ is the stock of money, and this $(V)$ is velocity, but written so as to show what the factors are which influence velocity. . . . What velocity is depends on what the rate of interest is on bonds in general, what the rate of return is on stocks, that is, equity yield, what is happening to the rate of change of prices, what fraction of people's wealth is in the form of property, what is their real income, and this "u" is a symbol to remind you that there are some other things associated with the utility which the people attach to the holding of cash balances, such as about how readily available banks might be, how fast the mail is, and things like that, which need to be taken into account in a full analysis.[55]

To put it differently, aside from the host of "some other things" affecting $(V)$, or its reciprocal $(M/Y)$, the main factors affecting the real stock of money the public wishes to hold are: (1) the level of real income and the "fraction of people's wealth in the form of property" represented by the symbols $(Y/P)$ and $(w)$, respectively; and (2) the alternative cost of holding money symbolized by bond yield $(r_b)$, equity yield $(r_e)$, and the rate of change in prices $(1/p\ dP/dt)$.

According to Professor Friedman, the level of real income and wealth affects the desired real cash balances in the following way:

> In the first place, a change in real income affects the total volume of transactions to be affected. . . . This effect would lead to a

---

[54] Friedman, p. 8.

[55] *Employment, Growth, and Price Level,* report to the Joint Economic Committee, 86th Cong., 1st sess., 1959, p. 634.

change in the desired real stock of money in roughly the same proportion as in output.

In the second place, if there is a change . . . in per capita income, it means that people are at a higher or a lower level of living. With such a change in the level of living, they may want to increase their stock of money more or less than proportionately, just as an increase in the level of living means a less than proportionate increase in expenditures on bread but a more than proportionate increase in the stock of durable goods. It turns out empirically that in this respect money is like durable consumer goods rather than like bread, so that an increase in real level of living is on the average associated with a more than proportionate increase in the real stock of money.[56]

Furthermore, "the income to which cash balances are adjusted is the longer term level of income that can be expected, rather than the income currently being received."[57] All these factors point to the empirical hypothesis that the income elasticity of the demand for money is greater than unity. This means that over the long run, income velocity appears to be falling.[58] It also implies long-run stability of the demand-for-money function.

With regard to the cost of holding money, Professor Friedman observed:

Empirical evidence suggests that interest rates have a systematic effect in the expected direction but that the effect is not large in magnitude. The experienced rate of change in prices has no discernible effect in ordinary times, when prices are not expected to change by much. On the other hand, the rate of change in prices has a clearly discernible and major effect when price change is rapid and long continued, as during extreme inflations and deflations.[59]

---

[56] *Ibid.*, p. 610.

[57] *Ibid.*

In his "The Demand for Money: Some Theoretical and Empirical Results," *Journal of Political Economy*, Vol. LXVII (August, 1959), Professor Friedman points out:

If money holdings were adapted to permanent income, they might rise and fall more in proportion to permanent income, as is required by our secular results, yet less than in proportion to measured income, as is required by our cyclical results [p. 334].

[58] Professor Friedman observes:

In countries experiencing a secular rise in real income per capita, the stock of money generally rises over long periods at decidedly higher rate than does money income. Income velocity—the ratio of money income to the stock of money—therefore declines secularly as real income rises.

"The Demand for Money: Some Theoretical and Empirical Results," *Journal of Political Economy*, LXVII (August, 1959), 327. In this article, Friedman (basing his estimate on annual national data from 1869 through 1957) estimates the income elasticity of the demand for money to be 1.8.

[59] Friedman, *Employment, Growth, and Price Level*, p. 610.

These observations reinforce the empirical hypothesis that the long-run demand-for-money function is highly stable. In other words, the interest elasticity of the long-run demand function for money is negligible. This interest-inelasticity hypothesis is further strengthened by Professor Friedman's definition of the money supply. He defines money as currency plus demand and time deposits held by the public in commercial banks.[60] By including time deposits in the money stock, the effect of the interest rate on the demand for money is greatly reduced.

Now we see the link between the pre-Keynesian quantity theory and the modern quantity theory.[61] The distinguishing features of the "crude" form of the quantity theory are: (1) unitary income elasticity of the demand for money, or, what is the same thing, constant income velocity;[62] and (2) zero interest elasticity of the demand for money. The modern restatement retains the distinguishing features but with important qualifications.

In the first place, the modern quantity theory is no longer strictly a theory of the value of money. Its central emphasis is on the demand for money. Specifically,

> The quantity theorist not only regards the demand function for money as stable; he also regards it as playing a vital role in determining variables that he regards as of great importance for the analysis of the economy as a whole, such as the level of money income or of prices. It is this that leads him to put greater emphasis on the demand for money. . . .[63]

The emphasis on the demand for money is further highlighted by Professor Selden in the following quotation.

---

[60] See Milton Friedman and Anna Jacobson Schwartz, *A Monetary History of the United States, 1867–1960*, a study of the National Bureau of Economic Research (Princeton: Princeton University Press, 1963), pp. 4–5.

[61] Professor Friedman in *Employment, Growth, and Price Level* points out: The modern version of the quantity theory that has been developed as a result of this work is more sophisticated and subtle than the earlier version. Like that earlier version, however, it attaches great importance to the quantity of money as a determinant of prices and like it, also, it is consistent with centuries of experience [p. 608].

[62] This can be demonstrated by using the quantity equation, $M = kPY$. It should be noted that Professor Friedman uses the symbol $(Y)$ to represent money income $(PY)$; whereas in our previous discussions, we have used $(Y)$ to denote output. By definition, $k = M/PY$. If $(k)$ is assumed to be constant, then $k = \Delta M / \Delta PY$. The definition of income elasticity is:

$$e = \frac{\Delta M/M}{\Delta PY/PY}, = \frac{\Delta M}{\Delta PY} \cdot \frac{PY}{M}$$

$$\therefore e = k \cdot \frac{1}{k} = 1$$

[63] Friedman, *Studies in the Quantity Theory of Money*, p. 16.

Hicks, in his famous 1935 article, and Keynes, in the *General Theory*, deserve much credit for getting velocity theory back on the main track—although, paradoxically, both go out of their way to denounce the concept. The great merit of these works is that they view the demand for money in terms of the alternatives sacrificed by the holders of cash. Once the dust settled after the "Keynesian Revolution," it became increasingly apparent that there was no conflict between this way of looking at money and the traditional velocity approach.[64]

Secondly, although the modern quantity theorist "accepts the empirical hypothesis that the demand for money is highly stable," he rejects the mechanical constant-velocity (unitary-income-elasticity) assumption of the crude version of the theory. As mentioned earlier, modern quantity theorists have suggested that the income elasticity of the demand for money is greater than unity, or, alternatively, $(V)$ is subject to a long-term downward drift. Furthermore, they have pointed out that this downward drift of $(V)$ is subject to aberrations when interest rates and the expected rate of change in prices both change drastically.

As pointed out by Professor Friedman, "Almost every economist will accept the general lines of the preceding analysis on a purely formal and abstract level, although each would doubtless choose to express it differently in detail. Yet there clearly are deep and fundamental differences about the importance of this analysis for the understanding of short- and long-term movements in general economic activity."[65]

Thus, the modern quantity theorist rejects the "neo-Keynesian" thesis that the demand for money is infinitely elastic at some small, positive rate of interest. This, of course, is the famous liquidity trap, which negates the effect of a money-supply expansion on the interest-rate level during depression. In contrast, the modern quantity theorist argues that even in the Great Depression (1929–1933), monetary changes should be considered as a causal factor.[66] This contention has been powerfully corroborated by Friedman and Schwartz in their monumental work, *A Monetary History of the United States, 1867–1960.*

---

[64] Richard T. Selden, "Monetary Velocity in the United States," in *Studies in the Quantity Theory of Money*, M. Friedman, ed. (Chicago: University of Chicago Press, 1956), p. 233.

[65] Friedman, *Studies in the Quantity Theory of Money*, p. 15.

[66] In the Preface of the paperback reprint of the chapter in *A Monetary History* on *The Great Contraction 1929–1933* (Princeton, N.J.: Princeton University Press, 1965), the authors wrote: "We concluded that the wrong inference had been drawn from the experience of those four years, that the experience was a tragic testimonial to the importance of monetary forces, rather than evidence of their unimportance."

Professor Friedman's restatement and the Friedman-Schwartz's *A Monetary History* have exerted a marked impact on the development of macroeconomics. They have compelled monetary theorists to take another close look at the basic premise of *The General Theory* as a monetary theory.[67]

Professor Friedman's findings also have important policy implications. "The first is the closeness, regularity, and predictability of the relation among the stock of money, the level of price, and the level of output over any considerable period of years."[68] This proposition "means that in order to attain a reasonably stable price level over the long pull, we must adopt measures that will lead to a growth in the stock of money at a fairly steady rate roughly equal to or slightly higher than the average rate of growth of output."[69]

The second major policy implication "is our present inability to predict at all accurately this same relation over very short periods, from month to month, quarter to quarter, even year to year."[70] This means "that in the present state of our knowledge we cannot hope to use monetary policy as a precision instrument to offset . . . short-run forces making for instability. The attempt to do so is likely merely to introduce additional instability into the economy, to make the economy less rather than more stable."[71]

---

[67] For instance, Professor Culbertson observed:
The ambitious Friedman-Schwartz interpretation of United States monetary history provides a test of the state of monetary theory. What the test discloses is that the theory is in a terribly unsatisfactory condition.
Friedman also commented:
Although economists, from further thought and the pressure of evidence, have been swinging away from anti-monetary theoretical views, a thorough-going reinterpretation of the Great Depression that requires discarding economic maturity, liquidity trap, and "pushing on a string" will still be quite a wrench. Perhaps it will require "a long struggle of escape . . . from habitual modes of thought and expression." This is the more true in that it will require admitting that the "Keynesian Revolution" just conducted with so much enthusiasm and flying of banners was, in a basic theme, erroneous. Its premise was in error. The starting point of the Keynesian revolution was a version of the banking-school fallacy.
See "United States Monetary History: Its Implications for Monetary Theory," in *The National Banking Review*, I, No. 3 (March, 1964), 378 and 369.

[68] Friedman, *Employment, Growth, and Price Level*, p. 611.

[69] *Ibid.*

[70] *Ibid.*

[71] *Ibid.*

It should be noted that this is Professor Friedman's position and not necessarily inherent in the quantity theory of money. For a more complete statement of his position, see "A Monetary and Fiscal Framework for Economic Stability," *American Economic Review*, Vol. XXXVIII (June, 1948).

Professor Shaw seems to have accepted this position. See Edward S. Shaw, "Money Supply and Stable Economic Growth," in *United Monetary Policy*, The

What is the quantity-theory approach to the theory of inflation? The answer is that modern quantity theorists believe that inflation can be explained in terms of the demand for money. Professor Phillip Cagan's comparative study of seven hyperinflations and Professor Richard T. Selden's criticism of the cost-push thesis are two illustrations of this [72]

Professor Cagan believes that "hyperinflations at least can be explained almost entirely in terms of the demand for money. This explanation places crucial importance on the supply of money."[73] Money does matter, because past and current increases in the money supply tend to accelerate the rate of increase in prices. Professor Cagan's findings show that during hyperinflation the demand for real-balances ($M/PY$) falls drastically. "Only one of the variables that determine this demand has an amplitude of fluctuation during hyperinflation as large as that of the balances and could possibly account for large changes in the demand. That variable is the cost of holding money, which during hyperinflation is for all practical purposes the rate of depreciation in the real value of money or, equivalently, the rate of rise in prices."[74] Professor Cagan further points out: "To relate the rate of price rise to the demand for the balances, it is necessary to allow for lags. There are two lags that could delay the effect of a change in this rate on demand. First, there will be a lag between the expected and the actual rate of price rise; it may take some time after a change in the actual rate before individuals expect the new rate to continue long enough to make adjustments in their balances worthwhile. Second, there will be a lag between the desired and the actual level of the balances; it may take some time after individuals decide to change the actual level before they achieve the desired level."[75] "Thus the large changes in the balances during hyperinflation correspond to large changes in the rate of price change with some delay, not simultaneously. The demand function that expresses this correspondence can be interpreted to represent a dynamic process in which the course of prices through time is determined by the current quantity of money

---

American Assembly, Columbia University (Englewood Cliffs: Prentice-Hall, Inc., 1958).

[72] See Phillip Cagan, "The Monetary Dynamics of Hyperinflation," in *Studies in the Quantity Theory of Money*, M. Friedman, ed.; and Richard T. Selden, "Cost-Push and Demand-Pull Inflation, 1955–57," *Journal of Political Economy*, February, 1959.

[73] Cagan, p. 91.

[74] Cagan, pp. 86–87.

[75] Cagan, p. 87.

and an exponentially weighted average of past rates of changes in this quantity."[76]

Professor Richard T. Selden argues that the 1955–57 inflation can be adequately analyzed with the traditional tools of monetary theory, and that the role of costs has been greatly exaggerated. "In a proximate sense the 1955–57 inflation was caused by one or more of the following: an increase in the stock of money, an increase in monetary velocity, or a decrease in real income."[77] The role played by increases in the quantity of money during the 1955–57 inflation is revealed by the fact that, using 1954 as a base, the stock of money rose by 7.2 per cent for the entire period. However, the rate of growth of the money stock failed to keep pace with the rising tempo of economic activity. Real *GNP* for the period as a whole rose by 12.1 per cent. Hence the stock of money per unit of output fell by more than 3.5 per cent. This reduction was more than offset by an increase in velocity. The arch villain was, therefore, velocity, which increased 10.4 per cent over the three-year period. This increase in velocity, according to Professor Selden, could be attributed to five factors: (1) the increase in the stock of money, (2) the higher cost of holding money, (3) the expansion of substitute sources of liquidity, (4) the increase in government expenditures, and (5) the general rise in confidence, particularly on the part of businessmen.

The role of costs in this inflationary episode was not a major one. Why? The answer given by Professor Selden is as follows. In the first place, "the only plausible link between costs and inflation is the possibility that, when wages rose, wage-earners may have increased their expenditures more than stockholders reduced theirs, not because of different marginal propensities to hoard for the two classes of income recipients, but because of an asymmetry in the degree of awareness of income changes. However, even this could not have been an important factor in the recent inflation, since the most intense pressure on prices was experienced in capital goods rather consumer goods."[78]

Secondly, Professor Selden observes that velocity did not adjust passively to cost pressures as assumed by the cost-push theorists. Instead, the principal determinants of velocity were quite independent of costs. This is evidenced by the fact that, although the optimism of earlier years had dampened greatly by 1957, interest rates, the volume of money substitutes, and government expenditures continued to in-

---

[76] Cagan, p. 88.

[77] Selden, *op cit.*, pp. 5–6.

[78] Selden, p. 20.

crease. The pressure of costs also continued to increase. However, "velocity turned downward sharply in the final quarter of 1957, presumably because of a crisis in confidence. It does not seem reasonable to ascribe more than a minor part of these velocity changes to cost pressures."[79]

The quantity-theory position is brought into even sharper contrast by Professor Selden's reply to Professor Ball's criticism.[80] Methodologically, "both the equation of exchange and the Keynesian income identity consist of a set of pigeonholes within which monetary phenomena are classified. There appear to be several criteria for deciding which set is best for analysis of a particular problem."[81] The important ones are: (1) simplicity, (2) measurability, (3) the extent to which factors assigned to different pigeonholes are in fact independent, and (4) regularity—the extent to which the sum total of forces summarized within each pigeonhole behaves consistently in accord with some easily discerned hypothesis. Professor Selden points out that the Keynesian framework is less desirable in terms of the first, second, and third criteria. "With respect to the fourth criterion it is too early to give a definite answer. However, it is fair to say that no evidence has yet been produced, by Ball or any one else, to suggest that the variables of the equation of exchange are less predictable than those of the Keynesian system. At least for the present, therefore, no one need apologize for using the concept of velocity in the analysis of inflation."[82]

### The Choice of a Definition of Money

The choice of a definition of the money supply is fundamental to monetary theory—partly because "a particular choice of definition may facilitate or blur the analysis of the various motives for holding cash,"[83] and partly because a particular choice of definition has important policy implications, since it indicates the "area over which the monetary authorities under given institutional conditions are assumed to exert direct influence."[84] Broadly speakng, one may distinguish three alternative views regarding a definition of the money supply: (1) The Quan-

---

[79] Selden, p. 20.

[80] See Selden, "Cost Push Versus Demand Pull: A Reply," *Journal of Political Economy*, LXVIII (June, 1960), 297–300.

[81] *Ibid.*, p. 300.

[82] *Ibid.*, p. 300.

[83] R. J. Ball, *Inflation and the Theory of Money*, p. 166.

[84] *Ibid.*

tity-Theory view, (2) The Keynesian view, and (3) Radcliffism and its variants.[85]

The modern quantity theorists insist that a clear distinction be made between money and credit. Professor Friedman defines the quantity of money as follows:

> By the stock of money, I mean literally the number of dollars people are carrying around in their pockets, the number of dollars they have to their credit at banks in the form of demand deposits, and also commercial bank time deposits. That is the stock of money at any moment of time.[86]

Credit, on the other hand, is defined by Professor Friedman as "something that flows, loans outstanding for 3 months, or for 9 months, and with any given stock of money you can have widely different amounts of credit."[87] Professor Friedman further points out:

> The two are, of course, very closely connected. They are connected by what from one point of view is a historical accident, that creation of money has been combined in commercial banks with the lending and investing of funds. That isn't a technical necessity. You could have the stock of money completely separated from credit. For example, if, let's say, gold coins were the only money being used, there would be no connection between them in any direct way. Under our present system, they are very closely connected. Because of this close connection, there is a tendency to confuse two different kinds of effects of monetary policy. One effect of monetary policy is on the number of these pieces of paper [bank-notes] around to be used. Another effect is on interest rates through changes in the amount of credit or availability of credit, and these two effects need to be distinguished.[88]

The modern quantity theorists reject the Keynesian view that the link between the stock of money and output is the rate of interest.

---

85 Professor H. G. Johnson distinguishes four main schools of thought in this particular area: (1) Those who continue to find the distinguishing characteristic of money in its function as medium of exchange, and define it as currency plus demand deposits adjusted; (2) The Chicago quantity theorists, who define money as currency plus total commercial bank deposits adjusted; (3) Radcliffism—This school does not so much advance a theory as assert a position that implies a highly elastic, complex, or unstable velocity function; and (4) The Gurley and Shaw thesis —They have developed an analysis of the role of finance and particularly of non-bank financial intermediaries in economic development which has important implications for monetary theory. See "Monetary Theory and Policy," in *American Economic Review*, pp. 351–354.

86 Friedman, *Employment, Growth, and Price Level*, p. 621.

87 *Ibid.*

88 *Ibid.*

When they say that "money matters," they mean the first effect of monetary policy as stated by Professor Friedman in the preceding passage. More explicitly, they insist that a change in the stock of money "influences economic activity more directly because of the desires of the people to make the stock of money they hold conform to their other items of wealth, to their income, and to their situation in general. Thus a change in the stock of money, independently of its effects on credit, will have effects on the rate at which people seek to spend or the rate at which they seek to accumulate cash." [89]

According to the quantity theorists, the central bank's function should logically be confined to controlling the stock of money and not credit. Professor Friedman observes:

> Credit is of many kinds. Most credit in this country does not derive from banks. It derives from personal loans to others in the form of mortgages, or holding of stocks. It derives from transactions by financial intermediaries such as life insurance companies, investment trusts, and the like. There is no reason in principle, it seems to me, why those transactions should be controlled by legislation. [90]

The Keynesian view of what constitutes the money supply is the traditional view—i.e., money is defined as currency and demand deposits. It is generally recognized that, according to both traditional and Keynesian thinking, the supply of money is crucially important to monetary policy. [91]

Analytically, however, the Keynesians tend to highlight the indirect influence of the quantity of money on economic activity. It was unfortunate that certain features of *The General Theory*, such as the liquidity trap, underemployment equilibrium, autonomous investment and the multiplier, etc., "diverted attention from the influence of money and of price expectations on spending." [92] This is the origin of the anti-monetary doctrine of the "vulgar Keynesians." The point that we wish to bring forth, however, is that the choice of a definition of the money supply influences the analysis of the demand for money. By defining money as currency plus total commercial-bank deposits, modern quantity theorists minimize the interest elasticity of the demand func-

---

[89] *Ibid.*, p. 622.

[90] *Ibid.*

[91] See R. S. Sayers, "Monetary Thought and Monetary Policy in England," *Economic Journal*, Vol. LXX, No. 280 (December, 1960); and H. G. Johnson, "The General Theory After Twenty-Five Years," *American Economic Review*, LI (May, 1961), 15.

[92] Johnson, p. 15.

tion for money; by excluding commercial-bank time deposits from the definition of the money supply, the Keynesians are able to place greater emphasis on the interest elasticity of that function. The Keynesian definition of the money supply is implicit in *The General Theory.* There are four major classes of assets in Keynes's model: cash, bank deposits, bonds, and others. Cash and bank demand deposits are classified as money, and the rate of return on money is set at zero. With this definition of money, Keynes formulated his working model which, in turn, pointed out the way for shaping monetary policy.[93]

Turning now to Radcliffism and its variants, the break from the Keynesian view is best seen in the following excerpt from the *Report of the Committee on the Working of the Monetary System* (The Radcliffe Report):

> Though we do not regard the supply of money as an unimportant quantity, we view it as only part of the wider structure of liquidity in the economy. It is the whole liquidity position that is relevant to spending decisions, and our interest in the supply of money is due to its significance in the whole liquidity picture. A decision to spend depends not simply on whether the would-be spender has cash or "money in the bank," although that maximum liquidity is obviously the most favorable springboard. There is the alternative of raising funds either by selling an asset or by borrowing; and the prospect of a cash flow from future sales of a product both encourages commitment beyond immediately available cash and makes borrowing easier.[94]

According to the Radcliffe theory, the velocity of circulation of money is a meaningless concept.

> The artificiality of the concept lies, in short, in its reliance on a distinct and identifiable category of money; and one danger in using it lies in its encouraging us to overlook the relevance, to the pressure of total demand, of sources of credit outside this defined category. A further danger is that the definition normally used being either bank deposits plus notes, which (particularly the notes)

---

[93] James Tobin in his "Money, Capital, and Other Stores of Value" makes the following comments on the Keynesian model:

Though there are four or five assets in this model, there are only two yields: the rate of return on money, whether demand debt or bank deposits, institutionally set at zero, and *the* rate of interest, common to the other two or three assets. For the nonmonetary assets of his system, Keynes simply followed the classical theory of portfolio selection in perfect markets . . . that is, he assumed that capital, bonds, and private debts are perfect substitutes in investors' portfolios. The marginal efficiency of capital must equal *the* rate of interest [p. 30].

[94] *Report of the Committee on the Working of the Monetary System* (London: Her Majesty's Stationery Office, 1959), p. 132.

come fully into action only late in productive process, a rise in the velocity of circulation is a phenomenon that lags behind a rise in the disposition to spend. The existence of this lag should warn us against undue reliance on any corrective mechanism set up by "a rise in the velocity of circulation."[95]

With regard to monetary policy, the Radcliffe view is that "the authorities thus have to regard the structure of interest rates rather than the supply of money as the centre-piece of the monetary mechanism. This does not mean that the supply of money is unimportant, but that its control is incidental to interest rate policy."[96] The rationale is that "a movement of interest rates implies significant changes in the capital values of many assets held by financial institutions. A rise in the rates makes some less willing to lend because capital values have fallen, and others because their own interest rate structure is sticky. A fall in rates, on the other hand, strengthens balance sheets and encourages lenders to seek new business."[97]

The Radcliffe theory rejects the idea of controlling the entire range of financial institutions. "Such a prospect would be unwelcome except as a last resort, not mainly because of its administrative burdens, but because the further growth of new financial institutions would allow the situation continually to slip from under the grip of the authorities. The fact that operations on the structure of interest rates do, for institutional reasons, change the liquidity of financial operators throughout the economy should make it possible to avoid any such complex direct controls."[98]

The Gurley and Shaw analysis discussed previously in this chapter may be considered either a variant of the Radcliffe view or a fourth school of thought. Unlike the Radcliffe view, Professors Gurley and Shaw appear prepared to contemplate an extension of the central bank's control to include the liabilities of nonbank financial intermediaries.[99]

---

[95] Professor R. S. Sayers is a chief exponent of the Radcliffe view. See his "Monetary Thought and Monetary Policy in England," *The Advancement of Science*, No. 68, Nov. 1960, p. 306.

[96] *Report of the Committee on Working of the Monetary System*, p. 135.

[97] *Ibid.*, pp. 133–134.

[98] *Ibid.*, p. 134.

[99] Professors Gurley and Shaw observe:
The lag of regulatory techniques behind the institutional development of intermediaries can be overcome when it is appreciated that "financial control" should supplant "monetary control." Monetary control limits the supply of one financial asset, money. With a sophisticated financial structure providing financial assets, other than money and bonds, in increasing proportion to both, control over money alone is a decreasingly efficient means of regu-

## THEORY OF THE SUPPLY OF MONEY

In conformity with the post-Keynesian approach to studying the demand for money, contemporary monetary theorists generally treat the quantity of money as an endogenous variable in the context of a general theory of asset choice. It will be recalled that in the Keynesian analysis (for that matter, in the Patinkin system too), the money supply is considered a datum, with no reference to either the influence of non-bank financial intermediaries, or the link between the reserves created by the central bank and the profit-maximizing behavior of commercial banks. This new orientation completes the integration of value theory and monetary theory by introducing asset choice into the supply side of money. A supply-of-money function, relating the quantity of money to a number of independent variables, also emerges from this innovation in monetary theory, which, in turn, has implications for monetary policy. The Gurley-Shaw thesis outlined in the preceding section is one of the manifestations of this new line of thought.

In this section, we attempt to illustrate the above-mentioned points by providing the reader with a brief exposition of the works of some leading writers in this area. Our discussion is organized under two headings: (1) The effect of changes in income on the supply of money, and (2) the effects of changes in the demand for money and in central-bank actions on the supply of money.

### The Effect of Changes in Income on the Supply of Money

J. J. Polak and William H. White in 1955 first drew attention to a new relationship between inflation and the money supply with particular reference to countries with an open economy.[100] According to their observation, in countries with an open economy, a decrease in the volume of money may be a symptom of inflationary strains; on the other hand, an increase in the quantity of money may be associated

---

lating flows of loanable funds and spending on goods and services. Financial control, as the successor to monetary control, would regulate creation of financial assets in all forms that are competitive with direct securities in spending units' portfolios. "Tight finance" and "cheap finance" are the sequels of "tight money" and "cheap money."
"Financial Aspects of Economic Development," *American Economic Review*, XLV (September, 1955), 537.

100 See J. J. Polak and William H. White, "The Effect of Income Expansion on the Quantity of Money," *Staff Papers*, International Monetary Fund, Vol. IV, No. 3, August 1955.

with contractionary tendencies.[101] "It appears, then, that the direction of change in the quantity of money is by no means an unequivocal indicator of the direction in which the economy is moving. . . . It is necessary, therefore, to analyze the relation between changes in income and changes in the quantity of money in order to develop a theory of more general applicability."[102]

The essence of the Polak-White theoretical analysis may be summarized as follows.

Suppose the initial level of equilibrium income is disturbed by an autonomous increase in domestic spending either by the government, or private investors. Through the operation of the multiplier, income will start to expand. "When income expands in an open economy, the money supply will be subject to two different pressures."[103] On the one hand, there will be a tendency for the money supply to increase. The chain of causations leading to this result is: (1) the increase in income will cause an increase in the demand for transactions balances; (2) the demand for bank credit will also tend to rise; (3) the multiple expansion of derived deposits by the commercial banking system will increase the supply of money.

On the other hand, there will be a tendency for the money supply to decrease. "Higher incomes will lead to higher imports. Exports will tend to decline as more resources are absorbed internally. If the balance of payments was just in equilibrium before the expansion phase started, it will now show a deficit. The public will buy more foreign exchange from the banks than it sells to the banks and, in the process, will reduce its holdings of money by an amount equal to the net reduction in the country's foreign exchange holdings. As the reserves of the banking system decline, and the central bank takes no steps to offset this decline, the banking system will wish to have less money outstanding."[104]

*

---

[101] Polak and White based their initial observations on the Annual Reports of the Netherlands Bank for 1951 and 1952. The Reports drew attention to the following phenomenon:

> The period from the latter part of 1950 through the first half of 1951 was without doubt one of inflation in the Netherlands; but the money supply fell in the fourth quarter of 1950 and in the first two quarters of 1951. The economic position was reversed around the middle of 1951, and the second half of the year, as well as the whole of 1952, was characterized by disinflationary or mild deflationary conditions; during that period the money supply consistently rose.

*Staff Papers*, p. 398.

[102] Polak and White, p. 399.

[103] *Ibid.*, p. 400.

[104] *Ibid.*, p. 401.

The interaction of the two opposing tendencies will lead to an increase in the rate of interest (assuming that the central bank adheres to a neutral monetary policy). What of the supply of money? "There may be an increase or decrease of the money supply depending on a number of elements which can most conveniently be discussed by means of a chart."[105] In Figure 10-9, the rate of interest $(r)$, is plotted on the vertical axis and the quantity of money on the horizontal axis. Both the demand for money and the supply of money are considered in a schedule sense. Other things being equal, both the demand for money and the supply of money are treated as functions of the rate of

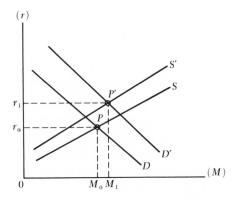

**Figure 10-9**

interest. (Note that a supply of money function has emerged.) The demand for money varies inversely with the rate interest. This is based on the assumption that the public "wants more money at a given rate of interest, but it will squeeze its holdings of money as they become more expensive."[106] The supply of money is considered a decreasing function of the rate of interest. The reason is that the banks "want a smaller money supply, but they are willing, within limits, to give in to the pressure for more money by squeezing their reserve ratios as the rate of interest goes up."[107] Point $(P)$ in Figure 10-9 represents the initial equilibrium position with the initial money supply $(M_0)$ and the equilibrium rate of interest $(r_0)$. When income expands, the demand schedule

105 *Ibid.*
106 *Ibid.*
107 *Ibid.*

(D) will shift upward and to the right to (D′), and the supply schedule (S) will shift upward but to the left to (S′). The distance of the shift of the demand schedule will be determined mainly by the magnitude of the income velocity of money, whereas the distance of the shift of the supply schedule will depend upon the loss of international reserves and on the reserve ratio (the ratio of reserves to deposit liabilities plus currency in circulation) of the commercial banks. At the new equilibrium position (P′), the rate of interest will undoubtedly be higher (from $r_0$ to $r_1$). However, the change in the money supply is not at all certain. Other things being equal, "the following five factors will determine whether changes in the quantity of money and changes in income are in the same or in opposite directions: (1) the income velocity of money, (2) the marginal propensity to import, (3) the reserve ratio of the banking system, (4) the elasticity of demand for money with respect to the rate of interest on the part of the public, and (5) the elasticity of supply of money with respect to the rate of interest on the part of the banks."[108]

If an approximately equal horizontal shift of the demand and the supply curves occur, the result, as far as the money supply is concerned, depends on the relative elasticity of the two curves. In Figure 10-9, the supply curve is drawn as more elastic than the demand curve. Hence, (P′) lies to the right of (P). If the supply curve is less elastic than the demand curve, (P′) will lie to the left of (P).

Symbolically, the preceding analysis may be represented by a system of five equations:

$$M_d = a(Y) + b(r) \qquad \text{Eq. (10-6)}$$
$$M_s = c(R) + d(r) \qquad \text{Eq. (10-7)}$$
$$Y = \frac{1}{1 - c + m}(A) \qquad \text{Eq. (10-8)}$$
$$R = [-t(Imp)] = -t(mY) \qquad \text{Eq. (10-9)}$$
$$M_d = M_s \qquad \text{Eq. (10-10)}$$

Equation (10-6) is the demand-for-money function. It states that the demand for money $(M_d)$ is a function of national income $(Y)$ and the rate of interest $(r)$. The symbols, $(a)$ and $(b)$, in the equations are parameters. Equation (10-7) is the money-supply equation. The main point here is that the money supply is no longer treated as an exogenously given variable. It is now treated as an endogenous variable, which is functionally related to commercial-bank reserves $(R)$ and the rate of interest $(r)$. The symbols $(c)$ and $(d)$ are also parameters. Equa-

---

[108] *Ibid.*, p. 404.

tion (10-8) is a reduced form of the truncated Keynesian model of an open economy, and is derived from the following system of equations:

$$Y = C + I + X - Imp \qquad \text{Eq. (10-11)}$$
$$C = cY \qquad \text{Eq. (10-12)}$$
$$I = I_0 \qquad \text{Eq. (10-13)}$$
$$X = X_0 \qquad \text{Eq. (10-14)}$$
$$Imp = mY \qquad \text{Eq. (10-15)}$$

Equation (10-11) is the definition of equilibrium income. Equations (10-12) and (10-15) are the consumption and import $(Imp)$ functions respectively. Consumption $(C)$ is related to $(Y)$ through the marginal propensity to consume $(c)$, and Imports $(Imp)$ are also related to $(Y)$ through the marginal propensity to import $(m)$. Both domestic private investment $(I)$ and exports $(X)$ are treated as known constants. The reduced form of the system is derived by substituting equations (10-12), (10-13), (10-14), and (10-15) in Equation (10-11):

$$Y = (cY) + (I_0) + (X_0) - (mY)$$
$$Y - cY + mY = I_0 + X_0 = A \text{ (where } A \text{ is autonomous expenditures)}$$
$$Y (1 - c + m) = A$$
$$Y = \frac{1}{1 - c + m}(A)$$

Turning now to the Polak-White model, Eq. (10-9) is a behavioral equation which functionally relates bank reserves $(R)$ to imports. It states that an autonomous expenditure $(A)$ will lead to a change in national income $[Y = (1/[1 - c + m]) (A)]$ which, in turn, will lead to a change in commercial banks' reserves $(R)$ equal to the annual increase in imports multiplied by the period $(t)$, during which the changed level of $(Y)$ persists. The negative sign indicates, of course, the inverse relationship between imports and reserves.

Equation (10-10) in the Polak-White model is the definition of equilibrium in the money market.

The first conclusion, that a change in $(Y)$ will lead to a change in $(r)$ in the same direction, may be stated more rigorously as follows. By substituting Eq. (10-9) in Eq. (10-7), we have

$$M_s = c (-tmY) + d (r)$$

If we substitute this new expression for $(M_s)$ in Eq. (10-10) and also substitute Eq. (10-6) for $(M_d)$ in the same equation, we have

$$a(Y) - b(r) = -tcm(Y) + d (r)$$

Solving for $(r)$:

$$a(Y) + tcm(Y) = d(r) + b(r)$$
$$Y(a + tcm) = r\,(d + b)$$
$$r = \left(\frac{a + tcm}{d + b}\right) Y$$

We have now expressed $(r)$ in terms of $(Y)$. In the above expression, all coefficients are positive, and a change in $(Y)$ will cause a change in $(r)$ in the same direction.

The second conclusion concerning the effects of changes in $(Y)$ on the quantity of money $(M_s)$ can be stated by expressing $(M_s)$ in terms of $(Y)$:

$$M_s = -tcm(Y) + d(r)$$

Substituting the expression $[r = ([a + tcm]/[d + b])\,Y]$ in the above equation, we have

$$M_s = -tcm\,(Y) + d\left(\frac{a + tcm}{d + b}\right) Y$$
$$M_s = -tcm\,(Y) + \frac{daY + dtcmY}{d + b}$$
$$M_s = \left(\frac{da - btcm}{d + b}\right) Y$$

Now we have expressed $(M_s)$ in terms of $(Y)$. Will a change in $(Y)$ lead to a change in $(M_s)$ in the same direction? It is not at all clear, because the numerator of the preceding expression is of uncertain sign. For $(t = 0)$, the numerator is positive; for sufficiently large values of $(t)$, it must become negative. In other words, for small time periods, $(M_s)$ will deviate from its original position in the same direction as $(Y)$; for long time periods, the deviation of $(M_s)$ from $(Y)$ will be in the opposite direction.

The preceding analysis clearly shows that the supply-of-money function is a crucial element in post-Keynesian monetary theory. In the Polak-White model, the supply of money function is:

$$M_s = -tcm(Y) + d(r).$$

This function is derived from one set of behavioral assumptions for both the public and commercial banks. It follows that different formulations of the function can be obtained from different sets of behavioral assumptions for the parties concerned. Such a money-supply function clearly facilitates the prediction of the effects of changes in the public's demand for money as well as the effects of changes in central-bank actions on the money supply.

## The Effects of Changes in the Demand for Money and Changes in Central-Bank Actions on the Money Supply

The effects of changes in the demand for money on the money supply have been discussed by Professors Gurley and Shaw. As mentioned earlier, they introduced the influence of nonmontary financial intermediaries as an important determinant of the demand for money. The link between the demand for money and the money supply is described by them as follows:

> The more adequate the non-monetary financial assets are as substitutes for money in transactions, precautionary, speculative, and diversification balances, the smaller may be the money supply for any designated level of national income. For any level of income, the money supply is indeterminate until one knows the degree of substitutability between money created by banks and financial assets created by other intermediaries. How big the monetary system is depends in part on the intensity of competition from savings banks, life insurance companies, pension funds, and other intermediaries.[109]

They further point out that financial competition may inhibit the growth of the monetary system, hence the growth of the money supply, in several ways. In the first place, "given the level of national income, a gain in attractiveness of say, savings and loan shares vis-à-vis money balances must result in an excess supply of money. The monetary authority may choose to remove this excess. Then bank reserves, earning assets, money issues, and profits are contracted. This implies that, at any level of income, the competition of nonmonetary intermediaries may displace money balances, shift primary securities from banks to their competitors, and reduce the monetary system's requirement for reserves."[110]

Secondly, even if the central bank does not choose to destroy the excess money created by the competition of nonmonetary financial assets, the growth of the money supply may still be retarded. The explanation is that the excess money "may be used to repay bank loans

---

[109] See J. G. Gurley and E. S. Shaw, "Financial Intermediaries and the Saving-Investment Process," reprinted from *Journal of Finance*, Vol. II (March, 1956), in *Monetary Theory and Policy*, R. S. Thorn, ed. (New York: Random House, Inc., 1966), p. 367.

[110] *Ibid.*

or to buy other securities from banks, the result being excess bank reserves."[111] But cannot banks use these excess reserves to make loans and investments? "They can do so by accepting a reduced margin between the yield of primary securities they buy and the cost to them of deposits and currency they create. But this option is not peculiar to banks: other intermediaries can stimulate demand for their debt if they stand ready to accept a reduced markup on the securities they create and sell relative to the securities they buy. The banks can restore the money supply, but the cost is both a decline in their status relative to other financial intermediaries and a reduction of earnings."[112]

Lastly, "the banks may choose to live with excess reserves rather than pay higher prices on primary securities or higher yields on their own debt issues. In this case, as in the previous two, a lower volume of reserves is needed to sustain a given level of national income."[113]

The trend of post-Keynesian analysis regarding how central-bank actions affect the money supply is clearly reflected in the writing of Professor Ronald Teigen.[114] In order to take account of the fact that the money supply is determined both by the policy actions of the central bank and by decisions of commercial banks, Professor Teigen introduces the following behavioral assumptions for the monetary system:

> Commercial banks act in a profit-maximizing way in response to changes in the return from lending relative to cost. Both the return and the cost are represented by short-term interest rates: in principle, the return is the yield on loans, and the cost is measured by the cost of acquiring the reserves necessary to support the new loans. When it becomes more profitable to make loans, banks are assumed to be willing to supply more deposits and to increase the money stock. However, member banks are constrained in supplying deposits by the reserve requirements imposed by the Federal Reserve System, and if excess reserves are scarce, member banks will tend to increase their borrowing.[115]

On the basis of this behavioral assumption, Professor Teigen formulates a money-supply function in the following equation.

---

[111] *Ibid.*

[112] *Ibid.*, p. 367–368.

[113] *Ibid.*, p. 368.

[114] See Ronald L. Teigen, "The Demand and Supply of Money," in *Readings in Money, National Income and Stabilization Policy*, pp. 44–76.

[115] Reprinted with permission from Ronald L. Teigen, "The Demand and Supply of Money," in *Readings in Money, National Income and Stabilization Policy*, W. L. Smith and R. L. Teigen, eds. (Homewood, Ill.: Richard D. Irwin, Inc.), p. 60.

$$\frac{M}{M^*} = f[(r - r_d)]$$

where $(M)$ is the stock of money; $(M^*)$ is defined as the amount of money which could be supported by unborrowed reserves (i.e., reserves created at the initiative of the Federal Reserve System instead of by borrowing), based on existing reserve requirements and other institutional charactristics of the system; $(r)$ represents the short-term interest rate; and $(r_d)$ measures the cost of lending.

It should be noted that Professor Teigen does not treat the money stock $(M)$ as the usual dependent variable. Instead, he uses the ratio $(M/M^*)$, in order "to take account of the fact that either the member banks or the System can initiate reserve changes."[116] $(M^*)$ is derived by Professor Teigen in the following way:

First, he introduces the following definition of total member banks reserves:

$$R = R^u + B = R^r + R^e \qquad \text{Eq. (10-16)}$$

$R$ = total reserves of member banks
$R^u$ = unborrowed reserves held by member bank
$B$ = borrowings from the Federal Reserve by member banks
$R^r$ = member bank required reserves
$R^e$ = member bank excess reserves.

"To avoid complications, time deposit required reserves are omitted from these definitions."[117] In view of the impact on bank reserves of the currency in the hands of the nonbank public, Professor Teigen introduces another variable $(R^*)$, which is defined as the sum of member-bank reserves supplied at the initiative of the Federal Reserve System and the currency stock in the hands of the nonbank public $(P)$:

$$R^* = R^u + P \qquad \text{Eq. (10-17)}$$

The stock of money is defined to consist of: currency in circulation $(P)$; demand deposits in member banks $(D')$; and demand deposits in nonmember banks $(D'')$:

$$M = P + D' + D'' \qquad \text{Eq. (10-18)}$$

It is further assumed that both currency in circulation $(P)$ and nonmember bank deposits are proportional to the money stock:

---

116 Reprinted with permission from Ronald L. Teigen, "The Demand and Supply of Money," in *Readings in Money, National Income and Stabilization Policy*, W. L. Smith and R. L. Teigen, eds. (Homewood, Ill.: Richard D. Irwin, Inc.), p. 60.

117 Reprinted with permission from Ronald L. Teigen, "The Demand and Supply of Money," in *Readings in Money, National Income and Stabilization Policy*, W. L. Smith and R. L. Teigen, eds. (Homewood, Ill.: Richard D. Irwin, Inc.), p. 60.

$$P = pM \qquad 0 < p < 1 \qquad \text{Eq. (10-19)}$$
$$D'' = hM \qquad 0 < h < 1 \qquad \text{Eq. (10-20)}$$

The next step is to substitute Eqs. (10-19) and (10-20) in Eq. (10-18); we have:

$$M = pM + hM + D' \text{ or} \qquad \text{Eq. (10-21)}$$

$$M = \frac{1}{1 - p - h} D' \qquad \text{Eq. (10-22)}$$

If the average reserve requirement is symbolized by $(g)$, then $R^r = gD'$, or

$$D' = \frac{1}{g} R^r \qquad \text{Eq. (10-23)}$$

By substituting Eq. (10-23) in Eq. (10-22), we get:

$$M = \frac{1}{g(1 - p - h)} R^r \qquad \text{Eq. (10-24)}$$

From Eq. (10-16), we may define member-bank required reserves as: $R^r = R^u + (B - R^e)$. By substituting this equation in Eq. (10-24), we obtain:

$$M = \frac{1}{g(1 - p - h)} [R^u + (B - R^e)]$$

If members' excess reserves were zero, the last equation tells us that the largest possible money stock at any point of time, given the institutional framework, is based on two types of reserves. First, part of this maximum possible money stock is based on unborrowed reserves, or on reserves which arose at the initiative of the Federal Reserve System. This part of the money stock is defined by $(M^*)$; that is

$$M^* = \frac{1}{g(1 - p - h)} R^u \qquad \text{Eq. (10-25)}$$

The second or remaining part of the maximum possible money stock is based on borrowed reserves $(B)$. $(M^*)$, of course, is a monetary-policy variable. Through open-market operations, or changing reserve requirements, the Federal Reserve System can affect $(M^*)$.

Turning now to Professor Teigen's money-supply function, $M/M^* = f[(r - r_d)]$, the effect of central bank actions on the money supply is represented by $(M^*)$. Given the $(M^*)$, the money supply will increase at the initiative of the commercial banks, when $(r)$, the return on lending, is greater than $(r_d)$, the cost of acquiring reserves from the central bank.

The effects of central-bank actions on the money supply have been analyzed by Professor George S. Tolley from a different standpoint.[118] He has suggested a simple framework for analyzing decisions concerning the money supply. First, a basic identity is introduced in the form of the familiar Cambridge equation of exchange:

$$M = kPY \qquad \text{Eq (10-26)}$$

Next, he brought forth the definition of member-bank reserve base:

$$R = gM \qquad \text{Eq (10-27)}$$

where $(R)$ is the reserve base, which is comprised of currency in circulation plus member-bank reserve; $(g)$ represents the member-bank average reserve ratio, which is the ratio of the reserve base to the money supply $(R/M)$; and $(M)$ is the money supply. It follows that $M = 1/g(R)$.

By substituting Eq. (10-27) in Eq. (10-26), we obtain:

$$R = g(kPY) \qquad \text{Eq (10-28)}$$

The basic identity sets out a few important variables on which attention may usefully be centered in analyzing the behavioral relationship concerning the money supply. "An advantage of the framework is that it permits a simple summary of the factors relating the money supply to government."[119] For instance, the central bank can affect the average reserve ratio $(g)$ by changing the legal reserve requirements. The central bank can also affect the reserve base $(R)$ by open-market operations. The important point brought forth by Professor Tolley, however, is that "decisions concerning the growth of the quantity of money may both affect and be affected by broader choices concerning the level of taxes and government expenditures and the management of the national debt."[120] The interrelationships between central-bank actions, the money supply, and the national debt are described by Professor Tolley as follows:

> If we momentarily neglect changes in the gold stock, we see that the Federal Reserve banks in the normal course of their opera-

---

[118] See George S. Tolley, "Providing for Growth of the Money Supply," reprinted from *Journal of Political Economy*, Vol. LXV (December, 1957), in *Monetary Theory and Policy*, R. S. Thorn, ed. (New York: Random House, Inc., 1966), pp. 382–409.

[119] *Ibid.*, p. 405.

[120] *Ibid.*, p. 382.

tions—open-market operations and the like—must find themselves accumulating earning assets, mainly government bonds. Increases in earning assets of the Federal Reserve banks are a major part of the debt retirement associated with growth of the money supply. The view advanced here is that the holdings of securities of the Federal Reserve banks should be substracted from the nominal national debt if we are to get a meaningful picture of the debt.[121]

Having considered the money supply as a source of debt retirement, Professor Tolley points out that "the [basic] identity allows one to see what the implications of price level and income changes are for debt retirement."[122] There is only one unique value for the reserve base $(R)$ which is consistent with a given set of equilibrium values of $(g)$, $(k)$, $(P)$, and $(Y)$. These interrelationships of variables suggest that the choice of the reserve base and the average reserve ratio by the central bank should be explicitly related to debt-management policy.

---

[121] *Ibid.*, p. 385.
[122] *Ibid.*, p. 390.

# Author Index

# Subject Index